Lifestyle

English for work, socializing & travel

Inter~~mediate Teacher~~

D1475996

Jacky Newbrook

PEARSON
Longman

Pearson Education Limited
Edinburgh Gate
Harlow
Essex CM20 2JE
England
and Associated Companies throughout the world.

www.pearsonlongman.com/lifestyle

First published 2010
Third Impression 2011

ISBN-13: 978-1-4082-37151

Set in: Avenir Book 9/11pt
Printed in China
CTPSC/03

Picture Credits

The publisher would like to thank the following for their kind permission to reproduce their photographs:

(Key: b-bottom; c-centre; l-left; r-right; t-top)

4 Corbis: Tokyo Space Club (t). **4 Getty Images:** ColorBlind Images (bl).
Masterfile UK Ltd:

Who is *Lifestyle* for?

Welcome to *Lifestyle*, an international course in English for work, socializing and travel. *Lifestyle* is designed to meet the practical needs of adults who need English for a variety of reasons whether it be in their work or to mix socially with foreign nationals, or for travel and interaction with other travellers.

Lifestyle's syllabus encompasses both professional and general English, so it is particularly suitable for classes where students have mixed needs. You could use *Lifestyle* with any of the following student groups:

- Students who have both professional and social goals for learning English.
- Company classes where the students come from different sections of an organization and perform different jobs.
- Diverse groups of people with different jobs and professions. These groups might also include students embarking on their careers or people preparing for a career change.
- Students who have not yet identified a career specialism but anticipate a need for professional English in their future.

The key goal of *Lifestyle*

Communication strategies

Lifestyle's key goal is to enable students to speak English with confidence. Conversation is unpredictable and we cannot rehearse all the different English conversations our students will have in our lessons. However, we can prepare them with coping strategies for a wide variety of situations. Communication strategies are techniques for overcoming difficulties in communicating. The communication strategies lessons in *Lifestyle* are designed to help students to explain what they mean, build relationships and use English effectively to get things done.

Functional language

In addition to practical techniques such as checking understanding and active listening, *Lifestyle* targets functional language. So it provides practice in language for making requests, offering, inviting, suggesting, thanking, agreeing, disagreeing, etc. But in addition to providing functional expressions, *Lifestyle* aims to provide usage information on when and how we use the expressions.

When we use functional language in English, we follow rules. Like grammar rules, we follow them subconsciously and we are often unaware of them until they are broken. To a large extent these rules are 'secret'. They cannot be uncovered by looking at lists of examples in the way we might discover grammar rules. They depend on context, social relationships and culture. In *Lifestyle*, we aim to uncover the rules.

The same sentence in English can perform different functions. For example, if someone says *Is that your jacket on the floor?* they could simply be enquiring if the jacket belongs to you. But in another context, they could be requesting that you move it. Meanings depend on context and along with understanding the words people say, students need to understand their intentions. To explain how functional language performs, *Lifestyle* looks beyond the literal meanings of the words that make up functional phrases to the intentions that lie behind them.

Culture and language

Language and culture are tied together in many ways and direct translations from one language to another are not always possible. An appropriate thing to say or do in one situation in one language may be inappropriate in another. Request forms are a good example. To get people to do things, English speakers often use expressions such as *Could you ...?* or *Would you ...?* where a bare imperative form (*Do it*) would be used in other languages. Translated directly into other languages the English phrases would sound peculiar. But failure to use them in English could make a speaker sound abrupt, uncaring, or even rude in many circumstances. *Lifestyle* aims to raise awareness of some of these cultural differences.

Appropriacy and directness

To communicate effectively, both grammar and appropriacy are important. If a student begins a discussion with *I am not agree*, there is clearly a grammar issue. *I don't agree* or *I disagree* would be the correct form. But there may also be an appropriacy issue. Disagreement is often signalled tentatively at the start of English discussions and it is possible that the student is sounding more forceful and argumentative than they intended. *Err, yes but ...* might better represent what they intended to say in English.

When students make grammatical mistakes in English, people generally recognize them as exactly that and they understand that they result from the language learning process. However, when students make mistakes like this, they are often interpreted on a social or personal level. People may attribute an inappropriate form to someone having a difficult personality.

There are many things we routinely say in English which are indirect. For example, if someone asks you *Are you busy?* it could be a genuine inquiry about your workload, or it could be a polite signal that they want your help or attention. Many people feel a direct style of communication would be better. Saying *I want your help* would certainly be clearer. However, indirectness is a regular feature in English conversation (as it is in many other languages) and it is not realistic to expect that students won't encounter it. Also, indirectness can have social benefits. *Are you busy?* can demonstrate a polite concern that *I want your help* lacks.

Lifestyle's approach to communication strategies

Critical incidents

To raise cultural awareness, *Lifestyle* includes critical incidents. These are short anecdotes about situations where cross-cultural miscommunication has occurred. The stories are generally told from two angles and illustrate two different ways of thinking. Both ways are logical and neither one is *right* or *wrong*. They are simply different. The incidents illustrate ways in which the social rules people follow can vary from culture to culture.

Conversational dynamics

Conversation is a dynamic process that involves turn taking. If A says *Hi, how are you?* we can expect that B will respond with something like *Fine thanks, and you?* It is a unit of conversation where one person says something that almost requires another to respond in a certain kind of way. In *Lifestyle*, functional language is generally presented in pairs of utterances rather than single-item lists. The goal is to equip students with units of conversation, which are the basic building blocks of conversation.

Communication strategies

Lifestyle highlights communication strategies that English speakers commonly use when they are getting things done. For example, when we're thanking someone, we might express delight, offer to repay them, say they shouldn't have gone to any trouble or exaggerate and say things like *You're my hero* or *You're a lifesaver*. Some of these strategies will be similar to the strategies students employ in their own language. Others may be different.

You will find further information on communication strategies in the relevant sections of the *Lifestyle* Coursebook and in the detailed teaching notes in this Teacher's book.

Working with *Lifestyle*

Flexible format

Teaching situations vary so *Lifestyle* has been designed to have a flexible format so that you can work with the units in different ways.

1 You can start at the beginning and work through from beginning to end. Following this path means students build on grammar structures and vocabulary that have gone before and steadily extend their skills. *Lifestyle* includes regular review and provides constant progression.

2 Each spread in *Lifestyle* is a stand-alone lesson. This means you can dip in and out, selecting particular lessons to meet the specific needs and interests of your class. This approach is most effective when time is short and you doubt there will be time to complete everything.

One-to-one classes

Lifestyle can be used for both small and large class sizes and many of the practice activities involve working in pairs or small groups. If you are teaching one-to-one, you can perform the pairwork activities by taking one of the roles yourself. Where

appropriate, you will find ideas and suggestions for adapting the group activities to one-to-one classes in the Teacher's book notes for each lesson.

Lifestyle is particularly appropriate for one-to-one situations as many of the activities in the course draw on a student's individual opinions and experiences which can be particularly fruitful areas to explore in one-to-one settings.

Components of the course

Coursebook

The Coursebook is the central component of *Lifestyle* and it contains the tasks and activities students will work on in class. The Coursebook units are divided into double-page lessons, each with a clear aim, which are designed to make the course flexible and easy-to-use. The number of units varies across the levels. See more detailed information on the structure of each level's Coursebook in *Lifestyle at a glance* on pages 7–12.

CD-ROM

The CD-ROM is attached to the back of the Coursebook. This component provides extra practice and self-assessment for students working alone through a variety of interactive activities, including listenings. It also contains a mini-dictionary and the complete set of Coursebook audio files in MP3 format.

Class CDs

Audio recordings are available on the two CDs that accompany the Coursebook and are also available as MP3 files on the Coursebook CD-ROM.

Workbook

The Workbook contains further practice of areas covered in the corresponding units of the Coursebook and introduces extra vocabulary to build lexis in the topic area. The Workbook is designed to provide practice activities for personal study, allowing students to practise the language they have learnt in class independently outside class. The answer key is included so students can check their own progress.

Workbook CD

Attached to the back of the Workbook, the CD contains all the Workbook listenings for extra practice.

Teacher's book

This provides all the support teachers need including detailed teaching notes, cultural, functional and background notes and extra photocopiable materials. The Teacher's book is accompanied by a Test Master CD-ROM.

Test Master CD-ROM

Attached to the back of the Teacher's book, the Test Master CD-ROM is an invaluable resource to accompany *Lifestyle*. The tests are based strictly on the content of the Coursebooks, providing a fair measure of a student's progress. The audio files for the listening tests are conveniently located on the same CD-ROM. The tests can be printed out and used as they are, or can be adapted using Microsoft® Word to edit them to suit different teaching situations. The Test Master CD-ROM contains the following: Unit Tests (one 'A' and one 'B' test for each unit); Progress Tests (one 'A' and one 'B' for every three units plus additional optional speaking and writing tests); a Final Test (one 'A' and one 'B' version).

Website

Further materials will be available on the Pearson Longman website: www.pearsonlongman.com/lifestyle. These will include free downloadable wordlists, MP3 files of the listening material for each unit of the course as well as videos explaining aspects of the course for the teacher's reference.

Unit sections

Speaking

Speaking is a top priority skill in Lifestyle and every lesson includes a substantial speaking task or activity. There are a wide variety of task types including roleplays, discussions, questionnaires, talks, games, etc. These tasks provide students with opportunities to experiment with new grammar, vocabulary or functional language and put it to use in a freer context.

Talking points

The input lessons in Lifestyle finish with Talking points – discussion questions which invite students to express their personal ideas and opinions on the topic of the lesson. They are positioned at the end of the lesson, but the Talking points can also be discussed earlier in the class if students bring them up (see Lifestyle at a glance pages 7–12).

Listening

Lifestyle listening texts include social conversations, telephone calls, professional meetings, discussions, talks, etc. Students will hear speakers with different accents in the audio recordings. They include British, American and other native speaker varieties and they also feature many foreign accents from around the world. The goal is to prepare students to operate in international contexts.

Audio scripts of all the recordings can be found at the back of the Coursebook on pages 142–159.

Reading

There are a variety of different reading texts in Lifestyle (articles, quizzes, emails, etc.) and they feature many real people, companies, products and dilemmas. They have been designed to provide a clear presentation of new language and also to prompt discussion. Reading texts are generally short and snappy to maximize opportunities for speaking practice in classroom time. More reading practice is available in the Workbook. Mini glossaries are provided with most of the reading texts. These mini glossaries give the student instant definitions for those words in a reading text that are not high frequency but that students would need to know to understand the text.

Grammar

Lifestyle takes a discovery approach to grammar. Multiple examples of grammar structures are presented in context in listening and reading texts and then students are encouraged to deduce the patterns and complete the rules for themselves.

The grammar points presented in these sections will be practised again later with speaking practice activities in new contexts. There is also a Grammar reference at the back of the Coursebook (see section on the Grammar reference).

Word focus

Lifestyle takes a systematic approach to vocabulary development. Each unit is built around a different theme and each lesson has a different topic. Together they cover a wide range of social and professional subjects. To help students fix words and phrases in their memory, each unit of Lifestyle contains one or more Word focus activities. Lifestyle pays special attention to collocations – words that are frequently used together in phrases.

Writing

Each unit of Lifestyle contains a writing task. Emails take priority but tasks such as writing PowerPoints, greeting card messages and reports on progress are also featured. These tasks provide students with an opportunity to use the language they have learnt to produce written messages for a variety of work and social needs.

Extra materials

There are three sections with extra materials at the back of the Coursebook. You might want to draw your students' attention to them at the start of the course.

Information files

These files contain information for pairwork and small group activities. Instructions for when and how to use them are provided in the Coursebook and are labelled 'Turn to File 00, page 00'.

Audio scripts

Scripts of all the listening materials are available on pages 142–159.

Grammar reference

There is a Grammar reference section on pages 160–175 of the Coursebook that draws the grammar information together and provides a comprehensive overview. Grammar is presented step-by-step throughout the lessons in the Coursebook and there are frequent cross-references to the Grammar reference section set within the grammar tables and in the Reminder box of each unit. There is also a list of irregular verbs at the end of the Grammar reference section on page 176.

Input lesson (1)

The teaching points for each unit are clearly labelled at the top of the opening page.

Lifestyle gets students speaking in English from the very beginning.

Content is presented in real modern text types such as websites and blogs as well as the traditional articles from magazines and newspapers.

Talking points draw on the students' views and ideas and round off the lesson topic.

1

A Tense review
B Present tense question forms
C Free-time activities
D Communication strategies Making suggestions
E Interaction Life coaching

Quality time

Tense review

Reading: Got things to do

1 Is your life busy at the moment or do you have plenty of free time?

2 Look at the to-do list. Do you have any similar jobs to do? Which other jobs are on your to-do list? Which jobs on your list will you enjoy doing and which will you dislike? Why?

to do
Complete tax form ✔
Take clothes to cleaners ✔
Submit expenses
Make dentist's appointment
Plan trip to Athens ✔
Look for cheaper car insurance ✔
Sell the old printer on eBay
Buy Jim and Jenny's wedding present ✔
Pay gas bill ✔
Clean out garage

3 Read the website. Would you like to use its services? Why? Why not?

Have you got too much to do and no time to do it?

Gottajobtodo.com helps thousands of people like you every month. It's as easy as one, two, three. Here's how it works.

1 Post a job ad on our site
It doesn't matter what is – no job's too big or too small. You can give all your boring chores to our assistants.

2 Choose your assistant
Individuals and companies reply to your ad and bid a price. You just select the one you want to do your job.

3 Sit back and relax
Let someone else get on with it. You can put your time and energy into more important projects instead.

In the past our assistants have done everything you can imagine. They've painted houses, filled in tax forms, researched better rates for car insurance, taught kids English, built websites, and even bought Aunty Freda's birthday gift. Last year more than 100,000 people found the help they needed at **Gottajobtodo.com**.

So tell your friends and family you're going to have a lot more time to spend together. We have thousands of assistants waiting to bid on your jobs, so you'll have time to begin those projects you've always wanted to do. You're going to love **Gottajobtodo.com**

4 Find words and phrases in the website text which match these definitions.
1 it's not important
2 routine boring tasks
3 advertisement
4 an offer made at a stated price
5 do something on your own without help
6 searched carefully for facts for a thing or person

5 Look at the three numbered paragraphs in the website. Which tenses are used? Past, present, future or a mixture?

Listening: Assistants

6 What do you think the people in these photos are thinking? What kind of assistant do you think they'd like to have?

7 🔊 1.1 Listen to the people in exercise 6. Find out if you are right.

8 🔊 Listen again and complete the sentences.
1 It always _____ longer to get home on Tuesdays.
2 I'm _____ exhausted but I'd better go.
3 I'm _____ the minutes this evening.
4 I think _____ these ones … or the other ones.
5 No, the other ones _____ my toes.
6 I'm _____ him at home next time.
7 Well, that new diet _____.
8 I've _____ good at dieting.

Grammar: Tense review

9 Look at the sentences in exercise 8. Which tenses are they talking about?
a past time
b present time
c future time
d mixture

10 Compare your answers with a partner. Do you agree? Then find examples of these verb forms in the sentences in exercise 8.

Grammar: Tense review
a the present simple
b the present continuous
c the will future
d the going to future
e the present continuous for future
f the past simple
g the past continuous
h the present perfect

>> For more information on the English tense system, see page 160.

Speaking: Past, present and future

11 Write an example of each of these things in the sections of the circle below.
• a routine job you do every day
• a job you didn't have time to do yesterday
• a project you're working on at the moment
• what you were doing at 6 p.m. last night
• a job you think you will do tomorrow
• something you've wanted to do for ages, but you haven't had time
• the name of a place where you've never been to but you've always wanted to go
• something you plan to do this weekend
• something you're going to do as soon as you get home
• something you hate doing but have to do

12 Work in pairs. Show each other your circles. Take it in turns to ask questions about the things you have written and develop conversations.
A: *Why have you written 'fix door bell'?*
B: *That's a job I plan to do this weekend. My front doorbell isn't working.*
A: *Is it broken then?*
B: *I'm not sure. I'm going to replace the batteries and see.*

TALKING POINT
• Are you good at organizing your time? Do you use any kind of planner?
• Do you think modern technology has helped people organize themselves better? Why? Why not?

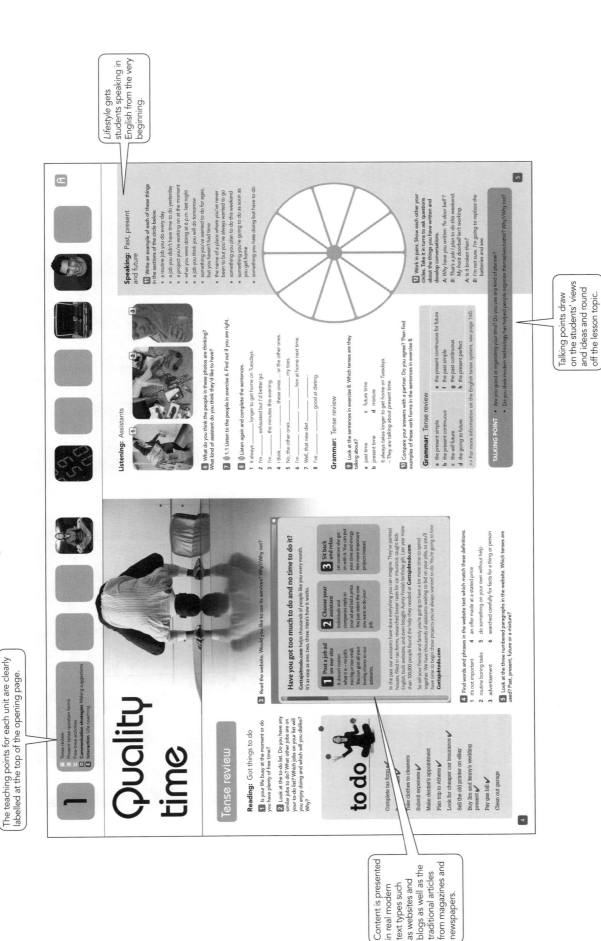

Input lesson (2)

Lifestyle Intermediate follows a traditional intermediate grammar-based syllabus that builds on the language structures students already know. The level of challenge increases as students progress through the course and there are many opportunities to put new grammar and vocabulary into action.

New language is presented in listening and reading texts.

1 Present tense question forms

Listening: Commuting

1 How do you get to work or school in the mornings? How long does your journey take? Is it generally stressful or peaceful? Why?

2 🔊 1.2 Listen to a radio interview with some commuters on a train. Make notes on the activities they mention.

Name	What they usually do	What they are doing now
Mario		
Alissa		
Steve		
Wanda		

3 Look at the questions the interviewer asked the commuters. <u>Underline</u> the present simple and present continuous forms. Which questions include both forms? Ask and answer the questions with a partner.

1 What do you usually do while you're commuting?
2 What book are you reading at the moment?
3 Does it take you long to get to work?
4 Do you listen to music while you're commuting?
5 What are you daydreaming about at the moment?
6 Are you studying for any exams at the moment?

Grammar: Present tense question forms

4 Look at the table and answer the questions.

Present tense question forms

Present simple

(yes/no questions)	(Wh- questions)
Do you usually **take** the train?	What **do** you usually **do**?
Does he usually **take** the train?	What **does** he usually **do**?

Present continuous

(yes/no questions)	(Wh- questions)
Is he/she **studying** for exams at the moment?	What **is** he **doing** now?
Are you **studying** for exams at the moment?	What **are** you **doing** now?

Which tense do we use to talk about:
a short-term or temporary activities?
b long-term situations?

>> For more information on the present simple and present continuous, see page 161.

5 Here are some things commuters sometimes do to pass the time on trains. Think of five more to add to the list.

• think about the day ahead
• eat snacks
• draw pictures
• study a language
• do crosswords and puzzles
• look out of the window at the scenery
• sleep
• chat with other travellers
• brush or comb their hair

6 Work in groups. What do you normally do on long journeys? Which are the best ways to pass the time and why?

7 Sometimes we just have to wait for things to happen. In your groups, discuss the best way to pass the time in these situations.

1 While you're standing in a long queue at the airport.
2 While you're waiting for red lights to turn green.
3 While you're listening to recorded music on the phone, waiting for someone to answer.
4 While you're waiting for your dentist to see you.
5 While you're waiting for your computer to boot up.

A: What do you usually do when you are standing in a queue at the airport?
B: I usually watch the other people in the queue.
A: What about you?
B: I sometimes close my eyes and meditate or I read something.

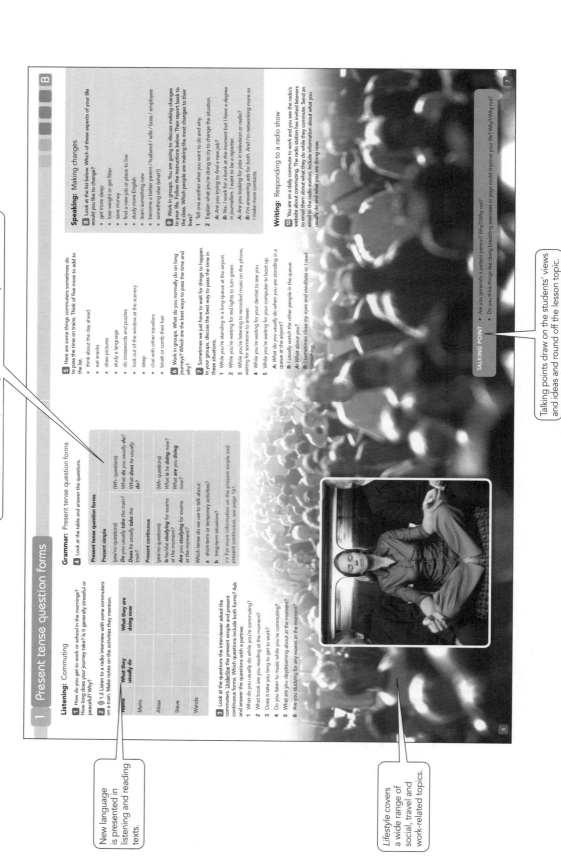

Speaking: Making changes

8 Look at the list below. Which of these aspects of your life would you like to change?

• get more sleep
• lose weight or get fitter
• save money
• find a new job or place to live
• study more English
• learn something new
• become a better parent / husband / wife / boss / employee
• something else (what?)

9 Work in groups. You are going to discuss making changes to your life. Follow the instructions below. Then report back to the class. Which people are making the most changes to their lives?

1 Tell one another what you want to do and why.
2 Explain what you're doing to try to change the situation.

A: Are you trying to find a new job?
B: Yes. I work for a bank at the moment but I have a degree in journalism. I want to be a reporter.
A: Are you looking for jobs in television or radio?
B: I'm answering ads for both. And I'm networking more so I make more contacts.

Writing: Responding to a radio show

10 You are on a daily commute to work and you see the radio's website about commuting. The radio station has invited listeners to email them about what they do while they commute. Send an email to the radio station. Include information about what you usually do and what you are doing now.

TALKING POINT
• Are you generally a patient person? Why?/Why not?
• Do you think things like doing breathing exercises or yoga could improve your life? Why?/Why not?

Talking points draw on the students' views and ideas and round off the lesson topic.

Lifestyle covers a wide range of social, travel and work-related topics.

A Tense review
B Present tense question forms
C Free-time activities
D **Communication strategies** Making suggestions
E **Interaction** Life coaching

Quality time

A Tense review

Aims and objectives

In this lesson Ss will:
- discuss and compare experiences
- read for specific information
- listen for specific information
- review and practise different tenses

Reading: Got things to do

Ex 1 Ask Ss whether they think their lives are busy or not. Do Ss think they have enough free time? What do Ss do in their free time?

Ex 2 Refer Ss to the to-do list. Ask them what they think of it. Ss work in pairs to discuss the questions. Take class feedback and discuss which are Ss' most and least popular chores.

Ex 3 Before they read the text, ask Ss discuss what kind of people they would like to help them with jobs on their to-do list (with reasons), and which jobs they would most like to have done for them. Ss read the text quickly to decide whether they would use the website services or not. Discuss ideas.

> **Possible answers:**
> **For:** convenient, easy to use
> **Against:** security issues of website

Ex 4 Ss read the text again to match words and phrases in the text with the definitions given. Check pronunciation of *chore*. Discuss Ss reactions to the text.

> | | | | |
> |---|---|---|---|
> | 1 | it doesn't matter | 4 | bid |
> | 2 | chores | 5 | get on with (it) |
> | 3 | ad | 6 | researched |

Ex 5 Ask Ss to work together to identify the tenses used in the paragraphs in the website.

> **Paragraph 1:** present tenses
> **Paragraph 2:** past tenses but also present perfect simple
> **Paragraph 3:** mixture: present, present perfect simple and future tenses

> Photocopiable notes 1.1 (page 116)
> How organized are you? (Group interviews page 123)

Listening: Assistants

Ex 6 Ss discuss photos in pairs, then share ideas with the class.

Ex 7 🔊 1.1 Ss listen to the people in the photos explaining what they are thinking. Play the recording for Ss to check their ideas.

> 1 I'd love to have a personal assistant.
> 2 I'd love to have a personal shopper.
> 3 I think I need a personal trainer.

Track 1.1: 1A, Page 5, Exercises 7 and 8

1

What a journey! It always takes longer to get home on Tuesdays. And there's a meeting at the kids' school tonight. It starts at eight. I'm feeling exhausted but I'd better go. I'm taking the minutes this evening. I'd love to have a personal assistant or maybe a butler.

2

I think I'll get these ones … or the other ones. No, the other ones were hurting my toes. Ted's been complaining for the last half hour. Why can't he give me some advice? I'm going to leave him at home next time. I'd love to have a personal shopper. They could help me decide what to buy.

3

Oh dear. Well, that new diet didn't work. I've never been good at dieting … or exercise. I haven't had a chance to get to the gym this week. If I had someone to help me, I'd feel more motivated. I think I need a personal trainer.

Ex 8 🔊 Ask Ss to read the sentences and discuss what they think the missing words might be, and which person might have said them. Play recording. Ss complete sentences and compare their ideas. Discuss which person Ss think needs most help and why.

> | | | | |
> |---|---|---|---|
> | 1 | takes | 5 | were hurting |
> | 2 | feeling | 6 | going to leave |
> | 3 | taking | 7 | didn't work |
> | 4 | I'll get | 8 | never been |

Grammar: Tense review

Ex 9 Ask Ss to work in pairs and decide which tenses were referred to in each sentence in Ex 8. How did they know?

> | | |
> |---|---|
> | 1 | b – present time |
> | 2 | b – present time |
> | 3 | c – future time |
> | 4 | d – present/future time |

1 Quality time

5 a – past time
6 c – future time
7 a – past time
8 d – past/present time

Ex 10 Ask Ss to underline the appropriate parts of the verb form in the sentences as they match the tense to the sentence.

a the present simple – takes
b the present continuous – 'm feeling
c the *will* future – 'll get
d the *going to* future – going to leave
e the present continuous for future – 'm taking
f the past simple – didn't work
g the past continuous – were hurting
h the present perfect – 've never been

Speaking: Past, present and future

Ex 11 Tell Ss that they are going to talk about themselves using past, present and future tenses. Refer Ss to the list and suggest what they could write in the circle, e.g. *I buy fresh bread every day. / I didn't have time to buy my friend's birthday present yesterday.* Ask Ss to write their own examples in the sections of the circle in the coursebook. Go round and monitor their work to check that they are using the correct tenses.

Ex 12 Ask Ss to work in pairs to share their ideas. Encourage Ss to ask detailed questions about what their partner has written, and to expand on their own answers when their partner asks them questions. After the activity, elicit the most interesting things they found out about their partner from each pair.

TALKING POINT
Ss discuss the questions and justify their ideas. They could run the Talking point as a formal debate.

Homework suggestions
• Ss think of three points for and against Talking point 2, and then write a short paragraph or essay. (120–150 words for the essay)
• Ss prepare their own 'to-do' list for the following week, and explain it to a partner next lesson.
• Ss choose one of the things their partner wrote in one of the circle sections in Ex 11 and they discussed together in Ex 12. Ss write an email to a friend telling them about their partner and giving more details of what they found out.

β Present tense question forms

Aims and objectives

In this lesson Ss will:
• listen to people talking about travelling to work and commuting
• think about ways of filling time
• study different question forms in the present tense
• do a speaking task using different tenses

Listening: Commuting

TALKING POINT
You could start with the Talking point to introduce the topic.

Ex 1 Ask Ss to work in pairs or groups. Elicit what Ss do on their own journey to work or college.

Ex 2 🔊 **1.2** Ss listen to people talking about commuting. Play the recording and ask Ss to identify the general attitude of each speaker towards commuting. (They generally don't mind it.) Play the recording again. Ss fill in the information, then compare their answers.

Name	What they usually do	What they're doing now
Mario	Works on laptop, checks emails on mobile phone and reads	People watching: (looking at other passengers and trying to imagine where they're going and what their life is like)
Alissa	Drives to work	Enjoying the train ride – closing her eyes and relaxing
Steve	Listens to podcasts or daydreams	Dreaming about winning the lottery
Wanda	Studies for an MBA course	Doing breathing exercises to help her relax

Track 1.2: 1B, Page 6, Exercise 2

I = Interviewer, **M** = Mario, **A** = Alissa, **S** = Steve, **W** = Wanda

I: Commuting! For many people it means delays, overcrowding and stress. The average British commuter spends nearly an hour travelling to and from work every day, and for some it's two, three or more. So how do they survive their daily journeys? Today we're talking to travellers on London's commuter trains to find out. With me now is Mario, that's right, isn't it?

M: Yes, I'm Mario.

I: And what do you usually do while you're commuting?

M: I generally work on my laptop – check emails on my mobile phone – and I read.

I: Ah. What book are you reading at the moment?

M: Well, I'm not actually reading this book. I'm people watching today.

I: People watching?

M: Yeah, I'm writing a novel in my spare time so I'm looking at the other passengers and trying to imagine where they're going and what their life is like.

I: Well, let's speak to one of them and find out. OK, here we have …

A: Alissa. Nice to meet you.

I: Does it take you long to get to work, Alissa?

A: Yes. I don't usually take the train but my car's broken down.

I: So you're taking the train today.

A: Yeah.

I: What's the traffic on the roads like normally?

A: Terrible, so I'm enjoying the train ride today. I can close my eyes and relax.

I: Well, you can't do that in your car! And here's someone else enjoying the ride …

S: Steve. Hi.

I: Hi, Steve. I see you have an mp3 player. Do you listen to music while you're commuting?

S: I mostly listen to podcasts or if I'm not doing that then I daydream.

I: What are you daydreaming about at the moment?

S: Oh the usual – winning the lottery.

I: No wonder you look so happy. And sitting next to you is …

W: Call me Wanda, though my real name is Wendaline. I usually study on the train.

I: Uhuh.

W: I have to use my time productively because I'm taking an MBA course.

I: Are you studying for any exams at the moment?

W: Yes, I am. It's a stressful time. … I'm doing breathing exercises at the moment. You know, to help me relax.

I: How does that work then?

W: I'm focusing on my breathing … in … out …

I: And there you have it. London's commuters are all finding ways to survive their journeys. So how do you manage to survive yours? Phone in and tell us about it …

Ex 3 Ss read the questions and underline the present simple and present continuous forms. Point out that sometimes they can use both forms. During feedback, ask them which questions used both forms. Then ask Ss to work in pairs to ask and answer the questions, and to share the most interesting answers with the class.

> 1 What <u>do you usually do</u> while <u>you're commuting</u>?
>   Both forms. Present simple, present continuous
> 2 What book <u>are you reading</u> at the moment?
>   Present continuous
> 3 <u>Does it take</u> you long to get to work?
>   Present simple
> 4 <u>Do you listen to</u> music while <u>you're commuting</u>?
>   Both forms. Present simple, present continuous
> 5 What <u>are you daydreaming</u> about at the moment?
>   Present continuous
> 6 <u>Are you studying</u> for any exams at the moment?
>   Present continuous

Optional homework suggestion
In pairs, Ss prepare a short dialogue to read to the class next lesson.

Grammar: Present tense question forms

Ex 4 Ss work through the questions in the box.

> **a** present continuous
> **b** present simple

Optional suggestion: Refer Ss to page 161 of the Grammar reference and go through the notes on present tense question forms. Allow time for Ss to discuss the examples and any problems they may have.

Ex 5 Ss work in small groups and share their suggestions.

> **Possible answers:**
> • read the newspaper/magazine or a book
> • work on a laptop

> • drink coffee
> • do homework
> • send text messages or phone on a mobile
> • listen to music

Ex 6 Ss discuss in groups. Make sure Ss discuss long journeys, not commuting. After the discussion, see if Ss agree on the best and worst way of passing the time.

Ex 7 Ss work in the same groups and share their ideas.

Optional activity: Ask Ss how people feel in these situations. You could do vocabulary work on adjectives of feeling – *nervous, frustrated, annoyed, impatient,* etc.

Variation: Ss write a four-line dialogue which they read to the class in pairs. For example:

A: What do you usually do …
B: I …
A: How do you feel in that situation?
B: I feel …

Speaking: Making changes

Ex 8 Brainstorm changes people sometimes want to make in their lives before Ss do Ex 8. Then ask Ss to discuss the list with a partner.

Ex 9 Monitor the discussion. Discuss any problems Ss may have had with question forms. Elicit which Ss are planning to make the most interesting changes to their lives.

Optional homework suggestion
After completing the task, Ss write a short report on their discussion for homework. They could include recommendations and advice if appropriate.

Writing: Responding to a radio show

Ex 10 Ss write the email. Ss then work in pairs to check and edit each other's email.

Sample answer:

> **To:** …
> **From:** …
> **Subject:** My daily commute
> Hi
> I often listen to your radio station while I'm travelling to work. I commute by train and it takes about an hour and 15 minutes. I usually listen to music on my mp3 player and check my emails on my laptop – I often get about 60–80 emails every day. Today I'm listening to the radio and doing my English homework.

TALKING POINT
If not used to start the lesson, Ss could interview each other about the kind of person they are and report back to the class.

Homework suggestions
• Ss write a short description of someone they know, explaining whether they are a patient person or not and why. (120–150 words)
• Ss write an email to a friend describing their own journey to work every day, explaining how they travel, why they travel in this way, how they feel about the commute and what they do while they are commuting. (120–150 words)

1 Quality time

C Free-time activities

Aims and objectives

In this lesson Ss will:
- read about popular activities in Europe
- study different uses of the *-ing* form
- read advertisements for popular activities
- write an email to a friend or family member

Reading: Activity Superstore

Ex 1 Ask Ss if they do any activities that are unusual or extreme and why they do them. Ask Ss to work in pairs to identify the activities shown in the photos. After they have identified the activities in the photos, ask Ss why they think people enjoy these types of activities.

A fashion shoot	**C** spy academy
B flying lessons	**D** aqua sphering

Ex 2 Ss work in pairs to read their adverts and match them to the activities.

1 aqua sphering	**3** fashion shoot
2 spy academy	**4** flying lessons

Ex 3 Ss continue to work in pairs and summarize the activities in their advert to each other.

Word focus: Free-time activities

Ex 4 Ask Ss to work in pairs or small groups and discuss how their free-time activities have changed. Ss should compare what they did as a child, what they do now and what they think they will do in the future.

Ex 5 Tell Ss that they are going to read about different ways young Europeans aged 15–30 spend their free time. Ask Ss what they think the most popular activities are. Then ask them to read the text to check their ideas. Were they surprised? Why?

> The most popular leisure activities are taking exercise and meeting friends.

Optional activity: Before they read the text, Ss work in pairs to make short notes on their ideas, then read the text and compare their notes with what they read.

Ex 6 Ss compare statistics with their own country. In a multi-national class, encourage Ss to ask each other questions about their ideas.

Ex 7 Tell Ss that the *-ing* form can be a verb, an adjective or a gerund. Ask Ss for any examples they can think of. Ss work in pairs to do Ex 7.

Optional suggestion: Refer Ss to page 172 of the Grammar reference and go through the notes on *-ing* forms.

> **1** reading **2** surprising **3** Watching
>
> **Other examples:**
> taking exercise, going for a walk, practising sports, meeting friends, eating, dancing, having a drink, hanging out, using the internet, playing video games, listening to music, going to the cinema

Ex 8 Ss work in small groups to discuss the leisure activities. After the activity, elicit any other suggestions for leisure activities and what the most/least popular class activity is.

Speaking: Choosing an activity

Ex 9 Point out the different ways of saying what hobbies or interests you like in the examples before Ss do the exercise.

Optional activity: Ss complete each sentence so that it is true for them or their family, then compare ideas.

Ex 10 Ss work in groups. Ss discuss the statements and explain their response to them.

Ex 11 Ss work in pairs. Ss can choose any activity as long as they can justify it. Take class feedback. Remind Ss of the number of different verbs used for *like* and point out that it is more interesting if Ss can use a range of vocabulary when they speak/write.

Optional activity: Tell Ss that the following activity will help them to extend their vocabulary. Dictate the following verbs in a mixed order without telling Ss how they are connected. Ask Ss to work in pairs and put the words into four groups. Take feedback or get Ss to write their groups of words on the board.

Ways of moving: run, walk, march

Ways of speaking: whisper, shout, call

Ways of looking: watch, stare, glance

Words for dislike: hate, dislike

Writing: Giving a dream

Ex 12 This exercise can be done in class or set for homework. (100–120 words)

Sample answer:

> **Subject:** Happy Birthday!
>
> Dear Auntie Mary
>
> Congratulations on your 50th birthday. I'm sorry I can't be with you on your special day, but I hope you have a fantastic celebration.
>
> You know you've always said you'd like to learn to fly. Well, I think now is a good time to start. As my birthday present to you, I've arranged for your first flying lesson. Click on this link to find out more details: www.livethedream.com
>
> What do you think? It looks really exciting, doesn't it? I'm sure you'll be a great pilot and it'll be an experience you'll never forget.
>
> Write and tell me all about it afterwards.
>
> All my love
>
> Suzie

TALKING POINT
Discuss the Talking points as a class.

Homework suggestions
- Tell Ss they are entering a competition in a magazine to write a short article explaining what dream activity they would like to receive as a present. (120–150 words)
- Ss write a short email to a friend about a new activity they have just started and are very excited about. (120–130 words)
- Ss research a new leisure activity they would like to recommend to their classmates. Next lesson they describe the activity to the class and explain why they chose it.

D Communication strategies
Making suggestions

Aims and objectives

In this lesson, Ss will:
- read an email about a work project
- listen for specific information
- study ways of making suggestions
- do an activity making and responding to suggestions

Culture and language
Making suggestions

Students may think that the way to make a suggestion, proposal or recommendation in spoken English is to say *I suggest …*, *I propose …* or *I recommend …* It seems logical.

However, we don't use the verbs *suggest*, *propose* and *recommend* much when we are speaking in English. When we do, it is generally because there is a particular need to be explicit. So, for example:
- we might use them to clarify something: *Are you suggesting that …?*
- we might use them to signal something we are going talk about: *We'd like to propose a different solution …*
- or we might use them to report what someone has said: *They recommended a change to the plans.*

So we generally use these verbs to 'talk about' suggestions, recommendations and proposals, and not to actually make them. And we generally restrict their use to contexts where there is conflict, and we need to be precise and formally go on-record about what is being said. If students use them outside these contexts in English, it could have the unintended effect of sounding formal, forceful or even argumentative.

In situations where we are collaborating with colleagues, we generally use more tentative expressions to make suggestions, such as the ones in exercise 8.

Listening: Issues with a project

Ex 1 Ss work in groups and discuss their attitude to deadlines. Do Ss think deadlines make them work more or less efficiently? Do Ss have problems meeting deadlines?

Ex 2 Ask Ss to read the email quickly to identify what work the deadline is for.

> a website project

Ex 3 Ask Ss to read the email again and find the words. These are useful topic vocabulary; do pronunciation work on them.

1	ready in time	4	delay
2	warn	5	launch
3	behind schedule		

Optional activity: Once Ss have identified the words, ask them to work in pairs and write their own sentences to demonstrate the meaning.

Ex 4)) **1.3** Ss listen to a conversation about the email. Play the recording. Ss compare their answers with a partner.

> 1 J 2 V 3 J 4 V

Track 1.3: 1D, Page 10, Exercises 4 and 6

V = Valerie, **J** = Jay

V: Hi, Jay. Have you got a couple of minutes?

J: Sure, Valerie. Is it about the new website?

V: Yeah, I got your email, thanks. So, we're two weeks behind schedule on this project. That's bad news!

J: Afraid so. There were lots of changes to the design and some people sent us new content very late. It's just one of those things.

V: I know, I know. Is there any way we can have the site ready for the first of May? It's very important.

J: How about asking someone to help us? What do you think?

V: Well, it's an interesting idea. Do you mean getting someone from another department?

J: No, I mean hiring an external contractor. We could have the site ready in time then.

V: Oh, I see.

J: My brother-in-law's a very good web designer. Why don't we ask him?

V: Um, I don't know. It sounds expensive.

J: I could talk to him today if you like.

V: Let's look at some other options first.

J: Oh, OK.

V: What about meeting a bit later to discuss this again?

J: Sure. I'm free after lunch.

V: Thanks, Jay.

Ex 5 Ss discuss the question. Encourage them to offer other suggestions.

Ex 6)) Ask Ss to try to fill in the missing words. Play the recording again for Ss to check their answers. Ss could read the final conversation aloud to lead in to Ex 7.

1	How about asking	5	don't know
2	interesting	6	could talk
3	mean	7	Let's look
4	Why don't we ask	8	What about meeting

Speaking: Making suggestions

Ex 7 Ss work in pairs and find five different expressions for making suggestions used in Ex 6. Ss should underline these so that they can find them easily.

> <u>How about</u> asking someone to help us?
> <u>Why don't</u> we ask him?
> <u>I could</u> talk to him today if you like.
> <u>Let's</u> look at some other options first.
> <u>What about</u> meeting a bit later to discuss this again?

Ex 8 Ss work in pairs. After the activity, go through the information in the box. Point out that there are five different ways of making suggestions in Ex 8.

> 1 delaying 2 add 3 get 4 meeting 5 look

Ex 9 Ss work in pairs, then share their ideas with the rest of the class.

Ex 10 Tell Ss that people don't always say exactly what they are thinking when they are being polite. Ask Ss to look back at Ex 6, and complete the table in pairs.

> Well, it's an interesting idea.
> I don't know. It sounds expensive.
> Let's look at some other options first.

Ex 11 Ask Ss to think about ways of rejecting and accepting ideas politely in their own language. Write ideas on the board. Do Ss think that it is important to be polite all the time? Why?

Ex 12 Tell Ss they are going to discuss four problems in pairs or small groups and suggest possible solutions. Monitor the discussions and make a note of good responses. Ask the whole class to present their solutions and give them a list of polite responses.

Homework suggestions

- Ss choose one situation and write an email to a friend telling him/her about the situation, what they did and how they feel about it. (120–150 words)
- Tell Ss that a friend is coming to visit their country, but is worried about behaving correctly in a new country. Write an email to your friend giving him/her some tips.
- Tell Ss to imagine that there is going to be a leaflet on appropriate behaviour that will be given to tourists arriving in their country. Ss write a short report making recommendations for what the leaflet should say and giving reasons why they think their tips would be useful for tourists. (120–150 words)

Ⓔ Interaction Life coaching

Aims and objectives

In this lesson Ss will:
- listen to interviews with a life coach and her clients
- read and discuss strategies for improving time management
- roleplay a discussion with a life coach
- write an email making suggestions for improving life issues

Refer Ss to the Reminder box and draw attention to the language that the lesson will focus on. Check Ss can use this language by looking at pages 161 and 162 of the Grammar reference and at the previous lessons of the unit.

Listening: Interview with a life coach

Ex 1 Ss discuss the questions in pairs. Ask Ss if anyone has had any help with making these kind of decisions.

Ex 2))) **1.4** Explain that Ss will listen to an interview with a life coach. Before you play the recording, ask Ss to read through the statements and check any unfamiliar vocabulary.

| 1 True | 2 False | 3 True | 4 False | 5 False | 6 False |

Track 1.4: 1E, Page 12, Exercises 2 and 3

P = Presenter, **N** = Nancy

P: Nancy Bailey is here with us today to talk about life coaching. Nancy, I'm sure many of our listeners want to know what this is.

N: Well, to put it simply, it's called coaching because in many ways it's similar to sports coaching. People often know they want to make changes in their lives, but then usually don't do anything about it. We help people to be clear about what they really want out of life, and we help them to make the changes they need to make.

P: So, who are your clients?

N: Coaching started out as a service for company executives, but now it's basically for anyone who wants to make changes in their lives. I work with small business owners, people who want to change careers, people who are planning for their retirement and managers who want a better balance between work and home life.

P: How much time do you spend with a client?

N: It's very flexible. We do all our coaching over the phone. Typically, we talk to clients once a week for 30 or 40 minutes and also communicate by email. The client can be anywhere in the world. Of course, most of the real action happens between the calls. Our clients can do as much or as little as they want to make those changes.

P: So how long do you work with clients?

N: It depends. I generally work with clients for three to six months and most see results in that time. It's a very fast process. The bottom line is when you work with a coach, you can identify clearer objectives and get results faster than if you work alone.

Ex 3))) Ss work in pairs to correct the false statements.

> 2 Clients are anyone who wants to make changes in their lives. Nancy says she's worked with small business owners, people who want to change careers, people who are retiring and managers who want a better work–life balance.
> 4 They usually phone clients once a week for 30 or 40 minutes and also communicate by email.
> 5 The client can be anywhere in the world.
> 6 Most clients see results within three to six months.

Ex 4))) **1.5** Ask Ss to read the information about the two clients and in pairs discuss briefly what they think the problem might be in each case. Play the recording and Ss check their ideas.

> Joe has problems at work. He says he feels more relaxed and in control so he was probably feeling stressed. He had a problem with time management because of interruptions. He says he's learning to say 'no' nicely when people give him jobs that aren't a priority for him.
>
> Kim doesn't want to continue working in her parents' business and she's investigating courses that she can do. She wants to be an interior designer.

Track 1.5: 1E, Page 12, Exercise 4

1

N = Nancy, **J** = Joe

N: Hi, Joe, how are you?

J: Hi, Nancy, very well thanks. And you?

N: Fine thanks. So, what do you want to talk about today? Shall we discuss your progress this week?

J: Yeah, sure. Things are definitely improving a lot at work. I'm feeling more relaxed and in control. The interruptions are becoming less of a problem – I'm using the strategies you suggested. And I'm learning to say 'no' nicely, when people ask me to do jobs that aren't a priority for me and my department.

N: Great! Tell me about the relationships with your team this week.

2

N = Nancy, **K** = Kim

N: Good evening, Kim. It's Nancy here.

K: Hiya, Nancy. Good to talk to you.

N: Do you want to talk about your homework for this week?

K: I'd love to. It was a really busy week, but I found the time to phone around a few colleges and get the information about courses.

N: Have you looked at it?

K: Yeah, I am so excited thinking about this. I really know I don't want to work in my parents' business forever, but it's taken me the longest time to decide what I really want to do. You know, the idea of being an interior designer really excites me.

N: That's great news, Kim.

Ex 5 Have a discussion with the whole class on what Ss do that waste time at work, and what they do about it. Ask the class what they think are the biggest time-wasting things at work, and collect suggestions on how things can be improved.

Ex 6 Ss read the text. Ss work in groups to make suggestions to help Joe. Make sure Ss use vocabulary of suggestion. Draw up a list of class suggestions.

Optional homework suggestion

Ss choose one of the 'Time Stealers' from Ex 6. Ss imagine that a friend has a problem with this and has asked them for help. Ss write an email to their friend outlining their suggestions. (100–120 words)

Ex 7 Ss prepare formal or informal presentations of one to two minutes taking two or three suggestions from the list and presenting them to the class, with justification and reasons why they are good ideas. Tell Ss not to write out their whole talk – they should work from notes or prompts so their presentation is natural.

Possible answer:
Perhaps you could answer the phone and emails at certain times of the days.
How about spending twenty minutes at the end of the day organizing your desk?
Maybe you should say 'no' more often to tasks that are not a priority for you.
You could just spend less time in meetings.
I would delegate more tasks to people in the team.

Speaking: Change we need

Ex 8 Explain that Ss are going to do a roleplay in pairs. One S will be a life coach and give advice to the other. Ss read the two comments and identify what the two clients want to change or plan.

Vikram wants to be able to manage his time better so that he can spend more time with his family. He would also like to cut down his commuting time.

Ruth is currently working as an admin assistant and wants to find more interesting and creative work but she is worried that she isn't very well-qualified.

Ex 9 Ss work in pairs (A and B) and roleplay the telephone call. Monitor the conversations and discuss with Ss the outcome and how they felt about the conversation. Do Ss think Vikram and Ruth will make the changes they hope for?

Ex 10)) **1.6** Play the recording and ask Ss to identify what has changed, and discuss what further help Vikram and Ruth might need. Tell Ss to keep a note of what advice they suggest as they will need it for their writing task in Ex 11.

Possible answer:
Vikram has help in the form of an assistant who is efficient but needs people skills. He could help her to understand how to deal with people.

Ruth followed Nancy's advice but the boss misunderstood her. She needs to go back to him and explain more clearly what she wants.

Track 1.6: 1E, Page 13, Exercise 10

Vikram

I took Nancy's advice and hired an assistant to deal with the day-to-day business. She's doing a good job, very efficient. The only problem is that, er … she doesn't have the same personal touch as me. You see, she doesn't get on with staff at all levels in the company.

Ruth

I talked to my boss at the advertising agency as Nancy suggested. I asked if there was anything more interesting I could do. He thought I was bored and he's just given me more admin work. It wasn't what I wanted at all!

Photocopiable notes 1.2 (page 116)
Meeting with lifestyle coach (Roleplay page 124)

Writing: A way forward

Ex 11 Ss use their notes to write an email to either Vikram or Ruth giving them further advice. They should use 120–150 words. This could also be done for homework.

Variation: Ss could draw up a proposal for either Vikram or Ruth suggesting a way forward.

1 Quality time

Sample answer:

> **Re:** Talking to the boss
>
> Dear Ruth
>
> It was good to hear that you took my suggestion and asked your boss for more stimulating work at the advertising agency. It's a pity but it seems he probably didn't understand you, which is why he gave you more of the routine admin work you don't like.
>
> The good news is that he seems prepared to listen and doesn't want to lose you. How about talking to him again and explaining what sort of work you want to do. You could also ask him how to get a more creative job in the company. Perhaps you could do a course in the evenings to show him you are serious and want to make progress in your career.
>
> Why don't we roleplay your conversation with your boss the next time we talk on the phone, so you are well prepared for the real thing?
>
> Best regards
>
> Nancy

Homework suggestions

- Ss write memo to their line manager describing two things they have noticed waste time at work, and making suggestions for improving the situation. (120–150 words)
- Ss write a short dialogue between two colleagues discussing a time-wasting situation at work and suggesting what could be done about it.
- Ss write an email to a friend describing a problem they have at work with time management. Ss bring their email to the next lesson and exchange it with a partner. Ss then write a reply to their partner, making suggestions for dealing with the problem.

2

A *will* and *going to*
B Present continuous for future plans
C Compound nouns
D **Communication strategies** Agreeing and disagreeing
E **Interaction** Five days in Dubai

Globetrotters

A *will and going to*

Aims and objectives

In this lesson Ss will:
- consider attitudes towards travel
- listen for gist and specific information
- discuss and compare experiences
- practise making plans using *will* and *going to*

Listening: Hong Kong Airport

Ex 1 Ask Ss to work in pairs to discuss the questions. Elicit other reasons for travel (e.g. to visit family, to watch a sporting event, to go to a cultural festival /event).

Ex 2 🔊 **1.7** Explain that Ss will listen to two travellers being interviewed for a passenger survey at an airport. Elicit reasons why people do surveys at airports, what they might do with the results, and what they might give as an incentive for people to take part in the survey. Play recording and ask Ss what the incentive was in this case.

> A complimentary voucher to spend in the duty-free shops.

Track 1.7: 2A, Page 14, Exercises 2 and 3

1
HL = Hong Li, **W** = Woman

HL: Excuse me. My name's Hong Li. I'm doing a passenger survey for the airport. I wonder if I could take a few minutes of your time.

W: Sure.

HL: Thank you. First of all, where are you travelling to today?

W: To London.

HL: For business?

W: Yes.

HL: Is business travel important for your job?

W: It is. I often travel for work. I'm going to meet the sales and marketing managers for my publishing company.

HL: Where are you going to stay in London? Near the airport?

W: No, in a hotel close to the city centre.

HL: What are you going to do at the airport today?

W: Well, there's free wireless internet access, so I'll probably check my email. Then, I'm going to charge my cellphone in the Business Centre. I forgot to do that last night.

HL: Technology follows us everywhere! Will you buy anything special for yourself?

W: Anything special! No, but I think I'll get a head and shoulder massage. I'm going to need it.

HL: Why's that?

W: Well, because my plane leaves early in the morning at around 5.30 and it's about 12 hours to London. I like to be relaxed on the flight.

HL: Thank you for talking for me today. Here's a complimentary voucher for the duty-free shops.

W: Thank you.

2
HL = Hong Li, **M** = Man

HL: Hello, my name's Hong Li. I'm doing a passenger survey for the airport. Can I ask you a few questions?

M: Yeah, sure. Why not?

HL: Thanks. So, where are you travelling to today?

M: To Malaysia, Kuala Lumpur.

HL: And what is the purpose of your trip?

M: See my family. I'm doing medical research in New York City, and I've been away from home for a year.

HL: Where are you going to stay?

M: Mostly with my parents and I'll probably visit other relatives, too.

HL: How long are you going to be there?

M: A whole month. It's a trip home. You know, I'm really looking forward to some home cooking.

HL: What are you going to do at the airport this evening? Will you buy anything special for yourself?

M: No! I am too tired. I'm in transit and my flight to KL doesn't leave until the morning. I don't want to pay for the round trip in to town and a room, so I'm going to stay here in the airport all night. Some restaurants are open 24 hours, so I'll get dinner. And I've found a lounge with comfy seats, and no armrests, near gate 61. But the airport's is quite cold. I think I'll ask one of the airline staff for a blanket and pillow.

HL: Thank you very much for your time. Here's a complimentary voucher for the duty-free shops.

Ex 3 🔊 Ask Ss to read the questions in the table before they listen to the recording. Ss listen again and fill in the missing information. Elicit answers from the class.

	Traveller 1	Traveller 2
1	London	Malaysia, Kuala Lumpur
2	Business – going to meet sales and marketing managers	See family
3	Hotel near city centre	With parents
4	Check email Charge cell phone	Stay overnight in one of the airport lounges and have dinner
5	No, but she'll get a head and shoulder massage.	No. Too tired.

Grammar: *will* and *going to*

Ex 4 Ss read the sentences in Ex 4 and discuss the differences between them.

> **1** a and c   **2** b and d

Optional suggestion: Refer Ss to page 166 of the Grammar reference and go through the notes on *will* and *going to*.

Ex 5 In pairs, Ss mark the uses of *will* and *going to* on the audio script. Ask Ss to decide why the speaker uses *will* or *going to* in each case.

> The second passenger uses a future form four times:
> 1 *I'll probably visit other relatives, too.*
> *will* to talk about intentions. (fairly certain – decision recently made)
> 2 *I'm going to stay here in the airport all night.*
> *going to* for firm intentions and plans (certain – plan already decided)
> 3 *I'll get dinner*
> *will* to talk about intentions (spontaneous decision/could be a decision recently made)
> 4 *I think I'll ask one of the airline staff for a blanket and pillow.*
> *will* for a spontaneous decision (not so certain)

Optional activity: Write the four uses identified from the listening on the board. Ss write a sentence that is true for themselves using each one, and then exchange with a partner to check that they have used it correctly.

Speaking: Plans and intentions

Ex 6 Ss work in pairs and share their ideas for extra questions. Write their ideas on the board.

> **Possible answers:**
> Who are you travelling with today?
> How long are you going to be there for?

Ex 7 Monitor the roleplays. Discuss any problems Ss may have had using the future forms.

Optional activity: Ss work in threes. Two Ss do the roleplay and the third S listens and gives feedback. Ss then change roles.

Ex 8 Encourage Ss to be imaginative in their discussion as this will help them remember the different uses of *will* and *going to*.

Ex 9 Ss share ideas and vote on the best plan.

Optional activity: Ss choose one of the situations discussed. Ask them to write an email to a friend describing the problem and explaining what happened.

TALKING POINT
Ss discuss the questions and provide examples.

Homework suggestions
- Ss write a short paragraph on what they like and what they dislike about travelling, and compare their ideas with the class at the start of the next lesson.
- Give Ss a city in another country. Ss find different websites that they would recommend to classmates for finding cheap flights to the city, finding hotel accommodation in the city and getting information about travelling round the city. Next lesson Ss present their websites to the class and explain why they think they are useful.
- Ss write an email to a friend telling them about a holiday they are planning, explaining what they are going to do and why. (100–120 words)

β Present continuous for future plans

Aims and objectives

In this lesson Ss will:
- read about attitudes towards exchanging houses
- learn how to use the present continuous for future arrangements
- do a communication activity

Reading: Home exchange stories

Ex 1 Introduce the topic of the lesson, exchanging homes. This topic may be new for some students. Explain that it is an increasingly popular way of getting cheap holidays, and that there are lots websites now devoted to it that Ss could look at after the lesson.

Give Ss time to discuss their ideas and experiences in groups. Write Ss' suggestions of advantages and disadvantages of home exchange on the board.

> **Possible answers:**
>
> | Advantages | Disadvantages |
> |---|---|
> | It's cheaper than hotel accommodation. | You don't know the people who will be in your home. |
> | It's an interesting way to experience another culture. | They might not look after your things. |
> | It has all the conveniences of your own home. | You might not like the home you go to stay in. |
> | You can cook meals at home. | You may worry about keeping it clean and tidy. |
> | You can experience the way of life in another country. | |

Ex 2 Tell Ss to compare their ideas with the experiences of people in the text.

Ss read both texts quickly for gist. Elicit the answer to the question.

Sandra had the more positive experiences.

Ex 3 Ss read texts again to list the advantages and disadvantages of home exchanges, and compare these with their own ideas on the board. Find out if Ss think the advantages outweigh the disadvantages.

Possible answers:

Advantages	Disadvantages
You can also exchange cars and save money.	Uneven swap – your home is better than the accommodation you get.
You can plan short trips.	Bad furnishings.
You have books and toys for your children.	Cold accommodation.
You don't have to eat out all the time.	Bad location.
It's fun to experience life in a different country.	No access to public transport.

Ex 4 Explain that Ss will read an advertisement for a home exchange. Ss read Carl's story again and write down what they think Carl and Shannon should look for in a home exchange. Ss look at Nicole's advertisement and discuss whether Carl and Shannon would like it, with reasons. Ss work in pairs and write down the questions they think Carl and Shannon should ask Nicole, and what her answers might be. Ss then write Nicole's email with her answers.

Possible questions:
Where is your apartment?
Is it near the city centre?
Is it near bus routes and a metro station?
Is there a lift/elevator?
Is there (central) heating and air-con?
Can you send me some more photos of the apartment?
Is it near shops and facilities?
Do you have any pets?

Possible answer:

Dear Carl and Shannon

To answer your questions:
The apartment is in a very central location. There are regular buses and a metro station five minutes away. There isn't an elevator, I'm afraid. We have central heating and fans. I've attached some photos of the flat for you. There are lots of shops in the local area and a great market. Our daughter has one pet – a hamster called Carla, but we'll leave it with my mother.

Optional activity: Ss roleplay Carl and Shannon's conversation.

Optional homework suggestions
• Ss write a short advertisement for their own home to put on a home exchange website.
• Ss write an email to a friend telling them about the home exchange website and recommending it to their friend for their next holiday.

Photocopiable notes 2.1 (page 116)
Exchange your home (Paired dictation page 125)

Grammar: Present continuous for future plans

Ex 5 Ss work in pairs. Ask them to read the information in the table. They look through the email to find the examples and complete the table.

Note: You write May 26th in AmE and 26th May in BrE.

a) present continuous
1 We're staying in a hotel in Piccadilly for three nights.
2 We're taking the Eurostar to Paris.
3 We're not arriving in Paris until about noon on May 26th …
4 We're leaving on the morning of June 6th.

b) *will*
5 We'll probably take a few day trips from Paris.
6 What time will you be home this evening?

c) *will*
7 I'll phone you for some first-hand advice …

Optional suggestion: Look at page 166 of the Grammar reference and go through the notes. For quick practice, ask Ss the following questions. They can answer using either form, but they must justify their choice: *What are you doing this evening? What will you do after this lesson? What are you going to study next?*

Ex 6 Ss work in pairs to complete the email. Elicit answers and get Ss to explain their choices.

1	're catching	7	're going
2	won't see	8	're spending
3	'll leave	9	'll probably visit
4	'll be	10	'll eat in
5	'll explain	11	'll be
6	're collecting		

Optional activity: Ss work in pairs. Student A reads Carl's email. Student B memorizes Nicole's arrangements in her email. Ss roleplay a phone call in which Carl and Nicole exchange information about their arrangements and intentions.

Speaking: Choosing a home exchange

Ex 7 Ss could work in pairs and plan a holiday.

Ex 8 Ss form new pairs and ask each other about their holiday choice.

Writing: Describing holiday plans

Ex 9 After the discussion in Ex 8, Ss write the email. Suggest that they use 120–150 words. With weaker groups, ask Ss to return to their original partner in Ex 7 and write the email together. Ss should help each other to check the grammar, spelling and punctuation.

Sample answer:

Subject: We're going to Peru

Dear Robert

How are you? How's the family? We're all very well. I'm very excited because I've just booked our holiday. We're flying to Peru in two months time. First we're visiting my family and friends in Lima. Then we're going to Cusco. We've arranged a home exchange with a family there for two weeks. They're staying in our apartment in New York at the same time.

The house looks wonderful. It has incredible views of the countryside and there are five bedrooms so we'll have lots of space. I've attached a few photos.
It's in a great location, close to Macchu Picchu. We'll definitely go there for a few days. I think we'll probably go trekking and horse-riding, too.
What about you? What are you guys doing this summer? Are you going anywhere exotic or staying close to home this year?

Write soon.
Love
Lilliana

TALKING POINT

Ss discuss the Talking point in pairs. Elicit ideas from the class beginning perhaps with your own reply to the questions.

Homework suggestion

- Ss research home exchange websites and chose one to recommend to the class next lesson. Ss should give a short presentation, explaining what the website is, what it says and why the S recommends it.

C Compound nouns

Aims and objectives

In this lesson Ss will:
- identify specific information in a reading text
- identify and practise making useful compound nouns

Reading: Unusual hotels

Ex 1 Ask Ss if they have ever stayed in any unusual places. How did they feel about them? Ask Ss to look at the photographs and guess what the hotels were used for originally. Write their ideas on the board. Ss read the texts quickly to see if they were right. Ss read the texts again to match the hotel to its description.

1 c – jailhouse (AmE)/prison (BrE) used for keeping prisoners
2 b – a lighthouse used to warn ships about bad weather
3 a – an aeroplane used for flying passengers

Ex 2 Ss work in pairs. Ss read the questions first and then scan the texts to find the answers.

1 a and c 2 a 3 c 4 b 5 a 6 b and c

Ex 3 Elicit Ss answers and the reasons for their answer.

Word focus: Compound nouns

Ex 4 Go through the information. Ask Ss to suggest compound nouns they already know.

Optional suggestion: Refer Ss to page 171 of the Grammar reference and go through the notes on compound nouns.

Ex 5 Ss work in pairs to match the words to make compound nouns. Check their answers before asking them to find other examples from the text.

bathrobe, toothbrush, honeymoon, newspaper, hairdryer (also hairbrush), laptop, lighthouse, seafood

Other examples:
Text a: businessman, jumbo jet, airport, ten-minute walk, check-in counters, Swedish krona, hotel rooms, hotel staff, flight attendant (uniforms), flat screen TV, bathroom, honeymoon (suite)
Text b: (150-year-old) lighthouse, bedroom, bathroom, hotel facilities, concierge service, (24-hour) room service, seafood restaurant
Text c: jailhouse, escape route, three-star hotel, hotel manager, strawberry jam, double beds, mini-bar, power shower

Ex 6 Ss work in pairs. Ask Ss to read through the list of nouns and underline the one in each list that does not go with the noun on the right to make a compound noun. Ss use a dictionary as a last resort. It is useful for them to recognize compound nouns for themselves.

1 economics (but *economy* or *economic hotel* is possible)
2 bed
3 bath
4 reception
5 heat
6 DVD
7 manager
8 facility
9 three (we say a *triple* room)
10 two (we say *twin beds*)

Speaking: Guessing hotel facilities

Ex 7 Ss work in pairs. For weaker groups, Ss could use a dictionary to give them ideas for their definitions. Monitor Ss and help when necessary.

In one-to-one classes, Ss prepare the definitions on their own.

Ex 8 Regroup pairs into fours. Each pair takes it in turns to read a definition for the other pair to guess the compound noun.

In one-to-one classes, Ss read out their definitions for you to guess.

Ex 9 Ss work in pairs and follow the instructions to guess compound nouns.

With weaker groups, brainstorm ideas for compound nouns connected to each place and write them on the board before asking Ss to work in pairs. After they have written definitions for the words, regroup pairs into fours. Each pair takes it in turns to read a definition for the other pair to guess the compound noun.

Possible answers:
Restaurant: waitress service, wine menu, seafood restaurant, main course, tablecloth, etc.
Airport: check-in desk, boarding card, boarding gate, passport, baggage claim, etc.
Modern office: air conditioning, photocopier, reception desk, meeting room, etc.
Shopping mall: rest room (AmE), coffee bar, department store, shoe shop, etc.

TALKING POINT

Ss discuss the questions in pairs.

Homework suggestions
- Ss write an email to a friend describing the most unusual place they have stayed in, and explaining how they felt about it. (120–150 words)
- Ss choose a hotel they have stayed in and write a description of it in the same style as the texts in Ex 1.
- Give Ss a city. Ss research on the internet and find a hotel they can recommend to the class next lesson. Ss present their hotel to the class, describing the hotel and explaining why they chose it.

D Communication strategies
Agreeing and disagreeing

Aims and objectives

In this lesson Ss will:
- understand people's opinions of low-cost airlines
- listen for attitude and opinion
- listen for agreement and disagreement
- express opinions, agree, disagree and negotiate an outcome

Culture and language
Agreeing and disagreeing

In some languages the word *agree* can be both an adjective and a verb. In English it's only a verb and we use do/does to form questions and negatives.
'Are you agree?' 'Yes, I am.' ✗
'Do you agree?' 'Yes, I do.' ✓

We noted earlier that English speakers use different verbs and expressions to talk about suggestions and to make suggestions. (See pages 10 and 11 on *Making suggestions* in unit 1.) The same is true with the verbs *agree* and *disagree*. We generally use these verbs when there is a particular need to be explicit. So, for example, we might use them to clarify something in the case of a misunderstanding:

No, you don't understand what I said. I disagree with that idea.

Or we might use them to signal the goal of a discussion:

We all need to agree on a solution for this.

Or we might use them to report what someone else has said:

Toby doesn't agree with us.

Students may think that the obvious way to express disagreement is to say *I don't agree* or *I disagree*. It seems logical. However, English speakers rarely do this. If students say, *I don't agree* or *I disagree* when there is no reason to be explicit, it could have an unintended effect of sounding argumentative. They're more likely to hesitate and sound uncertain saying, *Well, erm … maybe*, or they might also ask challenging questions, *Yes, but what if …?* or partly agree saying, *That's true, but …* and suggest alternatives. (See pages 20 and 21 on *Agreeing and disagreeing* in unit 2.)

Agreeing is generally straightforward in English. When someone says something that we agree with, we immediately give a short, positive response like *Yes, That's right,* or *Good idea,* etc. However, disagreeing is more difficult in English. We generally hesitate and we

might ask a question, say we partly agree, or suggest alternatives. So disagreements often emerge slowly as a conversation progresses. Initially, we tend to avoid stating our views directly. Once a disagreement is clear, we usually feel more comfortable about stating our views more forcefully saying something like, *I don't think that's true*, or *I don't think so*.

Background notes
Low-cost airlines

A low-cost carrier or airline (also known as a no-frills, discount or budget carrier/airline) offers low fares without traditional passenger services. The term originally referred to airlines with a lower operating cost structure than their competitors. Budget airlines frequently offer flights at very low prices (plus applicable taxes, fees and charges.) Roughly 10% of the seats on any flight are offered at the lowest price and are the first to sell. The prices then steadily rise to a point where they can be comparable or more expensive than a full-service carrier. Some examples of low-cost airlines include Ryanair and Easy Jet.

Reading: Low-cost travel

Ex 1 Introduce Ss to the topic of the lesson (low-cost travel) and discuss the questions with the whole class.

Ex 2 Tell Ss that they are going to read informal comments on a budget airline posted on the internet. Ask Ss what they know about budget airlines and what the posters might be saying. Do Ss think they will be generally positive or negative about the budget airline? Tell Ss that the postings are about extra charges. Ask Ss to read the text and identify the extra charges mentioned.

> Pay for checking in luggage
> Additional charges for sports/skiing gear
> Pay for food and drink on the flight
> Pay for boarding first
> Travel insurance
> Credit card charge
> Paying for a cab (AmE)/taxi (BrE) to the hotel

Ex 3 Ss discuss which comments they agree with and why.

Optional activity: Ss discuss each charge in groups and draw up a list of those they agree with and why.

Ss then work in pairs to write the next blog entry.

> **Photocopiable notes 2.2 (page 117)**
> **Compound nouns (Pelmanism page 125)**

Ex 4 Ss work in pairs to identify the compound nouns and identify the common factor in each group of words.

> **Compound nouns:** baggage claim, cabin crew, ground staff, flight attendant, take off (n), passport, boarding card, suitcase, backpack, hold-all, lost luggage
>
> 1 places in the airport
> 2 airport staff
> 3 verbs related to flying
> 4 documents
> 5 types of luggage
> 6 problems at the airport

Ex 5 Ss work in the same pairs to add words to the list. Weaker groups could use a dictionary.

Possible answers:
1 rest room, toilets, restaurant
2 pilot, security guard, shop assistants
3 fly, fasten, check-in
4 ticket, visa
5 handbag, briefcase, etc
6 overbooked, cancellation, etc

Listening: I don't think so

Ex 6))) 1.8 Ss listen to two friends at an airport. Ask Ss to read the questions before playing the recording.

1 K	2 B	3 B and K	4 B and K	5 B and K	6 K

Track 1.8: 2D, Page 21, Exercise 6

K = Keith, **B** = Beatrice

K: I don't believe it! The queue for boarding is already a mile long. We're never going to get a good seat.

B: Oh, no. That's what you get when you travel with a budget airline.

K: Absolutely. You get what you pay for.

B: Still, the tickets were really cheap.

K: That's right. We got a great deal.

B: Well … maybe. But, is it really cheaper? There are all those extras we have to pay for – the extra bag, the credit card charge …

K: Yes, and sandwiches on the plane.

B: Good point. I think these airlines should provide a better service.

K: Yeah, they should.

B: Shall we get in the queue?

K: It's twenty minutes till boarding. I think I'll buy a sandwich.

B: Good idea. I'll come with you.

Ex 7 This concept of strong and weak disagreement is rooted in cultures. Spend time on it so that Ss really understand what people mean. After checking the answer, explain that we often hesitate, sound uncertain and explain ourselves when we are disagreeing, and we often use single words or short phrases when we are agreeing.

agreeing

Ex 8))) 1.9 Tell Ss that they will listen to two managers discussing a business situation. Explain that they only need to identify what they disagree about, so should not worry about other words or information at this stage.

The two managers disagree that the cheapest flight, which has several stops, will save the company money. The main issue is that the cheapest flight will take much longer.

Track 1.9: 2D, Page 21, Exercises 8 and 9

A: We need a simple clear rule that everyone can understand.

B: Mmm.

A: So from now on, everyone has to take the cheapest flight they can find …

B: … Yes?

A: So? … What do you think?

B: Well … erm … I'm not sure. What if the cheapest flight has several stops?

A: They should take it. It's the cheapest flight.

B: Yes, but what if it takes ten hours instead of three?

A: It doesn't matter. We have to get our flight costs down.

B: That's true, but productivity's important, too. If people spend a day travelling, they're not going to be working.

A: Everyone has laptops and most airports have wifi.

B: How about setting a limit? They take the cheapest flight available, but not if it adds more than six hours to their journey time.

A: That makes the rule more complicated.

B: I'm sorry, but I think this rule could cost us more money in the long run.

A: The cheapest flight is the cheapest flight.

B: Yes, but what I'm saying is it won't always save us money.

A: It's a simple rule that everyone can understand. It has to save us money.

B: I don't think that's true.

Ex 9))) Ask Ss to read the notes and the example sentences from the recording. In pairs, Ss try to complete the sentences with the missing words, then listen to the recording to check their ideas.

1 I'm not	5 sorry, in the long run
2 what if	what I'm saying is
3 true, but	don't think that's
4 about setting	

Optional activity: Ss work in pairs. Student A makes a statement and Student B responds in one of the ways identified in Ex 9. Student A has to say which one Student B used.

Speaking: Hidden airline costs

Ex 10 Ss work in pairs to do this activity. Alternatively, Ss could work in groups of four. First, the group works in two pairs to prepare for the roleplay. One pair works with card A and the other pair prepares card B.

Ex 11 Tell Ss they are going to do a roleplay and that they should use expressions for disagreeing from Ex 9. To do the roleplay for Ss who worked in groups in Ex 10, Ss in each group divide into two pairs with one A and one B. The two pairs roleplay the situation, then compare what happened with the other pair. Take feedback from the whole class to see if there is a consensus on what should or should not be charged for.

Ex 12 Ss could present their ideas on how a business can introduce such charges without losing customers.

Homework suggestions

• Ss write a proposal for a plan to introduce the five most acceptable charges in the best possible way. Ss structure their proposal with recommendations and reasons, and present their proposal to the class at the start of the next lesson.

• Ss write an email to a low-cost travel company complaining about one of their charges, giving reasons and asking for a refund.

• Ss write an email to a friend complaining about a recent flight, telling them what happened when they travelled on a low-cost carrier and what they did about it.

E Interaction Five days in Dubai

Aims and objectives

In this lesson, Ss will:
- listen for attitude, opinion and detail
- express opinions, agree, disagree and negotiate an outcome

Refer Ss to the Reminder box and draw attention to the language that the lesson will focus on. Check Ss can use this language by looking at page 166 of the Grammar reference and at the previous lessons of the unit.

Listening: Change of plan

Ex 1 This exercise introduces Ss to the topic of the lesson (visiting Dubai). Ss discuss their ideas in pairs before they read the text.

Ex 2 This exercise prepares Ss for the listening. Ss work in pairs to ask and answer the questions. Point out the use of *going to* and *will* in the questions so that Ss use these in their answers.

> 1 They'll probably arrive between 9.30 and 10.00 p.m.
> 2 On Tuesday Fay is going to the Tourism Fair and on Wednesday she's going to interview some business contacts.
> 3 On Tuesday Martin is going to take photos of the city and on Wednesday he'll probably go on a desert trip.
> 4 On Thursday they're going sightseeing together.
> 5 They'll both be free to do sightseeing for two days. But Martin might have more free time because Fay is going to the Tourism Fair on Tuesday.

Ex 3))) 1.10 Ss listen to the recording and make the changes to the itinerary. Elicit answers from the class.

> There are three corrections.
> **12 Wednesday**
> Martin — desert trip? sightseeing
> **13 Thursday**
> desert trip together
> **14 Friday**
> Afternoon tea and watch sunset, Burj Al Arab hotel?

Track 1.10: 2E, Page 22, Exercises 3 and 4

M = Martin, **F** = Fay

M: So, while you interview your local business contacts, I'll go on the desert trip then, right?

F: Mmm, I'm not sure. Don't you think Thursday would be better for the desert trip? I mean together. I've got interviews all day Wednesday but we're both free on Thursday. I'd love to see the desert.

M: Well, I wanted to try sandboarding and maybe some er … dune bashing.

F: Dune bashing? What's that?

M: It's when you crash into sand dunes.

F: But won't you get a lot of sand in your eyes?

M: No, it's not like that, Fay. You're in a car, like a jeep or a four-by-four.

F: Oh, it sounds fun. I'd love to do that!

M: I don't know if that will be a good idea, Fay. I don't think it's your kind of thing. You know, you usually hate snowboarding and adventure sports.

F: No, I don't. Anyway, this is different. It's the desert! I'd love to go on a camel ride – you could take pictures of me. And we'll spend the night in a tent.

M: Well, all right then. But don't complain to me when you get covered in sand. There won't be any luxury bathrooms or hairdryers or anything.

F: Don't worry. I'll manage. So, will you change the booking to Thursday for two?

M: I suppose so. And I might do some more sightseeing on Wednesday.

F: Great. You know, Martin, we're visiting the Burj Al Arab hotel on Friday. It's seven stars and it's a fantastic building that looks like a sail. Shall we have dinner there?

M: Yes, but it's very pricey. To be honest, I don't think we'll be able to afford it. I've already got permission to take photos inside, remember? But I'd love to get some shots from the beach at sunset.

F: Mmm, I see they do afternoon tea. We don't need to have dinner there.

M: Well, you can schedule it in but let's see how it goes when we're in Dubai. I don't want to pay a huge bill just for a cup of tea!

F: All right. I'll pencil it in, OK?

M: Fine.

F: Friday – tea and watch sunset at the Burj Al Arab hotel.

Ex 4))) Before you play the recording again, tell Ss to listen for Martin's attitude towards the desert trip and his reasons for not wanting to go with Fay. Ss could discuss what they think the answers might be briefly.

> Martin probably wants to go on the desert trip by himself because he wants to do sandboarding and dune bashing and says Fay doesn't usually like adventure sports.
>
> Martin doesn't want to have dinner at the Burj Al Arab hotel because he says it's too expensive and they won't be able to afford it.

Ex 5 This exercise focuses on attitude and expressions that show how we really feel. Ss discuss the questions in pairs. During feedback, point out the difference in attitude between *fine* (agreement) and *well, all right then* (reluctant agreement).

> Martin isn't very happy to agree to Fay's ideas – he sounds reluctant. We usually use these expressions with people we know very well.

Speaking: What to do in Dubai

Ex 6 Ask Ss to do pronunciation work of the vocabulary in the box. After eliciting answers, Ss could say which countries they normally associate the activities with.

Ex 7 Ask Ss to scan the text and react to each activity. Ss explain their ideas, and say which their least favourite and most favourite activities would be. Is there a class consensus?

Ex 8 Ss plan their itinerary in pairs and present it to the class. Monitor and discuss the language used afterwards.

Ex 9 Ask Ss to work with a different partner and give them the new task. Monitor and discuss the changes made.

Optional homework suggestions

- Ss think of three things visitors could do in their town/country and write about them in the same way as the text in Ex 7. (120–150 words)
- Tell Ss to imagine that they took part in one of the six activities in Ex 7. They write an email to a friend telling them about the activity, what they did, how they felt about it and whether they enjoyed it. (120–150 words)

Writing: A budget increase

Ex 10 Go through the instructions with the class so that they know what they have to do, and ask them to discuss their ideas in pairs before writing the email. This can be set for homework or done in class in pairs. Suggest that Ss write 120–150 words.

Sample answer:

> Dear …
>
> I am writing to you about our trip to Dubai. As you know, the budget is US$450 per person. First, we're going on a bus tour of the city on Monday morning, and then we'd like to do a desert safari in the afternoon. On Tuesday evening we're planning to go on a dinner cruise along the Dubai river. These activities come to a total of US$215.
>
> We would also like to go hot air ballooning on Tuesday morning. We could take some great photos of the desert and put them on the company website. But the balloon trip costs US$245 per person, so it is US$10 over budget. Do you think the company could pay an extra US$10 for this special trip? Please let us know.
>
> We look forward to hearing from you.
>
> Best regards
>
> …..

Homework suggestion

Ss choose a city in their country that they think would be (or is) a good business centre like Dubai. Ss write a paragraph about their chosen city following the style of the text in Ex 1. (100–120 words)

3

A Base form with *to* or *-ing* form
B Food and entertaining
C Quantifiers
D **Communication strategies** Saying 'no'
E **Interaction** The visit (board game)

Be my guest

A Base form with *to* or *-ing* form

Aims and objectives

In this lesson Ss will:
- listen to two people talking about a meal
- read about dining etiquette in different countries
- study expressions using the base form with *to* and the *-ing* form
- roleplay a situation giving advice about dining out to people travelling abroad

Reading: Taking your food seriously

Ex 1 Ask Ss to discuss the question in groups. Make sure they understand the vocabulary. Do pronunciation work on key words.

Ex 2 🔊 1.11 Tell Ss they will listen to someone talking about a meal. Play the recording and ask Ss to identify the situation and what happened. Ask Ss how they would feel in the situation in the recording.

> **Situation:** The speaker went for an interview meal and was embarrassed because the potential boss had bad table manners. He dropped food on his shirt, ate with his fingers and made a terrible mess.
>
> **What happened:** The speaker was so shocked and distracted that she didn't talk during the meal and didn't get the job.

Track 1.11: 3A, Page 24, Exercise 2

I was applying for a really good job with a great company. My potential boss wanted to meet me at a restaurant for lunch. The interview was going well until they brought our food. This man had the most awful table manners I have ever seen. He was dropping food on his shirt, eating with his fingers and making a terrible mess! I was shocked. I didn't get the job and I'm sure it was because I couldn't speak. I was too distracted by his table manners.

Ex 3 🔊 1.12 Explain that there are always two sides to every story. Play the second recording and ask Ss to listen and compare the man's reason for his behaviour, and identify why the woman didn't get the job. Ask Ss the real reason why the boss behaved like this and why woman didn't get the job.

> The boss uses the restaurant experience to judge whether he would be able to work with the interviewee. He didn't like the way the interviewee reacted to the way he was eating his lobster and he thought he wouldn't be able to work with her.

Track 1.12: 2A, Page 24, Exercise 3

There's no tidy way to eat lobster. You have to break the shells and to work at it to get all the meat out. So I take job candidates to a seafood restaurant, order lobster and show great enthusiasm eating it. Then I watch their reactions. If they dislike my way of eating a lobster, I know I don't want to work with them. I want people who roll up their sleeves and get the job done. A lobster meal is a great way to find out who to hire.

Ex 4 Elicit the answer to Q 1. Ask how Ss feel about this technique used by the boss. How would they feel if they had an interview like this? Why? Can they suggest any other ways of finding out if an interviewee is suitable? Then ask Ss to discuss Qs 2 and 3.

> To watch their reactions to the way they eat lobster. The boss uses the restaurant experience to see if he could work with the interviewee and see if he/she doesn't mind getting messy to get the job done. The boss then decides if the person can do the job.

Ex 5 Before they read the text, ask Ss if they know anything about dining etiquette in the countries in the box. Write their suggestions on the board. Ss do the reading in pairs. Take feedback and check any unknown words. Ask Ss if anything surprised them and compare what they read with their own ideas on the board.

> **A** Germany **B** Japan **C** Turkey **D** Saudi Arabia

Ex 6 Tell Ss they will use the dining tips and relate the information to their own country. Ss work in pairs to rewrite the tips, then share ideas with the class.

Ex 7 Ss could work in groups and discuss other important aspects of good manners. During feedback, make a list of their ideas on the board. Ss rank them in order of importance.

Grammar: Base form with *to* or *-ing* form

Ex 8 Ss work in pairs to complete the information in the table.

1 eat	5 Asking
2 to use	6 laying, making
3 having	7 to rest, to try
4 eating, to talk	

Optional suggestion: Refer Ss to page 173 of the Grammar reference and go through the notes on the base form with *to* or the *-ing* form. For further practice, ask Ss to complete the examples so that they are true for their country. They can use information from their discussion in Ex 6 and Ex 7.

Ex 9 Ask Ss what they know about dining etiquette or manners in China. Ss work in pairs and complete the sentences. Ss read the sentences again and discuss whether any of the information is surprising.

1 entering
2 entertaining (or to entertain)
3 to eat, shouldn't serve
4 to revolve
5 Eating, to be
6 show, knocking
7 paying, refuse
8 to offer

Speaking: Copy your host

Ex 10 Ss work in groups of three. They read their texts and memorize the tips.

In one-to-one classes, choose two of the files.

Photocopiable notes 3.1 (page 117)
Natural spoken English (Card matching page 126)

Ex 11 Ss discuss the tips and make notes.

TALKING POINT

Ask Ss to discuss the first Talking point in pairs, and think about how they felt and whether there were any particular etiquette rules to be followed. Ss could discuss the second point in groups.

Homework suggestions

• Talking point 1 could be done as a writing exercise. Ss write an email to a friend covering the points mentioned. (100–120 words)
• Ss write a short story in which a visitor doesn't know about dining etiquette and makes some mistakes. Ss should explain what happened and what the consequences were. (120–150 words)
• Give Ss a country and ask them to research any dining etiquette rules that they can discover. Ss report their findings to the class next lesson OR write an email to a friend telling them about their findings.

β Food and entertaining

Aims and objectives

In this lesson Ss will:
• compare attitudes towards eating different or unusual food
• listen to people discussing and ordering food
• work with vocabulary around the topic of food
• do a roleplay describing and recommending food

Listening: What the locals eat

Ex 1 This exercise introduces Ss to the topic of food. Give Ss time to discuss their ideas in groups.

Ex 2 🔊 1.13 Explain the word 'blog' in case Ss are not familiar with it. They listen to the conversation and complete the travel blog.

Background information
Blog

The word *blog* is a contraction of the term 'weblog'. It's a type of website where a person can make regular entries on different topics, including comments, descriptions of events, or other material such as graphics or video. Other people may also contribute to a blog, so that ideas and opinions can be compared. The newest contribution to the blog is always at the top of the webpage. A person who writes a blog is called a blogger.

Before you play the recording, ask Ss to read the blog and try to predict the missing words. Ss listen and fill in the gaps. Check answers and explain any words that Ss do not know, e.g. *a pinch of salt* (a very small amount of salt that can be held between the first finger and thumb).

1 snack 2 street vendors 3 duck 4 egg 5 boiled
6 pinch of salt

Track 1.13: 3B, Page 26, Exercises 2 and 3

B = Barbara, **R** = Richie, **V** = Street vendor

B: Isn't this night market great?

R: Yeah. Hey, I've heard we should try the balut.

B: What's balut, Richie?

R: It's a popular snack here. Just look out for a street vendor selling them.

B: But what IS balut?

R: Ah look, here you go!

B: Ah, they're big eggs. What sort are they?

V: These are duck balut. Want to try? It's very tasty.

B: Are they cooked? I can't eat raw egg.

V: Yes, they're boiled. You want 12-day, 16-day or 18-day?

B: Sorry? What do you mean?

R: Look Barbara, I think I should warn you, it's a fertilized egg with an embryo inside.

B: What! Oh, no, not for me, thanks.

V: It's a local delicacy. Please, try it.

R: I'll give it a go. Which would you suggest?

V: 18-day is the king of balut. You crack open the shell like this and then eat it with a pinch of salt. …

R: OK, here we go. …

B: So, what's it like?

R: It's very good. It's quite chewy. It's like a normal boiled egg cooked with a bit of meat. Not bad at all for a midnight snack.

Ex 3 🔊 Ss listen again and underline the expressions they hear. Ask Ss to compare their ideas. Write the following language functions on the board and ask Ss to discuss what language function is used in each expression: *Suggestion, Compliment, Complaint, Asking for information, Description, Comparison.*

1 We should try the balut. (suggestion)
2 It's very tasty. (compliment)
3 I can't eat raw egg. (complaint)
4 What's it like? (asking for information)
5 It's quite chewy (description)
6 It's like a normal boiled egg (comparison)

Ex 4 🔊 **1.14** Ask Ss to look at the photo and discuss the following questions. *What kind of restaurant is it? What kind of food does it serve? What might be unusual about it?* Ss listen to a conversation between two diners at the restaurant and fill in the information on the waitress' menu pad.

Entrée: 2 crocodile carpaccios
Side order: 2 green salads
Main course: 1 grilled emu; 1 white fish

Track 1.14: 3B, Page 26, Exercises 4 and 5

R = Richie, **E** = Enrique

R: This is one of my favourite restaurants in Sydney. I hope you like it.

E: The location is fantastic. I really wanted to see Bondi Beach and it's nice to eat outside on the terrace. This menu looks interesting. I've never eaten crocodile or kangaroo before. What would you recommend?

R: For the entrée I usually have the crocodile carpaccio with a side order of green salad.

E: OK, that sounds good. I think I'll have the same.

R: For the main course, you could try the grilled emu or the kangaroo steak if you want to try something new.

E: What's emu?

R: It's a sort of big, funny-looking bird we have here. It can't fly. It's similar to an ostrich.

E: What does it taste like? Chicken?

R: No, it's like beef, only it's healthier. Apparently, it has, er … fewer calories and less fat.

E: Really? And what about the kangaroo?

R: That kind of tastes like beef, too, only it's tougher. The emu's more tender.

E: OK, I'll have the emu then.

R: Do you want to order any side dishes?

E: I don't know. What does it come with?

R: Um, you know, I don't remember. Let's get the waitress over and ask her.

E: What are you having for the main course?

R: Well, I've had a lot of red meat recently so I'm going for the white fish. Excuse me, hello …

Ex 5 🔊 Before playing the recording again, ask Ss to read the expressions. Ss listen and complete the expressions.

1 recommend	6 similar to
2 sounds	7 like
3 the same	8 like
4 could try	9 with
5 sort	10 Excuse me

Optional activity: For further practice, in pairs, Ss write short four-line dialogues choosing two expressions from the exercise and responding to them. Ss read their dialogues to the class.

A: *What would you recommend?*

B: *I think the kangaroo sounds good.*

A: *What does it taste like?*

B: *It tastes like beef, only it's tougher. It's very good!*

Ex 6 🔊 **1.15** Ask Ss if they are allergic to any kinds of food. Explain that Richie has invited Enrique to a barbeque at his house. What kind of information might Richie need to know about Enrique's eating habits? For example, *Does he have any allergies? What kind of food does he like/doesn't he like? What's his favourite food?* Ss read the four items the men discuss. Play the recording. Ss listen and put them into the order they are mentioned.

4, 2, 1, 3

Track 1.15: 3B, Page 26, Exercises 6 and 7

R = Richie, **E** = Enrique, **B** = Barbara

R: Glad you could make it to the barbie, Enrique.

E: Thank you for the invitation. I've heard a lot about the traditional Australian barbeque. People eat lots of meat, don't they?

R: Yeah, well, it's changed. It's more prawns than steak these days, mate.

E: Why's that?

R: Everyone's getting more health conscious. Hey, I'd like you to meet my wife. Barbara this is Enrique. He's here from the Philippines on business.

B: Hi, Enrique.

E: Pleased to meet you.

B: Did Richie tell you about the time we went to the Philippines and he tried that duck egg?

E: Balut? Did you like it?

R: Yeah, it was great. Listen guys, I'm going to check on the barbie.

E: Can I help you with anything, Barbara?

B: No, I'm fine thanks. Help yourself to the salads. Is there anything you don't eat?

E: Well, I'm not allergic to anything, but is there any onion in the salads? I can't eat it, you see, it repeats on me.

B: No worries, there isn't any.

E: This looks good. What's in it?

B: Ah, I wouldn't eat that with your salad, Enrique, it's the chocolate mousse for dessert. …

E: OK, thanks for warning me.

Ex 7 🔊 Play the recording again. Ss tick the expressions that are correct. Ss work in pairs to correct the expressions that are different.

1	Thank you for ~~inviting me~~ the invitation.
2	✓
3	✓
4	Help yourself to the ~~buffet~~ salads.
5	✓
6	Is there any ~~fruit~~ onion in the salads?
7	This ~~tastes~~ looks good. What's in it?
8	✓

Word focus: Food and entertaining

Ex 8 Ss could work in small groups to put the words into three sections. Take feedback, then do pronunciation work on the words.

A How food is cooked: boiled, grilled, roast, fried, baked, steamed, smoked, stewed
B Taste and texture: salty, delicious, sweet, spicy, chewy, rich, tasty, oily, tender, tough
C Things on a table: knife and fork, salt and pepper, oil and vinegar, chopsticks, serviette, plate, spoon, menu, glass

Ex 9 Before doing the exercise, explain that collocations are important because some words go together while others do not. Ask Ss to suggest some collocations about food using the words from Ex 8 and the words *meat* and *fish*. (Suggestions: *tough meat*, *chewy meat*, *tender meat* and *salty fish*, *fried fish*, *smoked fish*.) Ss do Ex 9 in pairs, then share ideas with the class.

1 g **2** h **3** d **4** f **5** b **6** e **7** c **8** a

Ex 10 Ss work in pairs to think of other combinations. Weaker groups could use dictionaries to help them.

Possible answers:
1 barbequed/fried meat
2 smoked/tinned fish
3 sirloin/grilled steak
4 pasta/tomato salad
5 fish/lamb stew
6 raw/seasonal vegetables
7 hot/mineral water
8 vanilla/yoghurt ice cream

Ex 11 Ss could discuss the questions in groups. After the activity, see if the whole class has a favourite food from Q 1, a food that nobody eats and a drink that is most popular.

Speaking: I'd recommend …

TALKING POINT
Discuss Talking point 1 to lead in to the roleplay. Extend it by asking *Why? What do you cook/order?*

Ex 12 Tell Ss they are going to do a roleplay about a business lunch. Ss work in pairs and follow the instructions to prepare their roles. Monitor and help if necessary. Give Ss five minutes to roleplay the situation. Monitor and give feedback on any problems.

TALKING POINT
Discuss these question with the whole class. Write the factors Ss suggest are important when choosing a restaurant up on the board and ask Ss to rank them. Talking point 2 could be done as homework.

Homework suggestions
• Use Talking point 2 for written homework. Ss write a short paragraph setting out the important factors and explaining why. (120–150 words)
• Ss write an email to a friend telling them about the lunch Ss roleplayed in Ex 12. Ss should say what happened, what they ate and how successful the meal was. (120–150 words)
• Ask Ss to look up more words connected with food, restaurants and cooking. Ask them to bring their words to the next lesson and share them with their classmates.

C Quantifiers

Aims and objectives

In this lesson Ss will:
• compare their own eating habits and what they know about healthy food in a quiz
• study the use of quantifiers in the context of food
• discuss what to say in situations connected with food

Reading: Food quiz

Ex 1 This exercise is an introduction to the quiz. Give Ss time to discuss their lists, then elicit feedback from the whole class.

Ex 2 Pre-teach important vocabulary so Ss can concentrate on answering the questions in the quiz, e.g. *saturated fat, artificial/processed sugar, high blood pressure, ready-prepared meals, teaspoon.* Ss work in pairs to complete the quiz, then ask them to check their answers in File 4 on page 132.

Optional homework suggestion
Ss write an email to a friend telling them about the quiz they did in Ex 2 and what their results were. (100–120 words)

Ex 3 Discuss any surprises with the class. Encourage Ss to give reasons for their answers.

Grammar: Quantifiers

Ex 4 Go through the information in the table with the whole class, asking Ss to choose the correct option.

1 uncountable, countable		4 –
2 large		5 more, less
3 uncountable, countable		

Optional suggestion: Refer Ss to page 171 of the Grammar reference and go through the notes on quantifiers.

Ex 5 Ask Ss to work in pairs to complete the sentences. With stronger groups, ask Ss to write a sentence of their own for each sentence for further practice.

1	much	7	Very few
2	many	8	very little
3	a lot of	9	too much
4	a lot	10	too many
5	a little	11	too
6	a few	12	enough

Ex 6 Ask Ss to suggest one or two questions using the information in the box before they work in pairs, so that they get the idea. Demonstrate one with a S if necessary.

Possible answers:
How much chocolate do you eat?
How many cakes and biscuits do you eat?
How much water/fruit juice do you drink?
Do you eat (too) many takeaway and ready meals?
Do you eat enough fruit and vegetables?
Do you drink much/enough water?
Is your diet varied enough?
Is there enough nutritional information on food labels?
Is there very little variety in your diet?

Optional activity: Ss feedback to the rest of the class on their partner's answers. The class produces a mini-report on their findings. For example:

Most of the class drink a lot of water but we also eat too much chocolate.

We don't think that there is generally enough information on food labels.

Speaking: It's all too much

Ex 7 This exercise focuses on politeness and anticipates the topic of the next lesson. After Ss have discussed the three situations in pairs, put them into new groups to discuss what their suggestions were and how important it is to be polite.

> **Possible answers:**
> In situation 1, it's very important to be polite because this is a working relationship. But you must not cause misunderstandings.
>
> In situation 2, it's important to be polite but also to stand your ground and not to be over-charged.
>
> In situation 3, politeness is less important as it is family. But you want your brother/son to become healthier so you must be diplomatic and tactful.

TALKING POINT

Use Talking point 2 to follow up Situation 3. Ss can make practical suggestions, such as encouraging competitive sport. Talking point 1 could be done as written homework. Ss write a letter to an international food magazine explaining how diets and eating habits have changed in their country and why. (120–150 words)

Homework suggestions
- Ss write an email to a friend in another country who is interested in healthy lifestyles. Ss explain the situation in their country, using the information from the quiz and class discussion.
- Ss choose one of the situations in Ex 7 and write a short dialogue. Ss read their dialogues at the start of the next lesson.

D Communication strategies Saying 'no'

Aims and objectives

In this lesson Ss will:
- discuss how to say 'no' in different situations
- identify ways of refusing politely
- listen to a telephone conversation to identify what was said
- roleplay different situations in which people say 'no'

> ### Culture and language
> #### Saying 'no'
> What makes a polite refusal can vary across cultures. When we turn down a social invitation in English, we generally provide a fairly concrete reason for why we won't be coming, and express our apologies and regret. Expressions of apology and regret are common in Japanese refusals, too, but excuses tend to be vaguer and a refusal might be signalled by incomplete sentences rather than an explicit *I can't*. In many South American countries, people may give an indefinite answer like *Of course I'll come if I can*, and they may hint at why it will be impossible. The person who is inviting them may continue to insist that they come, and they will continue to give indefinite responses. Failing to insist that your guest comes could be considered a little rude in some cultures, even if you realize they can't make it.
>
> This lesson looks at some of the common components of English refusals including giving an excuse, apologizing, hesitating, suggesting an alternative and saying 'thank you'. (See pages 30 and 31 on *Saying 'no'* in unit 3.) Be aware that your students may have different customs as you work through the situations in this lesson.

Speaking: Hosts and guests

Ex 1 Give Ss enough time to think about different situations. Ask Ss to discuss their ideas in groups. Encourage them to think about why it is polite to disagree in these situations.

> **Possible answers:**
> Some people don't like saying 'no' because they don't want to offend or disappoint people, or hurt their feelings. It can cause loss of face.
> People from Asian countries such as India, Indonesia or Japan think it's rude not to give a person what they have asked for. The word 'no' is considered impolite and is not often used directly in a business context.
> It's polite to insist when you are the host, especially in the Arab World or countries like Thailand, where it's also good etiquette for the guest to say 'no' before finally accepting something.

Ex 2 Give Ss time to think about what the people are saying and what they learn about the people from this.

> In Conversation 1 A is the guest. The guest would like to pay the bill (*check* is AmE for *bill*). In the end, they decide to split the bill between them.
> The guest is very generous offering to pay the bill. Students would probably respond well to this guest although it depends on the culture.
>
> In Conversation 2 A is the host. The host is trying to convince the guest that they need more food but the guest is politely saying 'no'. The host insists.
> The host is too insistent and is probably not one all students would respond well to.

Ex 3 Ask Ss construct their conversations in pairs. Ss then read them to the class. If the class is large, choose one or two pairs to do this. Encourage them to think about intonation and the way of speaking as well as the words themselves, as this can contribute to politeness. You may need to explain *doggy bag* – a container that you can ask for in a restaurant after a meal so that you can take any food you can't eat away with you.

> **Conversation 1:** 8, 6, 10, 2, 4
> **Conversation 2:** 7, 3, 1, 9, 5
> See complete conversations in the audio script on the next page.

Ex 4 🔊 **1.16** Play the recording so Ss can compare their ideas. Ss could look at the audio script at the back of the book and read it aloud as it is important to focus on how persuasive the first speaker is in each case. Ss should try to copy the intonation from the recording.

Track 1.16: 3D, Page 30, Exercise 4
Conversation 1
G = Guest, **H** = Host

G: Is that the check? Let me get that.

H: Oh no. This is on me.

G: No, no. Why don't we split it?

H: No, no I insist. You're our guest.

G: Are you sure?

H: Yes, the company's paying.

G: Well, that's very kind of you.

H: It's our pleasure.

G: Well, thank you very much. It was a terrific meal.

H: I'm glad you enjoyed it. Don't forget your doggy bag.

Conversation 2
H = Host, **G** = Guest

H: Have some more paella.

G: No, no. It was terrific, but I couldn't manage any more.

H: Some more shrimps then?

G: No really, I'm full. I'm trying to diet.

H: You don't need to lose weight!

G: I do!

H: Just a few more?

G: Well … maybe just a few then.

H: Good, and a little more paella?

G: No, really. I'll have to pass on that, but thank you.

Optional homework suggestion
Ask Ss to look at the audio script again and practise reading it aloud and try to copy the intonation they heard on the recording. You could suggest that Ss record themselves on their phones or mp3 players.

Ex 5 Ss discuss what makes a perfect host. Encourage them to think about a perfect host in their own country, but also what might be a perfect host in other cultures and any differences between different cultures.

> **Possible answers:**
> A perfect host is polite and sensitive to his/her guest's wishes.
> A perfect guest is polite and behaves well.
> It depends on the culture how a host or guest is expected to behave as ideas of polite behaviour vary.

Ex 6 Point out that English people tend to be uncomfortable when turning things down, which means that they often do more than just refuse. Ask Ss if they have noticed any of the things suggested in Ex 6. Then ask Ss to label the sentences.

> 1 I have to study
> 2 I'm so sorry, but
> 3 Oh …
> 4 Perhaps we can meet up another time?
> 5 It sounds great.
> 6 Thanks for thinking of me.

Listening: An invitation

Ex 7 This leads in to the topic of the listening. Ss should work in groups to explain the situation/event and their reasons for turning it down.

Ex 8 🔊 **1.17** Tell Ss they will hear one half of a conversation. Play the first part of the recording and ask Ss to listen for two things – what the event is and the reason Gabriella can't go.

> The event is a friend's birthday party. Gabriella can't go because she is studying for exams.

Track 1.17: 3D, Page 31, Exercise 8
G = Gabriella

G: Hello.

G: Sandy! Great to hear from you. How are you?

G: Not too bad. How's Peter?

G: Oh, nothing exciting. I've got some exams coming up so I'm studying all weekend.

G: Oh … I don't think I can. Sunday, you say?

G: It sounds great, but I have two exams the next day – Marketing and Accounting.

G: I'm really sorry, but I have to study.

G: Thanks for thinking of me. Look, when my exams are over, perhaps you and Peter can come over to my place for a meal?

G: OK, choose a restaurant you want to go to and it'll be my treat.

G: No, no. I insist. It'll be your birthday present.

G: OK, I will. And have a lovely birthday on Sunday.

G: Bye.

Ex 9 Ask Ss to work in pairs. Ss read the part of the conversation they have just heard. Ss discuss what Sandy might have said in response to Gabriella and make notes on their ideas.

Ex 10 🔊 **1.17** Ss listen to the second part of the recording, which is the complete version. They compare their ideas with what was actually said.

Track 1.17: 3D, Page 31, Exercises 10 and 11
G = Gabriella, **S** = Sandy

G: Hello.

S: Hi, Gabriella, it's Sandy.

G: Sandy! Great to hear from you. How are you?

S: Pretty good thanks and you?

G: Not too bad. How's Peter?

S: Oh, same as ever. Listen, what are you doing this Sunday?

G: Oh, nothing exciting. I've got some exams coming up so I'm studying all weekend.

S: Can you take a break? It's my birthday and I'm having a party.

G: Oh … I don't think I can. Sunday, you say?

S: Yes, we're just inviting a few close friends and Peter's cooking lasagne.

G: It sounds great, but I have two exams the next day – Marketing and Accounting.

S: Oh, what a pity.

G: I'm really sorry but I have to study.

S: It's OK, I understand.

G: Thanks for thinking of me. Look, when my exams are over, perhaps you and Peter can come over to my place for a meal?

S: That'd be nice. Or we could all go out to a restaurant together.

G: OK, choose a restaurant you want to go to and it'll be my treat.

S: Oh, no. We'll pay for ourselves.

G: No, no. I insist. It'll be your birthday present.

S: No, you don't have to do that. Let's talk about it later. Go and get on with your studying and make sure you pass the exams.

G: OK, I will. And have a lovely birthday on Sunday.

S: I will. Take care. Bye now.

G: Bye.

Ex 11 🔊 Ask Ss to work in pairs to try to remember the conversation and complete the notes with the words from the recording. After the activity, play the recording again for Ss to check their ideas.

1	are you doing	5	That'd, we could
2	take a break, having	6	ourselves
3	pity	7	don't have to
4	understand		

Ex 12 This exercise focuses on the words used to refuse politely. After Ss have underlined the words, get them to practise saying them in pairs.

> I don't think I can.
> It sounds great, but …
> I'm really sorry, but …
> No, no. I insist.

Ex 13 Ss compare the audio script with things people say their own culture. Discuss as a class and see if Ss can come up with anything they have noticed themselves, maybe from television programmes, if they haven't travelled to many other countries.

Optional activity: Tell Ss that they have been invited to lunch with a colleague but they don't want to go. They should call the colleague and leave a message on their answer phone refusing the invitation and making a good excuse. Ss compose their messages in pairs, and then read them to the class. The class decides which is the most convincing and polite message.

Speaking: Turning someone down

Ex 14 Ss work in pairs to think of ways of refusing and good excuses they could use in the five situations. With a weaker group, work with the whole class to suggest what could be said in the first situation before asking Ss to work in pairs.

Ex 15 Ask Ss to work with a different partner and think about what hosts and guests could say in the different situations. With a weaker group, elicit suggestions from the whole class for situation 1 before asking them to work with their new partner.

Ex 16 Ss work with their original partner and roleplay the situations in Ex 15. Encourage them to be polite at all times and to use some of the ideas suggested in Ex 6.

> **Photocopiable notes 3.2 (page 117)**
> **What do you do? (Situation cards page 127)**

Homework suggestions

* Ss write a dialogue for one of the situations in Ex 14 or 15. Ss read their dialogue to the class at the start of the next lesson.
* Ss choose one of the situations from Ex 15 and write an email to a friend telling them what the situation is and what happened. (120–150 words)

ℰ Interaction The visit

Aims and objectives

In this lesson Ss will:
* discuss giving and receiving gifts
* play a board game focusing on appropriate things to say in different situations

Refer Ss to the Reminder box and draw attention to the language that the lesson will focus on. Check Ss can use this language by looking at page 171 of the Grammar reference and at the previous lessons of the unit.

Speaking: Gift-giving

Ex 1 Ask Ss to discuss the questions in pairs. Elicit feedback from the class.

Ex 2 Ss work in pairs or groups. Make sure that they discuss gifts from a business contact and that they think of issues like suitability and practicality of the gifts.

Ex 3 In a multi-national class, put Ss into groups from different countries.

> **Examples:**
> **What to give**
> Safe options are good quality chocolates, books, pens and local handicrafts.
>
> **What not to give**
> People from France, Italy or Spain do not generally appreciate presents with large company logos. Do not give leather goods to a Hindu, a potted plant to a Japanese contact and never give knives or scissors as most people will think you want to sever the relationship.
>
> **Colours**
> Do not give flowers in Brazil; yellow flowers in Russia or white flowers in other countries, e.g. Japan, India and Indonesia.
> Gold or red wrapping paper is considered lucky in China; red, green or yellow paper in India.
>
> **Refusing gifts**
> People may refuse when you first offer them a gift. Just offer the gift again. If a gift is too expensive, the receiver may be embarrassed. It is policy in many companies to return extravagant gifts.

Board game: Entertaining

Ex 4 Explain that Ss are going to play a board game to practise politeness in different situations. Ss discuss the questions in pairs – this leads into the situations Ss will find in the board game.

Ex 5 Explain the rules, then give Ss time to play the game. After the activity, discuss the situations and any questions they may have. If the game is used in a one-to-one class, roleplay the situations with the student.

Writing: A thank-you note

Ex 6 Explain that Ss are going to write an email following an overseas visit to thank their hosts for the visit and for gifts they gave you. Ask Ss to work in pairs to think about what is important to thanks the hosts for, and what kind of gifts they were given. Ss can look back at Ex 2 for ideas for gifts. Ss should organize the email as introduction, thanks, extra details about the visit and food, final thanks and signing off. Ask Ss to work together to complete the email in class (or set it for homework) using 100–130 words.

Sample answer:

> **To:** …
>
> **From:** …
>
> **Subject:** Thank you
>
> Dear …..
>
> I'm writing on behalf of myself and my colleagues to thank you very much for all your hospitality and assistance during our visit to your company last week.
>
> I would also like to say thank you for the lovely gifts you gave us. I will always remember our trip when I use my beautiful Montblanc pen and pencil set. It is here on my desk right now.
>
> We all enjoyed the local fish restaurant you took us to on our last night. The cod was excellent. I hope we can go there again when we visit you next year.
>
> Best regards
>
> …..

Homework suggestions

● Tell Ss that a colleague from overseas is coming to visit their company. This colleague has emailed to explain that he/she is vegetarian and is worried about this being a problem. Ss should reply to the email, reassuring the colleague and explaining what they can eat and how the visit can be organized for them. (120–150 words)

● Ask Ss to research special meals in different countries. Ss should choose the food they think is most interesting and tell the class about it next lesson.

● Tell Ss that they have been given a gift of chocolate from a friend. Unfortunately they don't like chocolate, although they appreciate the kind thought. Ask Ss to write an email thanking their friend and saying something nice about the gift.

Review 1-3

The Review checks work covered in the previous three units, including grammar, vocabulary, communication strategies, collocations and pronunciation. It can be approached in a number of different ways, depending on classroom size and situation and time available, for example:

- as a whole-class activity
- with Ss in pairs or groups, followed by class feedback
- as a test to be marked
- as homework

1
1 d **2** c **3** e **4** h **5** f **6** g **7** b **8** a

2
1 offer **2** have become **3** carries **4** is increasing/have increased **5** have decided **6** uses **7** took **8** 've always been **9** makes **10** isn't

3
1 c **2** e **3** a **4** h **5** f **6** b **7** d **8** g

4
1 having/to have **2** taking/to take **3** to meet **4** getting up **5** leave **6** to get **7** say **8** to meet **9** be **10** cost

5
1 should **2** kind **3** taste **4** cooked **5** served **6** made **7** sort **8** napkin **9** mess **10** course **11** grilled **12** dessert

6
1 tender **2** baked **3** spicy **4** homemade **5** low-fat **6** still

7
1 enough **2** too early **3** few **4** too much **5** much **6** little **7** big enough **8** a lot of, many

8
1 a – because there is no specific plan or arrangement
2 a – a timetable or scheduled event, and b – an arrangement
3 b – an arrangement or plan, and c – firm intention or plan that has been made
4 a – firm intention or plan that has been made, and c – decision that has just been made.
5 b – decision that has just been made
6 a – firm intention or plan that has been made

9
1 f **2** a **3** b **4** c **5** e **6** d

10

Oo	oO	Ooo	oOo
survey	*career*	*passenger*	*assistant*
knowledge	commute	management	appointment
stressful	delay	sightseeing	suggestion
schedule	exchange	chocolate	arrangements
business	hotel	etiquette	departures
healthy	dessert	restaurant	delicious

37

A *can, could* and *be able to*
B Personal characteristics
C Comparatives and superlatives
D **Communication strategies** Building on ideas
E **Interaction** Training solutions

Learning curve

A *can, could and be able to*

Aims and objectives

In this lesson Ss will:
- assess their own abilities to do mental puzzles
- read an article about ways of improving people's mental abilities
- study ways of expressing ability (*can, could* and *be able to*)
- discuss things they would like to be able to do

Reading: Mental abilities

Ex 1 This introduces Ss to the topic of puzzles and ways of expressing ability. Ask Ss briefly about the kinds of puzzle they do. Do Ss like puzzles with numbers, words or pictures? Why do they think this is? How often do they do puzzles? Where do they do them?

Ex 2 Tell Ss that they can only use each letter once and that they have three minutes do the puzzle. Start Ss working at the same time and stop them after three minutes. Take feedback and write their suggestions on the board. This could be done as a competition – the winner has the most words that no one else found.

> **Common words:** no, on, one, in, into, an, not, and, end, ten, done, don't, ran, train, run, ruin, tune, tone, near, note, neat, dine, under, tuner, toner, train, trained, trend, turn, turned
>
> **Other words:** tan, tin, ton, dine, ant, anti, nod, tuna, dent, dune, Dane, den, donate, nut, dart, runt, rant, node, darn, torn, unite, united, untie, unto, tarn
>
> Excellent score: 20+
> Very good: 15
> Average: 10

Ex 3 Ask Ss how they felt about the puzzle and whether they think doing this kind of activity helps stimulate people's mental abilities.

Note: Research shows that in fact this is true – people who do 'mental gymnastics' in this way do stay mentally alert at an older age.

TALKING POINT
Use Talking point 1 at this point to introduce the idea of memory and natural ability.

Ex 4 Ask Ss read the title of the article and discuss in pairs what the article might say. Ask Ss to suggest some easy ways of improving brainpower. Take feedback.

Ask Ss to read the article and note down the six ways to improve mental ability suggested in the article. Tell Ss not to worry about words they don't understand for the moment. Take feedback and write the six ways on the board. Compare them with Ss' own ideas.

> 1 physical exercise
> 2 balanced nutrition
> 3 complex mental exercises
> 4 do things with the opposite hand you would normally use, e.g. using the mouse
> 5 make yourself remember things such as names and phone numbers
> 6 play games and activities such as sudoku and crosswords

Ex 5 Discuss the question with the whole class. Get Ss to explain and justify their ideas.

Optional activity: Get Ss to work in pairs and choose the way they think is most effective. Each pair presents their choice to the class. Class votes on the best idea.

Ex 6 Ask Ss to work in pairs to find the words in the article. Monitor them and explain any words they are not sure of. Weaker groups can use a dictionary if necessary, or alternatively do the exercise with the whole class so that Ss can discuss each one together.

> 1 boost   2 force   3 challenge   4 stretch
> 5 performance

Grammar: *can, could* and *be able to*

Ex 7 Go through the information in the box with the students. Ask Ss to suggest other example sentences as you go through it. Ask Ss to work in pairs to underline examples in the article. Ss explain to each other why these examples use *can, could* or *be able to*.

> **Paragraph 1:**
> I can remember the name of my first teacher but I can't remember what I did yesterday.
> I was able to learn things a lot faster when I was a child.
> Are you able to remember things easily?
> Could you learn things quicker when you were younger?
>
> **Paragraph 2:**
> What can we do to improve our memories?
>
> **Paragraph 4:**
> You can stimulate the brain just like your muscles …
> … last year I couldn't remember my mobile phone number.
> Now I am able to memorize phone numbers very easily.

Paragraph 5:
By playing games that involve some thinking you will be able to keep your brain in shape.

Optional suggestion: Refer Ss to page 167 of the Grammar reference and go through the notes on ability modals.

Ex 8 Ask Ss to work in pairs to choose the correct form of the verb. Point out that in some cases more than one answer is possible. Take feedback from the class and make sure that Ss explain their choices.

1   be able to
2   can't / won't be able to
3   Can / Could
4   can / are able to
5   will be able to
6   Being able to
7   weren't able to / couldn't
8   Will you be able to

Optional activity: Ask Ss to work in pairs. Dictate the six jobs. For example: *government minister, zookeeper, actor, driving instructor, air traffic controller.*

Ss discuss their ability to do the jobs, giving reasons. Each pair should rank the jobs in the order of their ability to do them: 1 = most able to do, 5 = least able to do. After the activity, Ss present their lists and compare with other pairs.

Speaking: I'd like to be able to sing

Ex 9 Explain that Ss are going to think about their own abilities. Refer them to the shapes in the coursebook and check that they know the words for each shape. Explain that they are going to write something in each shape. Ask Ss to look at Q 1 and suggest something that they could write in the first shape. Elicit several ideas, then ask Ss to complete the rest of the questions alone. Go round and monitor Ss and help if necessary.

Ex 10 Ss work in pairs to discuss their answers. After the activity, take class feedback and see if Ss have any abilities in common.

Optional activity: After discussing their sentences, Ss write a short report summarizing what their partner said about their abilities and what they'd like to be able to do in the future. This could also be done for homework.

TALKING POINT
Talking point 2 can be used to round off the topic as a discussion. It could also be done as written homework.

Homework suggestions
• Ss choose one of the shapes in Ex 9 and write an email to a friend telling them what they wrote in the shape and why. (100–120 words)
• Ask Ss to look at sentence 1 in Ex 8 and write an essay discussing the sentence. Ss should write two points supporting the sentence, two points against it and then a conclusion expression their own point of view. (120–150 words)
• Ss write an email to a friend telling them about a game or puzzle they enjoy playing and why. (100–120 words)

B Personal characteristics

Aims and objectives

In this lesson Ss will:
• listen to a recruitment specialist describing skills required by employers
• work with key adjectives describing personal characteristics
• match job skills with jobs
• consider and practise interview techniques

Listening: Life skills

Ex 1 Give Ss time to discuss their own jobs in detail. Take feedback and write the skills Ss suggest on the board. If any questions have not been discussed then do them with the whole class. Then refer Ss to the **Watch out!** box. The confusion between *job* and *work* is very common.

Optional activity: Do a quick practice by reading out the sentences below. Ss call out *job* or *work* to complete the sentences.

1   What's your _____? (job)

2   What do you do when you are at _____? (work)

3   Have you finished your _____ for today? (work)

4   What time do you start _____? (work)

5   What's your ideal _____? (job)

Ex 2 1.18 Tell Ss they are going to listen to advice being given to job seekers by a recruitment specialist and note down the seven skills she says are important. Play the recording and give Ss time to compare their answers. Take feedback and write the answers on the board. Do Ss agree that these are important skills?

Possible answers:
• communication skills
• interpersonal skills
• organizational skills
• ability to research
• analytical skills/logical thinking
• prepared to improve professionally

Track 1.18: 4B, Page 38, Exercises 2 and 3

RS = Recruitment specialist, **A** = Job seeker 1, **B** = Jobseeker 2

RS: We all know that employers are looking for job-specific skills when they advertise a vacancy. But there are also certain skills that they're looking for in all their staff. They're what we sometimes call 'soft' skills or 'people' skills. Can anyone suggest what some of these might be?

A: Good communication?

RS: That's exactly right. One of the most important soft skills is communication. Employers want people who are able to express their thoughts well, both when speaking and when writing. They don't want someone who can't spell or speak coherently. And let's not forget, the other part of communication is being a good listener. Any other ideas?

B: Getting on with people is important.

RS: Yes, isn't it? You know, there are all kinds of personalities in a work environment and you need to be able to communicate with all of them to work as part of a team. We're talking about good interpersonal skills here.

4 Learning curve

A: I think they'd want someone to be organized.

RS: I agree. Organizational skills are also essential. Employers rarely want someone who is messy or disorganized. If you're able to maintain a tidy workplace without leaving piles of paper everywhere, they know your work habits and time management will be more efficient. Great!

There are three more soft skills I would add: firstly, the ability to do research. If you can find out about the company and make a good impression at the interview, it can help you to get the job. But that's not all. In most jobs you'll need to be able to research answers to questions as well as find data for your manager. Companies basically want people who are self-sufficient when they get a task like this to do.

Next comes analytical skills and the ability to think logically. Being able to look at routine problems and using your common sense to make good decisions is a part of most jobs.

Finally, you know, employers want people who have thought about their career growth. I mean, someone who is prepared to improve professionally by learning new things. The good news is that if you think you're weak in some of these areas, you can always get some training to help you improve. Any questions so far?

Ex 3 🔊)) Before you play the recording again, ask Ss to read the notes. After listening, Ss compare their answers with a partner. Are there any sentences they do not agree with?

> 1 soft
> 2 their thoughts, listeners
> 3 kinds of personalities
> 4 tidy workplace
> 5 answers to questions, data.
> 6 your common sense
> 7 learning new things

Word focus: Personal characteristics

Background information

Positive and negative connotations

In this section Ss will consider the positive and negative connotations of different words. This is important because some words have a significance that is more than just the meaning, e.g. *fat* is always a negative word. If Ss understand this they will use words appropriately. As well as connotation they need to use words with the correct collocation. Collocations can be verb + preposition, adjective + preposition, verb + noun, etc.

Ex 4 This exercise gives Ss the meaning of the key words but not their connotation. Once Ss have done the matching exercise and understood the words, ask them whether they think the words are negative or positive. Then do pronunciation work on all the adjectives.

> **1** e **2** d **3** b **4** g **5** c **6** h **7** a **8** f
> All the words are positive.

Ex 5 This focuses Ss on the connotation of words and will help them use the adjectives appropriately. Give Ss time to think about the words carefully and identify the negative words. They can get help from the dictionary if they look at the examples given there. Ss could write sentences to show the connotation of the words.

> unreliable, messy, bossy, unpunctual

Optional activity: Tell Ss that people can misunderstand each other if they are insensitive to the connotation of words. Say the words below and ask Ss to call out positive or negative. If there is disagreement, then discuss the words with the class. Ask if the concepts are also negative or positive in their own language.

outgoing (positive)   *humorous* (positive)
pressured (negative)   *decisive* (positive)   *careless* (negative)
logical (positive)   *independent* (positive)

Optional homework suggestion

Ss write their own sentences using the words from Ex 5 to bring out their connotation.

Ex 6 In this exercise Ss look at verb + expression. Ss work in pairs to complete the mind map.

> **be a**
> team worker/player
> logical thinker
>
> **have**
> common sense
> good attention to detail
> a sense of humour
> an outgoing personality
>
> **have good … skills**
> problem-solving
> writing
> customer care
> decision-making
>
> **be able to**
> work on your own initiative
> think on your feet
> meet deadlines
> work well under pressure

Ex 7 You could give a different job to each pair and give them three minutes to come up with suitable skills from their mind maps. Each pair presents their words to the rest of the class, justifies their choices and answers any questions from the other Ss. They can add their own ideas it they wish.

> **Possible answers:**
> *civil servant* – be a team worker, have good attention to detail, have good writing skills
> *flight attendant* – have good customer care skills, be a team player, have an outgoing personality
> *journalist* – be able to work on your own initiative, have good attention to detail, be able to meet deadlines
> *sales rep* – be able to think on your feet, have an outgoing personality, have good customer care skills
> *lawyer* – be a logical thinker, be a problem solver, be able to meet deadlines
> *dancer* – have good attention to detail, have an outgoing personality, be a team player
> *chef* – be able to work under pressure, be a team player, have a sense of humour
> *surgeon* – have good decision-making skills, have good attention to detail, be able to work well under pressure
> *software engineer* – have good problem-solving skills, have good attention to detail

Optional homework suggestion

Ask Ss to write:
* a paragraph explaining why they do or don't have the skills for a particular job
* a statement as if they were applying for a job explaining their skills
* a paragraph about a job they would or wouldn't like to do
* an email to a friend suggesting they apply for a particular job

Speaking: Tricky questions

Ex 8 This introduces the idea of a job interview and interview techniques. Ask Ss if they remember the boss from Lesson 3A, who had a particular technique for choosing potential employees.

Ex 9 You could ask Ss to work in groups and share their own interview experiences.

Ex 10 Ss roleplay interviews. Monitor and take feedback.

Ex 11 Discuss any difficult questions with the whole class.

TALKING POINT

These could be done as class debates.

Homework suggestions

* Ss write a short report on their interview in Ex 10, recommending their partner for the job or not. (120–150 words)
* Ss write a short essay answering the question in Talking Point 1. (120–150 words)

C Comparatives and superlatives

Aims and objectives

In this lesson Ss will:
* compare ways of learning different skills
* listen to a man talking about his own and his son's experiences of education
* study comparative and tlative adjectives and adverbs
* read about the experience of e-learning and discuss it

Listening: Getting an education

TALKING POINT

Start the lesson with the Talking points to introduce the topic.

Ex 1 Ss discuss the questions in pairs.

Ex 2 🔊 1.19 Tell Ss they are going to listen to a father talking about his own education and his son's. Before you play the recording, ask Ss to read the statements. Ss listen and decide if the statements are true. Encourage Ss to compare their answers before you take feedback.

| 1 False | 2 True | 3 False | 4 True | 5 True | 6 True |
| 7 False | 8 False |

Track 1.19: 4C, Page 40, Exercises 2 and 3
Mark

I never enjoyed studying when I was at school. I failed most of my exams and left at sixteen. I became a driving instructor and I've never needed many qualifications. But when my children started going to school, I wanted to be able to help them with their homework, so I started studying again.

I studied on my own at first. I got into computers, and taught myself how to do some programming and how to upgrade the hardware for the business.

Going from that to studying online was a natural progression. I've always been fascinated by law, so I signed up for a law degree with the Open University two years ago. I can't take time off work and studying online is much more flexible than attending full-time classes.

I can choose how much I want to study every year, which is a big advantage. It's also a bit cheaper than a traditional course.

Last year, our oldest son, Nathan, got a place at one of the best universities in the country to study law as well. We're very proud of him. So, you see, there are two students in our family at the moment!

Nathan says the worst part for him is all the exams. My course is less stressful because it's mostly continuous assessment.

I don't learn as quickly as him, as you can imagine. Let's face it, studying for a degree when you're young is easier than at my age. Fortunately, I can take it more slowly. I'll probably retire before I graduate.

It would be easy to give up. I'm just doing it for fun and to encourage my kids to be good students. But I'd like to carry on. I hope Nathan completes his course, but if he does drop out, he knows he can study online, like his dad, if he wants to.

Ex 3 🔊 Before playing the recording, tell Ss they are going to compare the two courses. Give Ss time to compare their answers before taking feedback. Which person do they think enjoys their course the most? During feedback ask Ss if their own experiences of courses, or education in general, are similar or different.

> **Possible answers:**
> They are both law degrees.
> Mark is studying online and Nathan is going to a traditional full-time university course.
> The OU course is more flexible than the full-time course.
> The OU course is cheaper than the full-time course.
> The OU course is mostly continuous assessment. The full-time course is assessed by exams.
> The full-time course is more stressful than the OU course.

Optional activity: Read out the following phrases. Ss look at the audio script on page 147 and identify phrasal verbs that mean the same.

1 began to be interested in something (got into)

2 put your name on a list for something because you want to participate (sign up)

3 have a holiday from work on a particular day (take time off)

4 continue doing something (go on/carry on)

5 stop doing something that you do regularly (give up)

6 leave school or university before your course has finished (drop out)

4 Learning curve

Grammar: Comparatives and superlatives

Ex 4 Before you play the recording ask Ss to read the sentences and try to complete them. Ss listen to check their answers.

1	more flexible	5	less stressful
2	cheaper	6	easier
3	the best	7	more slowly
4	the worst		

Ex 5 Go through the information about adjectives in the box. Ask Ss to write a sentence for each form, then show it to their partner to check that they have used it correctly. Then go through the information about comparative and superlative adverbs and ask Ss to complete the examples.

Comparative and superlative adjectives
1 longer … than, the longest
2 easier than, the easiest
3 more flexible than, most flexible

Comparatives and superlative adverbs
1 faster than, the hardest
2 more slowly
3

adjective	adverb	comparative	superlative
good	well	better	the best
bad	badly	worse	the worst

Optional suggestion: Refer Ss to page 172 of the Grammar reference and go through the notes on comparatives and superlatives.

Ex 6 Ss work in pairs to choose the correct option to complete the article. Check the answers, then ask Ss to read the whole text again. Do Ss agree with the writer? Ask Ss to explain their opinions.

1 than **2** better **3** actively **4** less **5** more **6** more **7** more **8** more difficult **9** less **10** harder

Optional activity: Ss read the complete text again and debate whether e-learning is actually better than face-to-face learning.

Speaking: What do you think?

Ex 7 Ss could work in groups to decide whether they agree with the statements. Encourage debate and discussion but make sure Ss justify their opinions.

Optional homework suggestion

Ask Ss to think about the discussion they had in Ex 7, Q 3, and to write an essay discussing the statement. They should write an introduction, two points for the statement, two against and then write their own opinion. (120–150 words)

Ex 8 Ss continue the discussion. Make sure that they focus on learning online not face-to-face teaching. It could be done in pairs, with Ss reporting back to the rest of the class.

Writing: Asking about a new course

Ex 9 This writing activity could be set for homework. If it is done in class, ask Ss to work in pairs to think of the questions they need to ask in the email and the best way of phrasing them before they write the email. Tell Ss to write 120–150 words.

Sample answer:

To: …

From: …

Subject: English courses

Dear …..

I'm writing to ask for more details about the online English training that your organization offers.

I work for a multi-national company in the Finance department and use English on a daily basis. I deal with suppliers by phone and via email and sometimes I attend meetings in English.

Due to my family and work commitments, I can't attend face-to-face classes on a regular basis so I'm very interested in e-learning.

Can you send me more details about both the three-year and the six-month intensive courses? I'd particularly like to know the following:

• Does the material include business English content?
• How many hours a week of study are required for each course?
• How much support is there from the tutor?

I would be very grateful if you could provide me with this information.

Many thanks in advance for your assistance.

Best regards

…..

TALKING POINT
Discuss the questions with the whole class if they were not used to start the lesson.

Homework suggestions
• Ask Ss to go online and find an e-learning website that they could tell other Ss about at the start of the next lesson.
• Tell Ss that a friend has emailed them for advice. He/She is considering learning a new language, but is not sure whether to join a class, have private lessons or study online. Ss should write an email to their friend, explaining the advantages and disadvantages of the different ways of studying, and recommending the best type of course for their friend.

42

D Communication strategies
Building on ideas

Aims and objectives

In this lesson Ss will:
- consider how they feel about improvisation by doing a quiz
- read an article about the skill of improvisation
- identify different ways of accepting and rejecting ideas
- roleplay a situation

Culture and language
Building on ideas

How people handle disagreements varies greatly across cultures. In some cultures, consensus is very important. In others it is OK to agree to disagree. In Brazil, a passionate argument may demonstrate healthy enthusiasm for an idea. In Singapore, displaying too much emotion may be seen as signs of weakness and a lack of control. In Japan, people might signal they disagree by asking a string of questions. Israelis may build closeness and trust by expressing their disagreement more bluntly. Similarly, in Germany, people may appreciate a long, frank exchange of views that enables them to become more informed of the issues.

English speakers soften disagreements in many ways, but most commonly we say *Yes, but ...*. We also tend to balance disagreement with agreement fairly regularly. So we don't disagree for very long before we mention something we can agree about.

This lesson looks at ways we build on one another's ideas (see pages 42 and 43 on *Building on ideas* in Unit 4) and provides practice in balancing disagreement with agreement using expressions like, *Yes, I'll go along with that and ...*, or *Great idea! And what we could do is ...*, etc.

Reading: Improvisation skills

Ex 1 Ask Ss if they think they are planners or improvisers. Tell Ss that they are going to find out by doing a quiz. Ask Ss to answer the quiz for themselves and the check their answers on page 132.

Optional homework suggestion

Ss write an email to a friend telling them about the quiz they did in Ex 1, what they found out about themselves and whether they were surprised or not. (100–120 words)

Ex 2 Ss could discuss the questions in groups. After the activity, elicit their main ideas.

Ex 3 Discuss the question with the whole class. Ask Ss to read the text quickly to identify the writer's opinion.

The writer believes it can be learnt.

Optional homework suggestion

Ss read the article in Ex 3 again, and write an email to a friend telling them about the article and explaining whether they agree with the writer or not. (120–150 words)

Ex 4 Ss could discuss the questions in groups. Take brief feedback from the whole class.

Ex 5 Ss read the article again. Discuss any vocabulary items Ss are not sure of. Ask Ss to identify and underline the expressions.

If you like an idea:
Yes ..., and ...
That's a good idea
Sounds great to me.
I'll go along with that.

If you don't like an idea:
Yes, but ...

Ex 6 Ss work in pairs. Do an example with a student if necessary so that Ss understand the activity. Monitor and help as needed.

Ex 7 Discuss these questions with the whole class as a way of checking their work in Ex 6.

Possible answers:
1 The second conversation with 'Yes ..., and ...' should generate more ideas.
3 **Other possible expressions for resisting ideas:**
More forceful:
I don't like that idea.
Really? Do you think so?
That's a crazy idea!

Less forceful:
I don't know...
Mmm, (hesitating) that's an interesting idea.
Let's look at some other options first.

Speaking: Improvising and organizing

Ex 8 Point out that people expect to hear certain things after certain words and that this can influence the way a conversation goes. For example:

I'd love to come, unfortunately/but/however ... (negative idea)

I'd love to come, and/so/as well as ... (positive idea)

Ss work in pairs and report back to the class.

Ex 9 Discuss the questions with the whole class.

Ex 10 Ask Ss to look at the information on page 141 and discuss which prize they would like.

Photocopiable notes 4.1 (page 117)
Accepting and rejecting ideas (Card activity page 127)

Homework suggestion
Ss write a dialogue building on ideas that they read to the class at the start of the next lesson.

€ Interaction Training solutions

Aims and objectives

In this lesson Ss will:

- listen to people talking about courses they have attended
- read an advertisement giving course information
- listen to someone talking to her manager about courses
- roleplay a negotiation about going on and paying for a training course

Refer Ss to the Reminder box and draw attention to the language that the lesson will focus on. Check Ss can use this language by looking at pages 167 and 172 of the Grammar reference and at previous lessons of the unit.

Background information
NLP

Neuro-linguistic programming (NLP) is an approach that educates people in self-awareness and effective communication, and to change patterns of mental and emotional behaviour. It emphasises people's potential through overcoming learned limitations, well-being and healthy functioning. It has had an influence in management training, life coaching and the self-help industry.

Listening: Staff training needs

Ex 1 Give Ss a short time to reflect on their own experiences in pairs. The key point here is what was good about the course they did – how did it help them?

Ex 2 🔊 **1.20** Tell Ss they are going to listen to three people talking about their own work experiences. Ask them to write down what training they think the three people need.

> **Possible answers:**
> **Karen's training needs**
> She is shy/lacks confidence and needs to improve her communication skills for meetings.
>
> **Ricardo's training needs**
> He has no formal qualifications and his girlfriend says he should do a university degree and work part-time.
>
> **Nadia's training needs**
> She needs to improve her presentation skills in English because she goes to international conferences: the company has asked her to go to China for six months, so she might also need English and/or Chinese classes.

Track 1.20: 4E, Page 44, Exercise 2
Karen

I work in the R&D department. I think I'm very hard-working, but my boss tells me I'm a bit shy and lack confidence. She says I need to improve my communication skills. I always get nervous when I have to attend meetings. Actually, my boss doesn't speak very good English, so she always wants me to go with her when she has to negotiate product requirements with our clients. I prefer writing emails, although I know I need to be more confident when talking to people.

Ricardo

I help staff with any IT problems they have. I get on with everyone at work and I'm pretty good at what I do, but the job's getting a bit boring. The trouble is, I don't have any formal qualifications. I'm basically self-taught. But I'm 30 now and my girlfriend says it's a good idea to get a university degree. That way, I could get promoted and earn more money. I suppose I could work part-time and study but I'm not sure. If I study, I won't have much time to do sports – and I love skiing and playing golf.

Nadia

I think I have quite a lot of work experience at 46. I also speak fluent Swedish, Russian and German, but I really need to improve my presentations skills in English. I have to travel a lot for work, and I sometimes give presentations at international conferences in the languages I know. The thing is, the company has now asked me to go to China for six months and I don't speak Chinese! But I'm worried that if I say no, I might lose my job.

Ex 3 Ss read about different training courses. In pairs, they decide which course would be best for each one of the three speakers. Ss should justify their ideas.

> **Possible answers:**
> Karen could do the *Assertiveness* course, maybe *Presentations Across Cultures* and possibly *Advocacy and Mediation* because she attends negotiations with her boss.
>
> Ricardo could do the golf course, *Playing Golf with NLP* because he's interested in golf. The other courses are not really suitable for him because he is thinking of doing a university course.
>
> Nadia could do *Ex-pat Relocation* with some language classes and *Presentations Across Cultures*.

Optional homework suggestions

- Ss read the brochure in Ex 3 again and check that they understand all the vocabulary.
- Ss research NLP on the internet and explain it to the class the next lesson.
- Ss write an email to a friend telling them about the article and what they think of what it says. (120–150 words)

Ex 4 🔊 **1.21** Ss listen to see which course(s) Karen actually wants to do. Do they agree with her choice? Why?/Why not? What does Oskar promise to do?

> **Possible answers:**
> Karen would like to do two courses: *Assertiveness* training and *Presentations Across Cultures*. She doesn't have to do presentations at work at the moment but would like to improve her confidence when speaking in meetings, etc.
> Oskar agrees that she does both courses, but a&k will only pay for one them because they are cutting the training budget and she doesn't need presentations for her job at the moment. Oskar will confirm in writing.

Track 1.21: 4E, Page 45, Exercise 4

O = Oskar, **K** = Karen

O: Hi, Karen. As you know, I'm talking to everybody about their training needs and the courses you're interested in. Have you had any thoughts?

K: Well, I would like to do something to, er … improve my confidence and er … my communication skills.

O: Uhuh, so, which course do you want to sign up for?

K: Uh, my boss recommends the Assertiveness course, but I'm also interested in Presentations Across Cultures.

O: Yes, but do you have to give presentations in your job now, Karen?

K: No, not really.

O: Then it might be better to do a simpler course.

K: Yes, but I'd like to be able to participate more in meetings and be more confident when speaking in public, you know.

O: So you don't feel comfortable in meetings?

K: To be honest, I find it difficult but I know it's something I need to improve. Actually, I think it might be a good idea if I do both courses.

O: Two courses?

K: Yeah, if that's OK with you. Assertiveness and er … Presentations Across Cultures.

O: The thing is, a&k will definitely pay for one of the courses, but I'm afraid we won't be able to pay for both courses. You see, the situation is they're cutting the training budget this year and they're only going to pay for one course per employee for members of staff at your level.

K: Oh, so what happens if I want to do another course?

O: Well, one option is that you pay for the course yourself. Another possibility is that you wait until next year and do the presentations course then. What I'm saying is, you don't really need to do the presentations course at the moment, do you?

K: Not right now, no. I don't know. Maybe I could pay for the course myself?

O: Yes. That could be the best solution if you'd like to do both courses.

K: Yes, and it will benefit the company, too, because I think I'll be able to contribute more in meetings.

O: Great. So, we've agreed that you'll sign up for both courses, and we'll pay for one of them. I don't think there will be a problem with that. But let me check with the Human Resources Director and I'll get back to you.

K: Will you able to let me know soon, Oskar?

O: Yeah, sure. I'll put that in writing to the director and copy you in, OK?

K: Sounds good.

O: And if you have any more questions, Karen, you know where I am.

K: Thanks.

Ex 5 Ask Ss to read Oskar's email and decide what has happened.

Possible answer:
Karen has been promoted and has been asked to attend the annual a&k meeting in Copenhagen next month and present a&k's latest electronic card technology.
The company will pay for one of her courses.

Ex 6 Ss work in pairs to do the roleplay. The focus here is on the language of persuading and negotiating.

Ex 7 Discuss the question with the whole class.

Speaking: Persuading the boss

Ex 8 Give Ss five minutes to prepare their roles individually and five minutes to roleplay the situation in pairs. Monitor the Ss and help if necessary. After the activity, give feedback on how successful their negotiation was and whether they will be able to do their course or not.

Photocopiable notes 4.2 (page 118)
The appraisal meeting (Roleplay page 128)

Homework suggestion
Ss write an email to a friend telling them about a training course they have completed that they thought was either very good or very bad. In the email Ss should describe the course and give reasons for what they think of it. (120–150 words)

5

A Present perfect and past simple
B *used to*
C Conversation topics
D **Communication strategies** Socializing
E **Interaction** Choosing a candidate

Getting on

A Present perfect and past simple

Aims and objectives

In this lesson Ss will:
* read about famous talented people
* study uses of past simple and present perfect tenses
* study uses of *for* and *since*
* speak about talented people in their own country

Reading: Talented people

Ex 1 This introduces the topic of the lesson by getting Ss to think about talented people. Ask Ss what they know about the people in the photos.

1 Japanese writer Haruki Murakami
2 Spanish tennis player Rafael Nadal
3 Australian actress Cate Blanchett

Ex 2 Ss read the texts quickly to match the profiles to the photos. This could be done as a competition – the winner matches the texts first. This encourages Ss not to worry about unknown words.

Profile A: Rafael Nadal – photo 2
Profile B: Cate Blanchett – photo 3
Profile C: Haruki Murakami – photo 1

Ex 3 Ss discuss in pairs.

Optional homework suggestion

For homework Ss could research the celebrities and report back on their findings to the class the next lesson. Ss should use the present perfect tense in their reports.

Ex 4 Ss work in pairs to find the answers.

1 Cate Blanchett and Haruki Murakami
2 Rafael Nadal
3 Rafael Nadal and Haruki Murakami
4 Cate Blanchett and Haruki Murakami
5 Haruki Murakami
6 Rafael Nadal and Haruki Murakami

Ex 5 Ask Ss to work in pairs to list reasons for their choice of personality and what they would like to talk about.

Optional activity: Do the activity as a game. Ss think about the questions they would like to ask their chosen personality, then they tell the rest of the class, who guess which personality it is.

Ex 6 This exercise focuses on key vocabulary. Ss work in pairs and either list the words for each topic or produce a mind map of the topic areas on the board for the class to complete.

Sports: sportsman, tennis, professional, coach, win, singles titles, gold medal, French/US/Australian Open, Olympic Games, player, Grand Slam, clay court

Films: performer, cinema screens, play roles, starred, actors, acting awards, Academy Award, Best Supporting Actress, Oscar, director

Books: writer, literature, culture, author, novels, international bestseller, (Franz Kafka) Prize, writing, books, translator, works, translated, translations, languages

Optional homework suggestion

Ss research a personality they are interested in and produce a paragraph similar to the ones in the coursebook. Ss bring their paragraphs in to the next lesson for other Ss to read. Ss explain to the class why they chose this celebrity.

Grammar: Present perfect and past simple

Ex 7 Go through the information in the box with the class. Ask Ss to suggest other example sentences as you go through it. Ss work in pairs to underline the examples in the article, and explain why the sentence is in present perfect or past simple.

1 past simple – became
2 present perfect – hasn't received
3 present perfect – have been
4 present perfect – has just won

Optional suggestion: Refer Ss to pages 161 and 163 of the Grammar reference and go through the notes on present perfect and past simple tenses. Allow time to discuss examples and any problems Ss have. Provide further examples if required.

Ex 8 Ss work in pairs to find other examples in the texts. Ss explain to each other why these examples use the present perfect or the past simple.

Nadal
… sportsman has taken the tennis world by storm in recent years.
He has been especially successful on clay courts …

Both describe situations that started in the past and which are continuing now.

Blanchett

She has played diverse roles such as …
She has starred alongside famous actors such as …
She has won several acting awards.

These sentences describe life experiences in an indefinite time in the past.

Murakami

Since childhood, Western culture has influenced him …

This describes a situation that started in the past and which is continuing now.

… and has translated his own novels into English.
This describes the present result of a past action.

Refer Ss to the **Watch out!** box. Ask Ss if they know the difference in use between these three words and to suggest a sentence for each one. Go through the information in the box with the class. Ask Ss to suggest other example sentences as you go. If asked, point out that with some verbs like *live* and *work* there may be little difference in meaning between the present perfect simple and continuous, e.g. *I have lived here for five years. / I have been living here for five years.* There is more work on the present perfect continuous in Unit 11 and in the Grammar reference on Page 162.

Photocopiable notes 5.1 (page 118)
Talking about the past (Card activity page 129)

Ex 9 Ss work in pairs to discuss the uses of *for* and *since*. Ss could also write a sentence for each time expression.

for: many years, ages, two minutes, 15 years, a long time, months
since: 2007, May, he was 15, last Monday

Ex 10 Ss discuss the sentences in pairs.

1a, 2b – the event has happened sometime in the past.
1b, 2a – the event is expected in the future.

Ex 11 Ss work in pairs to find the true sentences. Ask Ss to write their sentences using *yet* and *already* in pairs, and then exchange their sentences with another pair to check.

1 a is true for Cate Blanchett
2 b is true for Rafael Nadal

Ex 12 Ss ask their partner their questions and choose the most interesting one. Each pair asks the class their most interesting question.

Answers and suggested questions:

1 Who has been Nadal's main rival since 2004? – Roger Federer
2 How have people described this special rivalry? – the greatest in tennis history
3 How long was Nadal World No. 2 behind Federer? – 160 (weeks)
4 Where has Cate Blanchett lived (with her family) for the last few years? – in Sydney
5 When did she/they renovate their mansion house? – in 2007
6 What has she been ambassador of since 2007? – an Australian conservation campaign for climate change
7 What (special edition) has she/Blanchett appeared in? – postage stamps

8 How many vinyl records has Murakami collected? – 7,000
9 When did he start running? – (when he was) 33
10 What is the name of his autobiography? – *What I talk about when I talk about running*

Optional activity: Play a True/false game. In this game, Ss write sentences about five events in their life. Three events must be true and two should be false. Ss work in pairs or groups. Ss take it in turns to ask each other three questions about each event. Their partner or the group then decides which events are true and which are false.

I've met a famous sports star.

Who did you meet? Where did you meet him/her? What did you say to him/her?

Speaking: 'A' list

Ex 13 Ss could also do this exercise in pairs and then exchange their sentences with another pair. Other categories could include: best film director, composer, dancer, artist, poet, TV presenter, politician, tennis player, etc.

Ex 14 Ss work in pairs or in groups of four to compare their ideas. If Ss don't want to vote for famous people from their own country, they could make a list of famous people around the world. For example:

Argentinean football player: Messi

American actress: Meryl Streep

British writer: J.K. Rowling

Italian opera singer: Andrea Boccelli

American business entrepreneur: Donald Trump

Catalan chef: Ferram Adria

British artist: Damien Hirst

America actor – Matt Damon

TALKING POINT

Talking point 1 could be used for written homework.
Talking point 2 could be done as a formal debate. Divide the class into two halves. One half should think of ideas to support the question and the other half should think of ideas to disprove it.

Homework suggestions

● Using Talking point 1, Ss write an email to a friend explaining who they suggest as the most talented personality of their generation and why. (120–150 words)
● After discussing their sentences in Ex 13, Ss write a short report on a celebrity of their choice or a short report on the class's chosen 'A' list. (100–130 words)
● Tell Ss that there is going to be a competition in which people can submit an article to a magazine describing a famous person and why they would like to meet this person. Ss should write an article. (120–150 words)

β used to

Aims and objectives

In this lesson Ss will:
- read an article about a person who changed his career
- study ways of expressing present and past habits (used to)
- discuss personal changes in their lives

Reading: Career change

Ex 1 To introduce the idea of choosing a career, ask Ss to discuss the question in groups.

Ex 2 This exercise helps Ss think about the topic of the reading text. Ss make notes of their ideas in pairs and then read the article to compare.

> **Possible answers:**
> An investment banker earns more money.
> A photojournalist travels more than an investment banker.
> A photojournalist has flexible working hours; an investment banker has to work long hours in an office.
> The life of a photojournalist is probably more exciting; the job of an investment banker might be more boring, but more secure.

Ex 3 Ss work alone to find the evidence, so that when they compare their answers with a partner, they have to explain and justify their ideas.

> **Possible answers:**
> 1 As an investment banker, Marcus Bleasdale used to earn £500,000 a year. By 30 he was the owner of two houses, a Porsche, and he spent weekends skiing in the Alps.
> 2 '… it's not that glamorous. I didn't want to be sitting in front of computer screens when I was 40. And when talking to a colleague about the Balkans, I knew I didn't want to be a banker any more.'
> 3 He suddenly decided to go the Balkans. Within 24 hours he was on a plane to the Balkans.
> 4 He won an award for best young photojournalist. Bleasdale has worked for *Time*, *Newsweek* and *National Geographic*.
> 5 He spent some of his savings on an orphanage in eastern Congo.
> 6 'I think I appreciate life a lot more. I think I'm more sensitive. I'm a nicer guy.'

Ex 4 Ss discuss in pairs. Extend the discussion by asking them which of the two jobs they would prefer to do and why.

Grammar: used to

Ex 5 Write three sentences on the board and ask Ss to explain the difference in meaning: *I used to smoke. I didn't use to smoke. I usually smoke after dinner.* Ask Ss to read the information in the box and choose the correct options.

> 1 past   2 past simple   3 present simple

Optional suggestion: Refer Ss to pages 164 of the Grammar reference and go through the notes on *used to*. Allow time to discuss examples and any problems Ss have. Provide further examples if required.

Ex 6 Ss complete the sentences, checking the information from the reading text.

> | | |
> |---|---|
> | 1 used to help | 5 used to wear |
> | 2 used to say | 6 didn't use to appreciate |
> | 3 used to eat out | 7 used to love |
> | 4 used to sit | 8 used to live |

Speaking: Guess what I used to do

Ex 7 Go through the instructions with the class. Tell Ss that they are going to read different texts and ask and answer questions about it. With a weaker group, do the first one together with the class as an example. Then ask Ss to read their own texts and write their own sentences. Monitor them and help where necessary. When all Ss have finished their sentences, ask Ss to work in pairs and ask each other questions about their sentences.

Ex 8 Ask Ss to think of three significant changes in their life. These changes should be things they are happy to talk about and share. Ss then work in pairs to ask each other questions about the change.

Optional activity: Tell Ss to imagine that they are attending a job interview and have been asked to present a short professional profile talking about your qualifications and previous work experience. Give Ss five minutes to prepare their presentations. Ss can then work in groups to present their profiles and ask questions.

TALKING POINT
This can be done for homework (see notes below) or discussed with the whole class.

Homework suggestions
- Using Talking point 1, Ss write an email to a friend telling them about a job they would like to do for a month or a year.
- Using Talking point 2, Ss write a short paragraph about a person they know of who has re-invented him or herself. This could be a celebrity rather than someone they know personally if they wish.
- Ss write an email to a friend telling them about a change they have made (or their partner has made) in their life, why they made the change, any further details about it and how they feel about the change. (120–150 words)

C Conversation topics

Aims and objectives

In this lesson Ss will:
- identify topics often involved in social conversation (small talk)
- read about someone explaining their favourite small talk topics
- listen to four people starting social conversations
- practise small talk with a partner

Background information
Small talk

In most English-speaking countries, people make 'small talk' in certain situations. This is a casual form of light conversation that 'breaks the ice' or fills awkward silences with people you don't know well. It can be difficult to do successfully, because people may not be confident about their conversational skills, or the person they want to talk to may not want to answer, or may have nothing to say on the chosen topic. There may also be cultural differences, so people may not want to start a conversation until they have established common ground. To make small talk easier:

• ask people about themselves. This is polite and gets the conversation going.

• listen carefully to what the other person says so that you can show interest and ask follow-up questions.

• ask about the other person's background, family, friends or acquaintances you may have in common, which will establish a relationship with them.

• keep yourself informed on a variety of different topics including what's in the news so you can converse with people from different backgrounds.

• keep the conversation casual and light. This may mean not always expressing your real opinion.

• avoid controversial topics which could make the other person feel defensive and lead to an argument. Topics to avoid include religion and politics. Good small talk topics include: current weather and climate change; hobbies and interests; sports; family and family life; recent television programmes or films; holidays; hometown and general background; general information about work and jobs; gossip about famous people; interesting events in the news (but not anything controversial).

Listening: Making small talk

Ex 1 Ask Ss what they think 'small talk' is. Explain that it may be used with acquaintances rather than friends and that this is important because the topics tend to be bland and unimportant. Ss look at the words in the box in Ex 1 and find the topics.

> **26 topics:**
> television, sports, politics, fashion, art, novels, family, architecture, the economic climate, music, pets, the weather, religion, food and restaurants, travel experiences, holiday plans, the news, salaries, your hometown, health, weekend activities, films and cinema, your job, hobbies, celebrity gossip, festivals

Ex 2 Ss compare their favourite topics in pairs. Then they make a list of unsuitable topics in local situations and discuss why there are unsuitable. Take feedback from the whole class and see if there are any common favourite topics.

> **Suggestions:**
> The topic may be controversial and cause arguments.
> It may be on a specialist area that not everyone can talk about.
> It may make someone look silly if they have nothing to say.
> It may demand personal information.

Optional activity: Ss could work in pairs to draw up a short list of five good topics and five unsuitable topics. For example:

Good: weather, food and restaurants, holiday plans, weekend activities, family, hobbies (all uncontroversial and people would have something to say)

Unsuitable: politics, religion, the news (could be controversial and polarizing), salaries, health (could be too personal)

Ex 3 Ss read the blog entry and answer the questions in pairs.

> Her favourite small talk topics are: weather, travel, books (what are you reading?), movies, kids, pets.
> She has a theory that everyone knows a beautiful place in their town.
> She asks her customers lots of questions.

Ex 4 Ss discuss their four situations in pairs. Take feedback with the whole class, and find out if there are any interesting or unusual topics of conversation that were not mentioned in Ex 1.

Ex 5 🔊 **1.22** Tell Ss they are going to listen to six people starting conversations and identify the main topic of each conversation. Before playing the recording, ask Ss to read the topics in the box.

> **1** weekend activities   **4** work
> **2** the weather   **5** the town
> **3** the news   **6** the physical environment

Track 1.22: 5C, Page 50, Exercise 5 and 6

1 Are you going to watch the match on Saturday?

2 Can you believe the rain we're having this week?

3 Have you heard the news about the physics experiment in Switzerland?

4 I hear that the big boss is coming from France next week.

5 What do you think of that new shopping centre?

6 Have you seen the beautiful spring flowers outside the office?

Ex 6 🔊 Ss read the questions and think about what the person might have said. Ask Ss to compare their ideas with a partner. Then play the recording for Ss to check their ideas and complete the questions.

> **1** going to watch   **4** I hear that
> **2** Can … believe   **5** you think of
> **3** heard the news about **6** Have … seen

Ex 7 Ss discuss their ideas in pairs.

> **Suggestions:**
> **1** You bet. / Absolutely. / I wouldn't miss it. / Who's playing?
> **2** I know! It's terrible. Still, it's good for the grass.
> **3** Yes, isn't it amazing! / No, I didn't watch the news. What happened?
> **4** Yes, we're all really nervous about it.
> **5** It's great. / I haven't been there yet. / It's an ugly-looking building.
> **6** Yes, aren't they wonderful! / Yes, I noticed them as I came in.

Ex 8 Ss work in pairs to practise some small talk conversations. Monitor and help where necessary. Take feedback and find out if Ss found it easy or difficult, and why.

Ex 9 🔊 **1.23** Tell Ss they are going to listen to two conversations to identify which one doesn't begin with small talk, and explain why.

> Conversation 2 uses small talk. Marco sounds friendlier than Paul because he asks personal questions and makes small talk, while Paul talks directly about work. When people are very busy and they feel small talk is a waste of time.

Track 1.23: 5C, Page 50, Exercises 9 and 10

P = Paul, **M** = Marco

Conversation 1

P: Hi, Marco, it's Paul. Sorry to call you first thing on a Monday morning. It's about a problem we're having with this new database.

M: I'm sorry to hear that. What seems to be the problem?

P: You see we can't get access to all the fields. Is some of it password protected?

Conversation 2

M = Marco, **P** = Paul

M: Hi, Paul, it's Marco here. How are you? I hear the weather's been bad up north recently.

P: That's right. It's been snowing heavily, and apparently some villages had no electricity.

M: Did it affect you?

P: No, not much, happy to say. Didn't play football on Saturday, that's about all. And yourself? Did you have a good weekend?

M: Fine, thanks. Just relaxed with the family, and I had lunch with my in-laws on Sunday. Anyway, Paul, I was just phoning to check if you've tried out the modified version of that database.

P: Yes, we're working on it now in fact. It all seems to be working fine.

Ex 10))) Ss listen for an expression that indicates the end of small talk and the start of work-related conversation.

> Marco moves from small talk to work talk by saying 'Anyway' to change the subject.

Word focus: Conversation topics

Ex 11 Ss identify the topics in pairs. Take class feedback and do pronunciation practice of any words Ss may be unsure of. This is important as they are key words for small talk.

> 1 Topic: weather. Exception: exhibition (this is an event)
> 2 Topic: fashion. Exception: flu (this is an illness)
> 3 Topic: films. Exception: main course (this is part of a meal)
> 4 Topic: (local) politics. Exception: author (an author is related to books in general)
> 5 Topic: travel. Exception: tie (this is a fashion item)
> 6 Topic: family. Exception: library (this is a building)

Optional activity: Write the words on the board that do not belong to each group. Ss could then suggest other words that could be connected to the words on the board and a topic that they could be used with.

Ex 12 Ss work in pairs. Again, do pronunciation practice of any words Ss may not be familiar with.

> 1 weather: freezing, shower.
> *Other suggestions:* rain, snow, wind, hurricane, drought
> 2 fashion: T-shirt, flip-flops
> *Other suggestions:* dressed up, sleeveless top, trainers, handbag
> 3 films: soundtrack, director
> *Other suggestions:* Oscars, comedy, cinema
> 4 (local) politics: politician, vote
> *Other suggestions:* council, civil servant, corruption
> 5 travel: check in, traffic jam
> *Other suggestions:* return ticket, vaccination, economy class, three-star hotel

> 6 family: niece, daughter
> *Other suggestions:* son, uncle, get-together, relatives, close family

Ex 13 Ss work in pairs. Tell them that they may use dictionaries. Do pronunciation practice of any unfamiliar words.

Speaking: Keep talking

Ex 14 Go through the rules for the game with the class and make sure they understand what to do. Then put Ss into pairs and give them the coins (or counters) they need to play the game with. Monitor the game and give help as needed. During feedback, discuss the subjects Ss talked about and any language problems which may have arisen.

> **Photocopiable notes 5.2 (page 118)**
> **Small talk (Card activity page 129)**

Optional activity: Ss work in groups. Give Ss a topic to talk about and dictate four words for the topic. One S in the group talks on the topic for one minute and must use the four words in the talk. The others in the group listen and give a point for each word used. After a minute, stop the discussion and give a new topic and different words for the next S to talk about.

Homework suggestions

- Ss write an email to a friend describing a conversation they had at work and what happened. (100–120 words)
- Ss write a short dialogue on one of the topics from the game in Ex 14 and read it to the class next lesson.
- Ss read the text in Ex 3 again. Then they write a short paragraph on a topic that they like talking about and explain why.

D Communication strategies
Socializing

Aims and objectives

In this lesson Ss will:
- discuss differences in social situation in different cultures
- listen to people greeting and responding to each other
- read a travel blog about social customs in North America
- roleplay social situations responding to compliments

> ### Culture and language
> #### Socializing (greetings and compliments)
>
> English speakers use compliments in many different contexts. For example, we might say *You look well* when we greet someone we haven't seen for a while, or we might say *That was a great meal* to our host when we are thanking them.
>
> In the US, compliments can also serve as an invitation to begin a conversation with a stranger. So, for example, someone might say *I love your bag* to a fellow passenger in an elevator (BrE *lift*) to signal they are willing to talk. This use of compliments may seem insincere to some students. Be ready to discuss the fact that compliments can be rituals (sets of actions that are always done in the same way) that fulfil a social function.

At a Chinese banquet, for example, a long exchange of compliments could be part of a greeting ritual. In the US, a compliment can be part of a greeting ritual, too, and it shouldn't be mistaken for fake friendliness.

Many languages have ritual greetings that can't be interpreted literally. For example, a Taiwanese speaker might greet someone by asking *Have you eaten yet?*, when they have no intention of sharing a meal. Similarly, a Tagalog speaker might greet a friend with *Where are you going?* and the appropriate answer would simply be, *Over there*. Rituals can play an important role in building and maintaining relationships.

Paying people compliments may seem like an easy way to win friends. After all, it is human nature to desire approval. But paying a compliment can also be problematic. In some contexts it could be an intrusion because the receiver may think 'What right have you got to pass judgement about me?' Or the receiver might wonder if we are expecting something in return, or feel obliged to pay us back. So we risk being seen as fishing for compliments ourselves.

Responding to compliments can be equally problematic because there are two competing social pressures. On the one hand, it is polite to be agreeable and not to contradict. Disagreeing with a compliment might suggest that we think someone is stupid to admire something that we don't. On the other hand, we want to appear modest. Accepting a compliment might make us appear conceited or bigheaded.

There are cultural differences in the way we give and receive compliments that relate to politeness. When asked, many AmE speakers say the polite way to respond to compliments is say *thank you* and accept them. However, research shows that in practice, they generally don't. The requirement for modesty is powerful, so like the rest of the world, AmE speakers use a variety of strategies to avoid accepting them. For example, they might downgrade the praise so it sounds less important or they may share the praise with other people. (See pages 52 and 53 on *Socializing* in unit 5.)

Be ready to explore ways in which English-speaking customs for complimenting may differ from your students as you work through the situations in this lesson.

Listening: Meeting and greeting

Ex 1 Give Ss time to think about each point in turn in groups. Ss could tell anecdotes if appropriate.

Ex 2 🔊 **1.24** Before playing the recording, ask Ss to read the responses. Explain that Ss are going to listen to six greetings and choose the best response. After listening, ask Ss to compare and explain their answers in pairs.

1 c 2 b 3 a 4 b 5 c 6 a

Track 1.24: 5D, Page 52, Exercise 2

1 Hi! How's it going?

2 You must be Günter. I'm Miriam from R&D. It's nice to finally put a face to a voice.

3 Hi. I don't think we've met before. I'm Sandra Mendelssohn.

4 Hey, what's up?

5 Hi, you're David, Carla's assistant, aren't you?

6 Hello, Irina. Mind if I join you?

Ex 3 Tell Ss that greetings and responses may be different depending on how close the relationship is. Ask Ss to discuss in pairs the relationship between the people they listened to in Ex 2.

Then refer them to the information in the **Watch out!** box and tell them that it is equally important to respond to a greeting appropriately.

The people in conversations 1, 4 and 6 know each other in person.
The people in conversation 2 are meeting face-to-face for the first time, but know each other probably from phone contact.
The people in conversation 3 are meeting for the first time.
In conversation 5 it seems that they are meeting for the first time, too, or David has forgotten meeting the woman before.
Conversations 1 and 4 are the least formal.

Ex 4 Ask Ss to work in pairs to complete the gaps and to discuss any other greeting they may know.

up?
it going?

Ex 5 Ask Ss to work in pairs to discuss the different responses and situations. Monitor and check ideas with the whole class.

Possible answers:
1 **b** *She's fine. Thanks for asking.*
   = When someone asks how a female family member or colleague is; e.g. *How's your wife?*
2 **a** *Yes, it's been a long time since the last conference.*
   = When someone comments they haven't seen you for a long time; e.g. *How are you? I haven't seen you for ages.*
   c *You haven't changed a bit either!*
   = When someone comments that you look the same as ever; e.g. *You don't look a day older than you did five years ago.*
3 **b** *Great to see you again, too, Sandra. How have you been?*
   = When you're responding to someone you already know in a greeting, and who says something like *It's good to see you again.*
   c *So, where are you working now?*
   = When you're responding to someone who has just told you they've changed jobs or left their old company; e.g. *I've moved on from Peterson's you know.*
4 **a** *No, it's old. I've had it for ages.*
   = When you're responding to someone who asks you if something you're wearing is new; e.g. *Like your shirt. Is it new?*
   c *No, I haven't watched the news today.*
   = When you're responding to someone who wants to comment on a news story and has said something like; *Did you hear about those terrible forest fires in California?*
5 **a** *Of course.*
   = When you're responding positively to someone who has made a short, small request; e.g. *Can I take this chair?*

b *Can I have your name, please?*
= When a visitor has arrived at the reception desk where you work and may say, e.g. *I have an appointment with Mrs Jones.*
6 b *Yes, I'll join you later.*
= When you're responding to someone who asks you to go somewhere with them; e.g. *Coming for lunch, Sue?*
c *I don't mind.*
= When you're responding to someone who asks you about your preference, e.g. *Do you want the pink one or the yellow one?*

Reading: Compliments

Ex 6 Remind Ss what a blog is. Ss read the text and discuss the similarities and differences in pairs. Ask Ss to underline the compliments and responses in the text. (*I love your coat. Thanks, I like your coat, too. Oh, it's old – nothing special, Thanks.*)

Optional homework suggestion

Ss read Ex 6 again and write a contribution to the blog about their own country or a country they have visited. (100–120 words)

Ex 7 Ask Ss to work in pairs and respond to the compliments. Point out that there is no right answer in this exercise. Ss could discuss why they think they would respond in this way. This discussion leads on to Ex 8.

Ex 8 Ss read about different strategies that are used to respond to compliments. Ss work in pairs to match the strategies to the responses they discussed in Ex 7.

Strategy	Examples
Accepting the compliment	1c, 3a, 4b
Responding with a compliment	2a
Questioning the compliment	1b, 2c
Sharing the praise with someone else	5a, 5b
Downgrading the praise so it seems less important	2b, 3b, 3c, 4a, 4c, 5c
Giving an explanation	3a, 4b
Joking	1a, 3c

Ex 9 Ss work in pairs to make up compliments and discuss when they could be used.

Suggestions:
1 Your apartment is beautiful. / Your hair is really nice.
2 That workshop was really great. / That meal was really good.
3 I really liked your presentation. / I love your accent.
4 That was a really fantastic/enjoyable party.
5 This is a good idea. / This is a nice restaurant.

Speaking: Social chit-chat

Ex 10 and Ex 11 Both these exercises are good for mingling and getting Ss to work with different people. Ss work in pairs to complete the roleplays, then move on to a different partner. After the activity ask Ss to discuss the strategies they used and give reasons for their choice, e.g. *I felt uncomfortable accepting praise so I downgraded the compliment.*

Homework suggestions

• Ss write a short dialogue from one of the situations in Ex 10 or 11, which they can read out to the class at the start of the next lesson.
• Ss prepare two compliments that they can pay to other Ss in the class the next lesson.

E Interaction Choosing a candidate

Aims and objectives

In this lesson Ss will:
• listen to people talking about social enterprise
• read an advertisement offering an award for social enterprise
• do a roleplay discussing the finalists for the award and choosing a winner

Refer Ss to the Reminder box and draw attention to the language that the lesson will focus on. Check Ss can use this language by looking at pages 161 and 163 of the Grammar reference and at previous lessons of the unit.

Background information
Social enterprises

Social enterprises are organizations which trade in goods or services for a social or environmental purpose. They often use blended value business models that combine a revenue-generating business with a social aim, which is central to what they do. They use their profits to further their social and environmental goals.

Listening: Social enterprise

Ex 1 🔊 **1.25** Ask Ss what they think social enterprises are. Give Ss a short time to discuss in pairs anything they might know about social enterprise. Before playing the recording ask Ss to read the definitions and discuss the missing words.

1	goods or services	4	profits
2	business strategies	5	pockets
3	social causes		

Track 1.25: 5E, Page 54, Exercises 1 and 2
Part one
P = Presenter, **Z** = Zahir

P: Zahir Rahman has received many social enterprise awards. I spoke to him earlier today. Zahir, what is a social enterprise?

Z: It's basically an organization that provides goods or services like any other business, and uses the same business strategies.

P: So, how are social enterprises different from a commercial business?

Z: Well, like the name suggests, they focus on social causes and needs. It's central to what we do. But er, one of the main differences is that with er, with social enterprise the profits generated are put back into the business rather than going into the pockets of owners or shareholders.

P: Can you give me some examples?

Z: Sure. For instance, it can be a company that promotes better health. There are lots and lots of examples all over the world. It could be a company that helps old people.

Another example is a company that provides transport for remote communities. Some people talk about 'not-for-profit' organizations, but I prefer to call it 'more-than-profit'. It doesn't mean not for money, but the money's going back into the quality of service.

Ex 2 🔊 Play the recording again so that Ss can make notes.

- a company that promotes better health
- a company that helps old people
- a company that provides transport for remote communities

Ex 3 🔊 **1.26** Tell Ss they are going to listen to the second part of the interview and correct the information. Ask Ss to read the sentences first before they listen to the recording.

1 Zahir Rahman has run his social enterprise for ~~twelve~~ ten years.
2 He has more than ~~118,000~~ 180,000 customers today.
3 He thinks that a social entrepreneur is an ~~inventor~~ innovator.
4 He qualified in ~~engineering~~ economics.
5 He ~~went to live~~ left the US twelve years ago.
6 He has just started a ~~clean water~~ low-cost mobile phone company.

Track 1.26: 5E, Page 54, Exercise 3

Part two

P = Presenter, **Z** = Zahir

P: You started selling solar panels to poor communities in your native Bangladesh ten years ago, and today you have more than 180,000 customers. You call yourself a social entrepreneur. What does that mean exactly?

Z: I like to think I'm an innovator. A social entrepreneur is someone who identifies a social problem and then organizes and manages a business that will make change.

P: You studied economics. So, what made you want to be a social entrepreneur?

Z: I wanted to do some good, something ethical. Just making money isn't enough for me. When I left the US twelve years ago and came back home, I had very little money. I moved to a rural area, and lived in a house without electricity because I wanted to find out what it was like in those conditions. That gave me the idea for my first business. Having very little money helped me to be more innovative.

P: What projects are you working on now?

Z: Well, I've just started a low-cost mobile phone company. The batteries are solar powered. It's a very exciting project.

Ex 4 Ss could discuss the question in groups.

Ex 5 Explain that there is a social enterprise award. Ask Ss to read the advertisement and answer the questions.

The *Daily Times* newspaper and the Northern Hibernia Bank are offering the award.
The prize includes £300,000 for the winner, £200,000 divided between the other three finalists, a consultation service from a leading social entrepreneurs and publicity in the *Daily Times*.

Speaking: Four finalists

Ex 6 The following exercises in this section lead to the final roleplay and writing exercise. Tell Ss that they are going to prepare for a roleplay. Ask them to work in pairs to read and ask each other questions to complete their information.

1 When did Top Note Orchestra start? – ten (years ago)
2 How many young musicians has Top Note trained? – 400
3 Where has the orchestra given concerts? – all over the country
4 What does TNO do with the money from the concerts? – buy more instruments
5 When did D'Silva Arts Centre start? – four (years ago)
6 When did Carla graduate from art school? – (in) 2005
7 What did she open with her prize money and government grants? – an arts centre
8 Who has the D'Silva Arts Centre helped? – thousands of mentally ill (people)
9 What did employees do after cuts in the service? – bought the centre
10 What type of policy does CLU operate? – a flexible pricing (policy)
11 How many jobs has CLU created? – 350
12 Who does CLU provide financial support for? – talented young sports (people)
13 How many restaurants does Jamie run? – three
14 How many cookbooks has he written? – eight
15 How long do they train apprentices for? – six (months)
16 What percentage of apprentices have found permanent jobs? – 80 (%)

Ex 7 Ss read the information and roleplay the small talk.

Ex 8 Ss work in pairs and decide on the strongest candidate. Give Ss time to explain the reasons for their choice to the rest of the class.

Ex 9 🔊 **1.27** Ss listen to the finalists talking to the judges and make notes on what they say. To help them, tell Ss to listen for the candidates' future hopes and future plans for the company.

David Horn
- hopes to get a contract with a music company
- plans to set up similar projects in poor communities in other parts of the country
- give concerts in other countries

Carla D'Silva
- wants to create sculpture gardens on neglected land
- expand the art therapy to prisoners
- open a café at the arts centre

Sally Warren
- They want to negotiate with other local councils to run their sports and leisure facilities and take sport to everyone in the community.

Jamie Barnes
- wants to continue expanding the chain of restaurants in London and set up a catering service
- He's also thinking of selling his own range of food. This will create more jobs.

Track 1.27: 5E, Page 55, Exercise 9

David Horn

We're hoping to get a contract with a music company. The idea is that sales from our music will go back into the orchestra. I also plan to set up similar projects in poor communities in other parts of the country. But the most immediate project for us is to give concerts in other countries. Can you imagine how exciting this travel experience will be for these youngsters?

Carla D'Silva

I would like to create sculpture gardens on neglected land, something the local community can be proud of. If I win this award and get publicity, the local council will be more interested in working with us. I would also like to expand the art therapy to prisoners and I've already had a lot of interest from the prison service. And I want to open a café at the arts centre to get more people coming here.

Sally Warren

This award will bring us a lot of prestige. We want to negotiate with other local councils to run their sports and leisure facilities for them. We have shown our ability to run a profitable business and cut costs without cutting quality in three centres already. But most of all, we want to take sport to everyone in the community.

Jamie Barnes

I want to continue expanding the chain of restaurants in London. And set up a catering service for companies and individuals. It will be run as a commercial business just like the restaurants, and we'll also train apprentices at the same time. I'm also thinking of selling my own range of food. This will create more jobs.

Ex 10 This discussion is divided into sections. Give Ss time to debate each part, but make sure that they can justify their ideas. Tell them that they should make notes on what is decided as they will have to write an article about it.

In one-to-one classes, discuss the ideas with the S.

Writing: Choosing the winner

Ex 11 This article should cover all of the points discussed in Ex 10. Tell Ss to write 120–150 words. It could be set for homework or done in class.

Sample answer:

Social entrepreneurs of the year

The Daily Times newspaper and Northern Hibernia Bank are pleased to announce the winners of our fourth annual Social Enterprise Awards. Every year we give away £500,000 to social enterprises that have innovative ideas to achieve social change.

This year the top award of £300,000 goes to Sally Warren and City Leisure Unlimited, a company that works to keep the whole community fit and health. People of all ages and income levels are welcome at their gyms. The organization also provides financial support for young sports talent. Everyone is a winner at CLU.

Runner-up prizes of £80,000 each go to the David Horn and Top Note Orchestra which brings joy to many people with their youth orchestra and Jamie Barnes whose restaurants teach apprentices how to work in the industry. Artist Carla D'Silva receives £40,000 for her innovative projects bringing art to the community.

Homework suggestions

• Ask Ss to research a social enterprise organization and write a short paragraph about the company and what it does. (100–130 words)

• Ask Ss to write a short essay discussing the statement 'The only purpose of business is to make money for shareholders'. Ss should think of two points to support the statement, two points against it and then give their own opinion. (120–150 words)

• Ask Ss to read the audio script for Ex 1 and record any useful vocabulary.

6
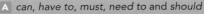

A *can, have to, must, need to* and *should*
B Obligation in the past
C Writing emails 1
D **Communication strategies** Giving advice
E **Interaction** Helping new people

Rule of thumb

A can, have to, must, need to and should

Aims and objectives

In this lesson Ss will:
- consider what makes a good workplace
- read about a successful company
- study uses modal verbs of obligation
- talk about unwritten rules of behaviour in different situations

Reading: Happy Computers

Ex 1 Ask Ss to discuss their ideas in pairs. Write suggestions from each pair on the board, so that they can compare them with the reading text.

> **Possible answers:**
> friendly boss, nice colleagues, good salaries, interesting work, career prospects

Ex 2 Ask Ss to read the texts quickly and find three good things about the company. Tell Ss not to worry about new vocabulary at this stage, but point out the glossed words to help them. Give Ss time to compare their answers with a partner before taking class feedback.

Add new good things to the list on the board. Ss rank the reasons and share their top five.

> **Possible answers:**
> Flexible working hours, freedom, responsibility, a trusting boss, team-based bonuses, openness about pay, staff participation in business and financial decisions.

Background information

Happy Computers

Happy Computers is a UK computer training company which believes that learning should be fun. It combines technical expertise and excellent training skills with an enjoyable learning environment. Its training is based around the principle 'tell me and I will forget, show me and I will remember, involve me and I will understand'. It is in the top 50 IT training companies for size and prides itself on its customer service and satisfaction.

Ex 3 Ask Ss to read the statements, which are all true. Ss read the text again in detail to find and underline the information in the text proving that these statements are correct. Ss work in pairs, discuss and justify their ideas before plenary feedback.

Ask Ss if there were any words they didn't understand. Before explaining, give Ss time to try to work out the meaning for themselves.

> 1 ' … There are no specific rules. The simple reason that you need to have flexi-time is good enough for us to give it to you.' There are no rules such as 'You should work from 9 to 5'.
> 2 'It worked out very well because he was much more productive on the other four days.'
> 3 Originally focused on IT training, the 50-employee company now also offers management and personal development courses as well.
> 4 He lets staff participate in business and financial decisions and allows them to vote on most major decisions. They can also have a say in pay rises and bonuses, which are all team-based and set by staff.
> 5 'Nothing is secret. We're very open about things like finances and people's salaries.'
> 6 Happy doesn't need to pay for recruitment agencies or job advertisements. It currently has about 2,000 people signed up to receive information when a position at the company becomes available.

Optional activity: Ss pick their own words from the text, put them in sentences and ask their partner to paraphrase or identify them.

Optional homework suggestions

- Ss produce a flyer that Happy Computers could circulate to companies to advertise its training courses. You could suggest that Ss look at Happy's website for ideas, but tell them not to 'lift' the language – they should paraphrase.
- Ss write an email to a friend telling them about Happy Computers and saying what they think of the company and why. (100–130 words)

Grammar: *can, have to, must, need to* and *should*

Ex 4 Go through the information in the table with the class. Ask Ss to suggest other example sentences. Make sure Ss understand the different functions. Then Ss work in pairs to underline examples of modal verbs of obligation in the article.

> 1 can
>   can also have a say
> 2 have to
>   have to be able
> 3 need to
>   you need to have
> 4 should
>   should be fun
>   should have the freedom

5	don't have to
	don't have to give
6	don't need to
	doesn't need to pay

Optional suggestion: Refer Ss to pages 167 and 168 of the Grammar reference and go through the notes on modals of obligation. Allow time to discuss examples and any problems Ss have. Provide further examples if required.

Ex 5 This exercise reinforces the use of just two modals of obligation. Ss complete in pairs.

1	mustn't
2	don't have to
3	mustn't
4	don't have to
5	don't have to
6	mustn't
7	mustn't
8	don't have to

Speaking: Unwritten rules

Ex 6 Ask Ss what they think an 'unwritten rule' is. They could try to come up with a definition to share with the class. Ask Ss to suggest situations in which there are unwritten rules, or examples of unwritten rules.

Ask Ss to work in pairs to complete the unwritten rules. Each pair reads their sentences to the rest of the class and explains their ideas.

Ex 7 Ask Ss to work in pairs to match the sentence endings to the unwritten rules in Ex 6. Ask them how similar they are to their own ideas. Are the rules true for Ss' own country? How are they different?

1 f	**2** a	**3** d	**4** e	**5** c	**6** b

Ex 8 Ask Ss to discuss the unwritten rules in pairs or small groups. One S should be the secretary and write the rules down.

Possible answers:
1   You should wait until you are sure no one else is getting into the lift before closing the lift doors. You should ask others which floor they are going to. You should move to the back of the lift if you are the last person out.
2   You shouldn't disturb other people's enjoyment of the film: you should turn off your mobile phone; you shouldn't talk while the film is showing; you shouldn't eat noisily.
3   If you want to talk about personal business, go somewhere private. You shouldn't talk for a long time on the phone on public transport. Turn your phone off in waiting rooms and other public places where you have to be quiet.
4   You should respect your friend. You should support your friend. If your friend needs help, you should listen to him/her.

Ex 9 Each secretary reads their rules to the class. Discuss the questions with the class.

Photocopiable notes 6.1 (page 119)
Social rules (Discussion cards page 130)

TALKING POINT
Ask Ss to work in pairs or small groups to come up with reasons why the Happy Computers model of working might or might not be good for their own organization. Ss could also come up with a list of the advantages and disadvantages of the Happy Computers model.

Homework suggestions
•   Ss write a proposal for their own organization recommending particular aspects of the Happy Computers model of working that they think would be appropriate. (120–150 words)
•   Give Ss the following situations and ask them to come up with two unwritten rules for each to share with the class next lesson.

In the theatre

In a supermarket

On a plane

Playing tennis with a friend

Using the internet

β Obligation in the past

Aims and objectives

In this lesson Ss will:
•   listen to people talking about their boss
•   study ways of expressing obligation in the past: *have to/ need to/be allowed to*
•   listen to people talking about a TV show
•   discuss working life in the past

Listening: A memorable boss

Ex 1 The lesson focuses on workplaces and working environments. To start Ss thinking about working situations, ask Ss to discuss their own best boss in pairs. What was so good about him/her?

Optional activity: Ss work in pairs and identify the qualities and kind of behaviour that make a person a good boss. Ask half the pairs to think about the positive qualities and the others the negative. Take feedback. Ss write their ideas on the board under + *Good boss* and – *Bad boss* columns. (Suggestions: Good boss: pulling their weight, supporting staff in crises, taking a lead, being a team player; Bad boss: telling workers off in front of others, taking long breaks, not rewarding good performance.)

Ex 2))) **1.28** Before you play the recording, tell Ss they are going to listen to five people talking about their boss. Play each recording, then allow Ss to discuss the questions in pairs.

Speaker 1: good boss
Speaker 2: good in some aspects and bad in others
Speaker 3: bad boss
Speaker 4: bad boss
Speaker 5: good boss

Track 1.28: 6B, Page 58, Exercises 2 and 3

1

My first boss was a doctor before she went into hospital management. I was only an admin assistant in the department, but she sometimes mentioned my research and contribution to her reports when we were in meetings with other managers. She didn't have to do it but she often thanked her staff and always shared the credit with us.

2

Our office manager encourages us to work independently so he's not keeping an eye on what we do all day long. The only problem is that my co-worker is really lazy and she keeps chatting on the phone to her friends and spending too much time on Facebook. Last week, we needed to prepare a presentation and I had to do most of it. I'm tired of doing her work as well as my own, but our manager doesn't seem to notice.

3

I once worked for a small marketing company and I shared an office with my boss, who just loved sending me emails. It was a bit strange. I could understand it when she was out of the office, but she didn't need to email me when she was sitting opposite me. Why didn't she just tell me the information I needed to know?

4

I once worked in a large open plan office, but our section head put lots of partitions and plants around himself – to hide from us I think. He only spoke to the supervisors and not the rest of his staff. And he had some strange rules. Like, we had to speak to each other very quietly, and we weren't allowed to laugh because he said it was unprofessional. As you can imagine, they didn't keep staff for long in that department.

5

My boss has young children herself and values her free time. She knows how to keep her team happy. We don't need to work late often, but when there is something urgent or really important, like the monthly sales figures, nobody minds too much staying to get the work done.

Ex 3))) Tell Ss they are going to listen for specific information about each boss. Ask Ss to read the statements. Play the recordings again straight through. Ss compare their answers in pairs and justify their ideas; they can look at the audio script on page 149 if necessary.

After checking answers, ask Ss for their own opinions about the bosses on the recording. If you did the optional activity in Ex 1, Ss can compare the ideas they have heard on the recording with their own ideas they identified in Ex 1.

> **1** b **2** a **3** d **4** c **5** e

Grammar: Obligation in the past

Ex 4 Remind Ss of different ways of expressing obligation in the past. Ask Ss to complete the table in Ex 4 in pairs. Tell them that they may have to change the form of the verb. If Ss ask, remind them that there is no past form of the verbs *must* and *should* (which also express obligation but not in the past). Instead we use the past forms of *have to* and *need to*.

> (See answers in Ex 5)

Optional suggestion: Refer Ss to page 168 of the Grammar reference and go through the notes on obligation in the past.

Ex 5 Ask Ss to read the audio script on page 149 and find examples to complete the table.

	Present	Past	Example
1	have to	had to	*I had to do most of it.* *We had to speak to each other very quietly.*
2	need to	needed to	*Last week, we needed to prepare a presentation.* *Why didn't she just tell me the information I needed to know?*
3	don't have to	didn't have to	*She didn't have to do it but she often thanked her staff.*
4	don't need to	didn't need to	*She didn't need to email me when she was sitting opposite me.*
5	isn't/ aren't allowed to	wasn't/ weren't allowed to	*We weren't allowed to laugh.*
6	1 had to, needed to 2 didn't have to, didn't need to 3 wasn't/weren't allowed to		

Ex 6 Ss work in pairs to rewrite the rules in the past. Ask pairs to exchange their answers with another pair so that they can check them.

> **1** I <u>had to</u> start work at 9 a.m. and finish at 6 p.m every day.
> **2** We <u>had to</u> wear a uniform and an ID badge for work.
> **3** We <u>weren't allowed to</u> surf the internet for fun.
> **4** I <u>needed to</u> leave my mobile phone on during meetings.
> **5** We <u>weren't allowed to</u> smoke anywhere in the building.
> **6** Sometimes everyone <u>had to</u> do some overtime.

Speaking: Those were the days

Ex 7))) 1.29 Ask Ss to discuss the photos that are taken from a TV show in pairs. Who do they think the people are? Where are they? What jobs do they think they have? When do they think the show is set? How do they know? What do they think the show is about?

Tell Ss they are going to listen to colleagues talking about the show. Before you play the recording, ask Ss to read the questions and predict the answers. Ss listen to see if they were right.

> **1** *Mad Men*
> **2** male executives and female employees at an advertising agency and their boyfriend/girlfriends and spouses
> **3** New York, Madison Avenue
> **4** in the 1960s
> **5** the dialogue, acting, clothes, the authentic feel, the female characters

Track 1.29: 6B, Page 59, Exercises 7 and 8

M = Marianne, **N** = Nicole

M: Did you watch *Mad Men* last night?

N: Is that the show about some advertising executives?

M: Yeah, that's the one. It's set in New York in the 60s.

N: Why's it called '*Mad Men*'?

M: They work in an ad agency on Madison Avenue.

N: Oh, yeah, I've heard of it. But I haven't seen it yet.

M: You must! It's great. It took me a few episodes to really connect with the show, but I love it now.

N: Why do you like it?

M: Lots of things; brilliant dialogues, amazing acting and it feels really authentic. You see what society was like in the 60s. In those days people were allowed to smoke at their desks, and everybody smokes a lot. And all the men had to wear smart suits, ties and hats to the office. The women's clothes and make-up are amazing, too. They're so glamorous.

N: Sounds interesting.

M: It is. The most interesting part is the lives of the female characters. You know, women were basically second-class citizens and had to fight a lot harder then. They usually had to work as telephone operators or secretaries, or be the perfect housewife and stay at home with the kids. And at work, the secretary had to make the coffee, and give the boss his hat and coat when he left for the day. It makes me realize how far we've come in society.

N: I'm glad those days are over!

Ex 8)) Ask Ss to read the statements and think about how to complete them. Play the recording again and ask Ss to complete the sentences.

Note: This gives Ss information about working life at that time, which will help them with the discussion in Ex 9 and Ex 10.

1	smoke at their desks
2	smart suits, ties and hats
3	fight a lot harder
4	telephone operators, secretaries
5	make the coffee

Ex 9 Ask Ss to complete the sentences on their own and then compare their answers with a partner. Ss should ask their partner extension questions to get them talking about the topic.

Optional activity: This could be done as a 'consequences' game. Ss write one sentence at a time on a different piece of paper. Ss write the first sentence and fold the paper so that their sentence is hidden but there is still space for the next S to write their own new sentence underneath. Ss pass their folded paper on to the S on their right for them to write sentence 2 in the space. Ss fold the paper again, hiding their second sentence, and pass it on to the next S (or back to their partner if the class is small). When all the sentences have been completed, the papers are opened and all the sentences read and compared.

Ex 10 Ss discuss each point in pairs and try to think of points for and against each one. If necessary, give Ss suggestions for the first point to give them ideas. The whole class then debates each point in turn.

TALKING POINT

Discuss this with the whole class. Ss could then make a list of rules that they think make any workplace a good place to work.

Homework suggestions

• Ss write a report on their own organization, describing the set-up and recommending it as a place to work. (120–150 words)

• Ss interview older people they know (family or friends) and find out what they think has changed about people's working lives. Ss report back to the class next lesson or write a short report for the class.

C Writing emails 1

Aims and objectives

In this lesson Ss will:
• identify informality in writing
• read an article about the effects of text messaging and email on language and punctuation
• discuss formal and informal styles in different situations
• rewrite an email in a more formal and informal style

Reading: Informality in writing

Background information

Text messaging

The main difference between text messaging and writing emails is that people shorten words to say more. It is also a more informal style. There are different ways of doing this:

• remove vowels:
  TEXT = TXT

• remove punctuation like apostrophes and hyphens:
  I'M = IM   CAN'T = CANT or CNT

• use symbols and numbers instead of words:
  FOR = 4   FORGIVE = 4GIVE or 4GIV

• think about the sound of the words. Use Y instead of I and remove unnecessary letters:
  RIGHT = RYT   TIME = TYM

• use sounds instead of words:
  WHY = Y   ARE = R   YOU = U   LATE = L8

TALKING POINT

Begin the lesson with the Talking point to get Ss to start thinking about different types of writing, which is the focus of the lesson.

Ex 1 Ss work in pairs. During feedback, get Ss to write their answers on the board so that everyone can see.

colon :
full stop .
semi-colon ;
comma ,
an exclamation mark !
B is a capital letter, the D and L are also in capital letters in *Dear Lucy*
a is a letter in lower case, the letters in *hi lucy!* are also in lower case.

Ex 2 After discussing the meaning of *C u l8r*, ask Ss to suggest where they would usually see this message and then to discuss any other places that abbreviations are used. Are they usually formal or informal? Point out the importance of pronunciation here. The numbers and letters are pronounced like words. Ask Ss to write the message in 'real' English.

> *C u l8r* = See you later. You usually see it in mobile text messages.

Optional activity: Write the following words from text messages on the board. Ss read them aloud and work out their meaning.
M8 = mate   B4 = before   BCZ = because   NE = any
RYT = right

Ex 3 Before doing Ex 3, point out that punctuation is vital in writing as it can change the meaning and give a negative impression. To demonstrate, write the following on the board and ask Ss to punctuate the sentence correctly: *Its a bit colder today so theyre going to work in their car's.* (Answer: It's a bit colder today so they're going to work in their cars.)

Ask Ss to work in pairs and punctuate the sentence, which introduces them to the topic of the reading text. Ask Ss to find and underline the sentence in the text and check their answer.

> I, sadly, will be late for our meeting; the Underground is running with long delays.

Note: good dictionaries such as the *Longman Exams Dictionary* give rules on basic punctuation. It is worth going through the basic rules with Ss to remind them of the importance of punctuation for both meaning and to create a good impression on the reader.

Optional homework suggestion

Type out one paragraph from the text in Ex 3 and then take out the punctuation (or write a short text yourself without punctuation). Ask Ss to punctuate it correctly.

> **Photocopiable notes 6.2 (page 119)**
> **Formal and informal styles (Dictation and punctuation page 131)**

Ex 4 Ask Ss to read the article quickly. Does the writer think that language is becoming more or less formal? (More formal.) Ss then work in pairs, read the text in detail and answer the questions. Finally, go over any unknown words in the text. Ask Ss whether they agree with the writer.

> **Possible answers:**
> 1 The writer probably prefers more formal emails from people she doesn't know, like the one she received from the UK Head of Internal Communications at Google.
> 2 She recently carried out research on 100 unsolicited emails and compared them with a similar study she did in 2000. She found that now people are not using informal expressions like *Hi, Hey* or *rgds*, but using more formal forms of address e.g. *Dear Ms Kellaway* and signing off with *Yours sincerely* and even *Yours faithfully*.
> 3 She thinks business writing is getting more formal. She also says that when people are losing their jobs, correct dress and usage of words is a good insurance policy, or a good idea.

Writing: Emails 1

Ex 5 Ask Ss to work in pairs to identify the conventions of writing emails. Take feedback from the whole class. With a weaker class, do this together with the whole class so that Ss can ask questions or compare with their own language.

> 1 At the end of a formal letter or email to someone we don't know, or don't know very well.
> 2 We use *Ms* for a woman when we don't know, or she doesn't want us to know, whether she is single, married or divorced; *Mrs* for a married woman.
> 3 Regards
> 4 Students' own answers. For example:
>   More formal = *Best regards, Regards, Best wishes*
>   Informal = *Take care, See you soon, See you, Cheers*
> 5 We use *Yours sincerely* at the end of a formal letter when we know the person's name and *Yours faithfully* for formal correspondence when we don't know the person name, that is, when we address them as *Dear Sir/Madam*.
> 6 The correct forms are: *Dear Ms Kellaway, Dear Lucy Kellaway*. We can say *Dear Mrs Kellaway* if we know she's married.

Ex 6 Tell Ss that the email has been written in an informal style. Ss work in pairs. Ask them to discuss the changes they would make to the email, using the points listed. Point out that there will be more than one possible answer.

Ex 7 Ss work in the same pairs to rewrite the email based on the ideas they have discussed in Ex 6. Take feedback, then write a final answer on the board that all Ss agree on. Ss can make suggestions and corrections to the email on the board as suggestions are made.

Sample email:

> Dear Lucy Kellaway
>
> I am writing to you because we would like you to speak at an event that we are organizing about how business writing is changing. It is going to be (held) on Thursday 21 February.
>
> We look forward to hearing from you (soon).
>
> Regards
>
> John Moore
>
> (+ position and company)

Ex 8 Ss read the message quickly for the main point. Take class feedback on their ideas for advice.

> The man has been unemployed for the last three years and wants advice about how to present his current situation and CV to a future employer.

Ex 9 Ask Ss to work in pairs to rewrite the email. Each pair reads out their rewritten version to the class for comments.

Sample answer:

> Dear Lucy (Kellaway)
>
> I'm writing to you as I'd like your advice. Three years ago I resigned as a manager and since then I have enjoyed gardening, fishing and writing. But recently I have been worried about my situation, so I went to a recruitment agency. When I explained the past three years to one of their staff, he was very shocked. I'm afraid any future employer will react in the same way. How should I present my situation and CV at the next interview?
>
> Regards
>
> MB, Unemployed, male, 41

Speaking: Formal and informal styles

Ex 10 Ask Ss to work in pairs or groups of three and discuss the first question. After they have finished, you could move one S round to the next pair/group and the new pairs/groups discuss the next question. Continue until all the questions have been discussed, then take class feedback.

TALKING POINT

If not already used to start the lesson, discuss the questions with the class. Continue the discussion of Talking point 1 by asking whether Ss feel that it is or isn't important to write correctly, and when it might be most important to give a good impression.

Homework suggestions

● Ss write a message to the class in informal text language. Ss write the message on the board next lesson and other Ss rewrite it more formally.
● Tell Ss to write an email to a friend talking about a business email they have received that they feel was badly written. In their email, Ss should tell their friend what was wrong with the email, how it made them feel and what they would like to do about it.

D Communication strategies
Giving advice

Aims and objectives

In this lesson Ss will:
● listen to people giving and receiving advice
● study ways of checking understanding, asking for opinions and suggestions, raising objections, responding to advice
● roleplay situations giving and receiving advice

Culture and language
Giving advice

Good advice can be very helpful, but giving it can be difficult. While giving advice can demonstrate that we care about someone, it can also mean we're intruding and interfering in their lives. Exercise 1 in this lesson raises some dilemmas of advice-giving for discussion.

In many languages, advice is generally given in the form of an imperative (*Do it*). Imperatives are used less frequently in English and they could sound harsh or dictatorial in the situations in this lesson.

Some of the English advice-giving expressions in this lesson are more forceful than others. We tend to select more forceful expressions when:
1 we think the actions we are suggesting are critical
2 we have a very close relationship with the person we're talking to

In other contexts we generally use tentative forms such as *You might want to …* or *What you could do is …* . (See pages 62 and 63 on *Giving advice* in unit 6.)

There is a close relationship between giving advice and giving orders in English. So for example, *Maybe you could tell him* could just be a suggestion when said by one colleague to another. But it could be an order when said by a boss to a subordinate. In situations where there is an unequal power relationship, we often use advice and suggestion forms to give orders in English.

Listening: What should I do?

Ex 1 As the lesson focuses on giving advice in different situations, start by referring Ss to the information in the **Watch out!** box so that Ss understand the grammatical use of *advice*. You could also point out that the verb form is *to advise*. Ask Ss to discuss the questions in groups. Take feedback from the whole class.

Ex 2 🔊 **1.30** Before you play the recording, ask Ss to read the topics of the two conversations. Ss compare their answers in pairs and explain the reasons for their choices.

1 b   **2** d

Track 1.30: 6D, Page 62, Exercises 2 and 4
Conversation 1
K = Kelly, **R** = Robert

K: Robert, I have a question. I want to ask Kristof for a few days off next month but I think he'll say no. It's one of our busy periods. I wonder what I should say to him.

R: Maybe you could just tell him why you need to have the time off.

K: OK, I'll try that.

R: And you might want to make sure your work is up-to-date before you go away.

K: Yes, that's a good idea. And I'll tell Kristof I'll do that.

R: And what you could do is leave information with me, you know, so I can cover for you. Tell Kris I'll take care of things, no problem.

K: Really? That's excellent. Thanks Robert. I'll do the same for you some day.

R: You're welcome. What do you need time off for, by the way?

K: I'm going away with my husband, without the kids. We need a break.

R: Well, good luck with Kristof.

Conversation 2
K = Kelly, **J** = Jake

K: You know that job interview I went for last week?

J: Yeah, did you get the job?

K: Well, I dunno. I haven't heard from them yet. But I thought the interview went really well. Do you think I should phone them?

J: No, don't do that yet. It'd be better to send them a thank-you note first.

K: A thank-you note? You must be joking!

J: No seriously, that's pretty standard in the States. An email will do. Then you follow up with a phone call.

K: Oh, no. I don't think that would work. We don't do that here.

J: Oh, OK. I think you should phone them then.

K: Yeah, perhaps. I'll give it another couple of days.

Ex 3 Note that these two questions are different. Ss need to think about clues that tell them the relationship, but the advice is specific. Ss discuss their ideas in pairs and compare with the class.

> **Possible answers:**
> 1 They are work colleagues. The woman's colleague suggests that she tell her boss why she wants time off and get all her work up to date before going away.
> 2 They are probably friends. The man advises the woman to write a thank-you note to the company that interviewed her.

Ex 4))) Ask Ss to read through the conversation before you play the recording. Ss listen, complete the sentences and compare their answers with a partner.

> 1 Maybe you could   4 don't do that
> 2 you might want to   5 be better
> 3 what you could   6 you should

Ex 5 Ask Ss to work in pairs to complete the ways of giving advice in the box.

> **Conversation 1**   **Conversation 2**
> You might want to …   You should …
> What you could do is …   No, don't do that …
> Maybe you could …   It'd be better to …

Ex 6 This introduces the idea of connotation and starts Ss thinking about contexts in which different kinds of advice is given. Ask Ss to discuss their ideas in groups. If necessary, play the recording again so that Ss can listen to the way the people are speaking.

> The phrases in Conversation 2 are more forceful.
> You should …
> No, don't do that …
> It'd be better to …

Speaking: If you want my advice

Ex 7 Tell Ss that they are going to practise giving and receiving advice in different situations. Ss discuss the situations in pairs and who they would go to for advice.

> **Possible answers:**
> Buying a car – car showroom/sales person
> Investing money – bank manager/financial advisor
> Feeling stressed or overworked – doctor/boss/friend
> Job and career options – teacher/job centre
> Where to go on holiday – the internet/travel agency
> A good place to eat out in your town – tourist information/friend
> What to wear on a special occasion – shop assistant/friend
> Ideas for decorating your home – builder/architect

Optional homework suggestion

Ask Ss to imagine that a friend has asked them for advice on one of the situations in Ex 7. Ss write an email to their friend, giving them advice and reasons why they think their friend should take the advice.

Ex 8 In the same pairs, Ss discuss what advice the people would give.

Ex 9))) **1.31** Tell Ss they are going to listen to six people receiving advice. As they listen they should make notes, then discuss the questions in pairs. Take feedback from the whole class. Make the point that the expression in Conversation 2 could sound negative and the interpretation depends on the speaker's intonation.

> 1 Improving your English (response sounds positive)
> 2 The best time to go on holiday (response sounds positive)
> 3 Someone checking your resume/CV (response sounds negative)
> 4 Buying a laptop instead of a PC (response sounds positive)
> 5 Moving house to send the kids to a better school (response sounds negative)
> 6 Writing a report in French (response sounds negative)
>
> **Expressions used to respond to suggestions:**
> 1 That's a great idea!
> 2 Yeah, perhaps we should do that.
> 3 Maybe, but I'm not sure who to ask.
> 4 That sounds like a good idea.
> 5 Yeah, but I don't think we can afford to move house.
> 6 Mmm … I'll think about it.

Track 1.31: 6D, Page 63, Exercise 9
Conversation 1

A: If you want to improve your English, I think you should study abroad for a couple of months. Maybe in San Diego. I know a family there you could stay with.

B: That's a great idea!

Conversation 2

A: What you could do is go on holiday in November. You can get really good deals at that time of year.

B: Yeah, perhaps we should do that.

Conversation 3

A: Ask someone to check your resume for you. It might help to get a second opinion.

B: Maybe, but I'm not sure who to ask.

Conversation 4

A: Well, it'd be better to get a laptop. You can take it with you wherever you go. No one uses PCs these days.

B: That sounds like a good idea.

Conversation 5

A: Maybe you could move to a better area if you want your kids to go to a good school.

B: Yeah, but I don't think we can afford to move house.

Conversation 6

A: You might want to write the report in French, seeing that it's a French client.

B: Mmm, my French isn't very good. I'll think about it.

Ex 10 Ask Ss to work in pairs or threes. If in threes, then two students should roleplay the situations, and the third listens and gives feedback on the following: Was the advice clear? Was it forceful or not? Was it convincing? Monitor the groups as they work and give feedback at the end.

Homework suggestions

• Ss choose one of the situations from Ex 10 and write an email to a friend telling them about the situation, what advice they were given and what the outcome was. (120–150 words)
• Ask Ss to think of three situations in which they need advice. Ss bring these to the class next lesson and discuss them in groups.

E Interaction Helping new people

Aims and objectives

In this lesson Ss will:
• read an article about starting a new job
• listen to people talking about their first day at work
• roleplay different situations to practise advising, explaining, suggesting, proposing, justifying, recommending and persuading.

Refer Ss to the Reminder box and draw attention to the language that the lesson will focus on. Check Ss can use this language by looking at pages 167 and 168 of the Grammar reference and at previous lessons of the unit.

Listening: First-day nerves

Ex 1 The discussion gives Ss ideas and vocabulary for the topic of helping new colleagues and problems that are connected with being new to a job. Ss should discuss their own ideas before reading the newspaper article.

> People worry about the unknown, strange surroundings and unfamiliar faces.

Ex 2 Ss discuss the questions to get them thinking about the topic and enable them to predict some of the language and ideas they will hear in the listening. Ss make a note of their ideas so that they can use them in the speaking activity later.

Ex 3))) **1.32** Tell Ss to listen and decide who has the more positive attitude to their first day at work and who enjoyed it the most. Play the recording and give Ss time to discuss their ideas. Discuss reasons for their opinions with the whole class.

> Julia seemed to enjoy her first day more as she was less nervous.

Track 1.32: 6E, Page 64, Exercises 3 and 5

Julia

I was really excited about my first day and a bit nervous, too, because I'd never had a job before. When I got there I was shown to my desk and given things to do, but I wasn't really shown around or introduced. It was a busy office so I decided it was up to me to get to know everyone. To break the ice I went round asking the people in my team if they wanted a cup of tea. We soon got chatting and my nerves disappeared! I think that the key to a good first day in a new job is to make

sure people know who you are. Don't be afraid to introduce yourself. It means you're included from the start, and even if not everybody's friendly at first, at least it's a start.

Saul

I could hardly sleep the night before my first day at the engineering firm. I was so tired that I kept getting things wrong when I was left to do something. Getting stuff wrong made me even more nervous and I couldn't really take in what was being said to me. I thought I was in trouble when my boss called me into his office, but he actually said that he could see I was nervous and that he would team me up with somebody the next day. Being partnered with someone more experienced was just what I needed. After that, it got loads better. Because I was being shown what to do by somebody I felt more included and learnt a lot more.

Ex 4 This exercise focuses on useful topic vocabulary. Ss do this in pairs. You could play the recording again for Ss to compare their answers with the recording.

> **1** g **2** a **3** d **4** b **5** c **6** e **7** f

Ex 5))) Ss read the questions before listening so that they listen effectively.

> **1** both **2** Saul **3** Saul **4** Julia **5** Julia **6** Saul

Ex 6 This prepares Ss for the roleplay in Ex 9, which is an important part of the lesson as it activates the ideas and the vocabulary. Give Ss time to plan their ideas in pairs.

> **Possible answer:**
> No, their companies did not do enough to help Julia and Saul on their first day. If would be a good idea to show staff around and introduce them to other people. It would also help some staff to be teamed up with someone on the first day.

Optional homework suggestion

Ss write a short report on what happened on their own first day at work, how they felt and what they did to make a good impression on their boss. (120–150 words)

Speaking: What should we do?

These exercises are a series of roleplays which lead to the group roleplay in Ex 9.

Ex 7 Ss work in pairs, read the roles and prepare a short dialogue. Each pair could roleplay their conversations in front of the class so that other Ss can make suggestions about language.

Variation: Group Ss into pairs, Pair A and Pair B. Ask the As to prepare their roles together and the Bs to prepare together. They can make notes to help them if necessary, and discuss ideas and useful vocabulary. Regroup Ss into new pairs, A + B and let them roleplay the situation. This regrouping is important as the Ss will not know what their partner will say, which makes the dialogue more meaningful. Ss can follow-up by writing a dialogue and reading it to the rest of the class.

Ex 8 Ss work in pairs and roleplay the situation. Monitor and give feedback. Ss share their ideas with the rest of the class.

Ex 9 Divide Ss into pairs. Explain that they are going to design an induction programme for new staff or students. Go through the agenda and ask Ss to discuss what should be included in the programme in detail.

Ex 10 In pairs, Ss prepare for the meeting and write notes. Remind Ss of the language they will need, including giving advice and expressing obligation.

In one-to-one classes, take the role of one of the students.

Ex 11 Ask Ss in each group to choose one person to lead the discussion. After the activity, take some quick oral feedback from Ss on how they felt during the discussion.

In one-to-one classes, hold the meeting with the S.

Ex 12 Ss present their ideas to the whole class. Ask pairs to join another pair to form groups.

In one-to-one classes, Ss can do this Ex for homework.

Homework suggestions
- Ss write up their PowerPoint slides and notes. Note: Ss don't need to actually do this homework in PowerPoint, Ss can summarize what their slides would be and write the appropriate notes.
- Tell Ss that a friend is starting a new job and has emailed them for advice on what to do on their first day. Ask Ss to email their friend, telling them what to look out for and what they might expect to happen.

Review 4–6

The Review checks work covered in the previous three units, including grammar, vocabulary, communication strategies, collocations and pronunciation. It can be approached in a number of different ways, depending on classroom size and situation and time available, for example:

- as a whole-class activity
- with Ss in pairs or groups, followed by class feedback
- as a test to be marked
- as homework

1
1 c 2 a 3 a 4 c 5 b 6 a 7 b 8 c

2
1 education 2 course 3 degree 4 online 5 attend
6 skill 7 trainer 8 career 9 e-learner 10 needs

3
1 used 2 more 3 better 4 use 5 cheaper 6 bigger
7 worse 8 longer 9 the same 10 than 11 much more
12 as 13 let 14 since 15 have

4
1 's played, was 2 retired 3 Did you learn, were
4 has just won 5 Have you seen
6 's already published 7 's lived, wasn't born
8 started, 's starred

5
1 b 2 h 3 f 4 g 5 c 6 e 7 a 8 d

6
1 a and b
2 b and c
3 a
4 a and c
5 a and b
6 a and c

7

Cinema	Sport	Books	Weather	Politics
movie	Grand Slam	novel	boiling	politician
leading actor	champion	author	changeable	vote
director	sportsman	bestseller	flood	government
screen	medal	literature	storm	local council
role	match	translate	freezing	mayor

8
1 Don't let staff choose their trainers.
2 I think you should do an online degree.
3 You might want to think about learning a new skill.
4 It'd be better to let everyone choose their courses.
5 Maybe you could let me know when you've passed.
8 What you could do is allow us to do courses in work-time.

9
1 relaxed (oO)
2 punctual (Oo)
3 efficient (oOo)
4 easy-going (ooOo)
5 logical (Ooo)
6 hard-working (oOo)

Tell us a story

A Past continuous

Aims and objectives

In this lesson Ss will:
• read an article about what three famous people did before they became well-known
• study uses of the past continuous tense
• compare uses of the past continuous with the past simple
• discuss personal experiences using past tenses

Photocopiable notes 7.1 (page 119)
Jobs (Matching activity page 132)

Optional activity: Start or finish the lesson with a true/false game. Write five statements about a job you have had in the past – three should be true and two false. Ss work in pairs to think of questions they could ask to find out if the statements are true.

To follow-up, Ss could write their own statements and repeat the activity in groups.

Reading: First jobs

Ex 1 Ask Ss to look at the photos and in pairs discuss who the people are, what they know about their early lives and what they know about their current lives. They then match the jobs to the famous people.

Ex 2 Ss read the article quickly to check if they were right. Tell Ss not to worry about any new vocabulary at this stage. To focus Ss on general comprehension and identification of attitude, ask Ss if anything surprised them in the texts. Ask them if any of the jobs related to what the people do now, how did these people feel about their early jobs and what did they like or dislike about them?

Brad Pitt – driver, removal man, promotions representative
Johnny Depp – musician, telemarketer
Michael Dell – dish washer, telemarketer

Ex 3 Ask Ss to read the questions and see if they can complete the answers from memory. Ss then work in pairs to read the text and complete the notes.

1 Brad Pitt and Michael Dell
2 Johnny Depp
3 Brad Pitt
4 Johnny Depp and Michael Dell

Ex 4 This exercise focuses on paraphrasing. Ss should try to find the words and expressions without using a dictionary.

1 humdrum
2 dropped out
3 pursue his (childhood) dream
4 the early days were tough
5 fake
6 recalls

Optional activity: Ss pick their own words from the text. They then write a sentence explaining each word (without using it). Ss work in pairs to read their sentences to each other to see if they can identify their partner's words.

Grammar: Past continuous

Ex 5 Ss should underline their examples from the text so that they can find them again for Ex 6.

Possible answers:
• Pitt did various part-time jobs while he <u>was taking</u> acting lessons.
• … when he <u>was working</u> for the Mexican fast food chain El Pollo Loco.
• Depp <u>was</u> still <u>selling</u> pens when his friend Nicolas Cage suggested that he try acting.
• At the age of 12, the founder of Dell computers, Michael Dell, <u>was washing dishes</u> …
• … by the age of 16 he <u>was selling</u> newspaper subscriptions.
• I discovered that people who <u>were moving</u> into new houses or apartments <u>were buying</u> more newspapers …

Ex 6 Ask Ss to look at the table. Ask Ss to work in pairs to match the uses of the past continuous to the examples in Ex 5, then share ideas with the rest of the class.

1 … <u>when</u> he <u>was working</u> for the Mexican fast food chain El Pollo Loco.
   <u>At the age of 12</u>, the founder of Dell computers, Michael Dell, <u>was washing</u> dishes …
   … <u>by the age of 16</u> he <u>was selling</u> newspaper subscriptions.
2 Pitt <u>did</u> various part-time jobs while he <u>was taking</u> acting lessons.
   Depp <u>was</u> still <u>selling</u> pens when his friend Nicolas Cage <u>suggested</u> that he try acting.
   I <u>discovered</u> that people who <u>were moving</u> into new houses or apartments <u>were buying</u> more newspapers than other people …
3 I discovered that people who <u>were moving</u> into new houses or apartments <u>were buying</u> more newspapers than other people …

Optional suggestion: Refer Ss to page 165 of the Grammar reference and go through the notes on the past continuous. Allow time to discuss examples and any problems Ss have. Provide further examples if required.

Ex 7 Ask Ss to explain what the difference between the past continuous and past simple is.

(Past simple is used for a completed action in the past and the past continuous is used for actions or situations in progress at a particular time in the past.)

Ask Ss to read the complete texts and discuss in pairs any other facts they know about these celebrities.

> 1 *was working*, was dancing, taking
> 2 was working, got, transformed
> 3 was sitting, occurred, could, was looking

Optional homework suggestion

Ss research one of the three celebrities and write a short quiz for other Ss to answer next lesson.

Speaking: Recalling the past

Ex 8 Ss work in pairs to ask and answer the questions. Remind Ss to listen carefully for the tense used in the question.

Optional activity: Divide Ss into groups of four or five. Give each group one blank sheet of paper and three sticky labels for each S. Ss write one date on each label that was important to them or their family. Ss stick all the dates in chronological order on their paper in a line.

Give each group a dice and a counter. Ss roll the dice and move the counter along the dates. For each date, that S explains why it was important, what happened, etc. Then the next S rolls the dice and moves the counter. The activity finishes when all the dates have been explained.

Ex 9 This exercise enables Ss to personalize the grammar by using the past continuous and past simple in natural personal conversation. Ask Ss to discuss the questions in groups.

TALKING POINT

Ask Ss to discuss the questions in pairs or small groups. Ss then share their experiences with the class. What was the most unusual job in the class?

Homework suggestions

* Ask Ss to write an email to a friend dealing with the three questions in the Talking point.
* Ask Ss to research a celebrity of their choice, and write a paragraph about their life in the same ways as the texts in Ex 3.
* Ask Ss to talk to their families and find out about any interesting or unusual jobs any family members may have done in the past. Ss write about these jobs giving the dates they are writing about and using the past continuous tenses, e.g. *In 1945 my grandfather was working in …*

β Past tenses

Aims and objectives

In this lesson Ss will:
* read an article about an entrepreneur who uses humour as a business strategy
* study uses of the past simple, past perfect and past continuous tenses
* discuss success stories
* write about a successful person or company using past tenses

Reading: Humour in hard times

Ex 1 Ask Ss what kind of bags they use and why. Do they buy designer bags? Why?/Why not? Ask Ss to look at the photos and discuss the questions in pairs.

TALKING POINT

Start the lesson with the Talking point. Ask Ss to suggest successful people and explain to each other what they know about them.

Background information

Anya Hindmarch

British designer Anya Hindmarch started designing handbags, shoes and small leather goods in 1991. She says all her products are based on high quality workmanship and is proud that they are British, humorous and bespoke. In 2007, she branched into eco-fashion and launched the popular limited edition canvas bag with the logo 'I'm Not A Plastic Bag'. She designs three collections annually, which could include handbags, shoes, luggage, small leather goods, a beach collection, a small range of ready to wear – even an iPod carrier. Her collections are regularly featured in leading fashion magazines including *Vogue*, and are popular among celebrities including Sienna Miller and Reese Witherspoon.

Ex 2 Ask Ss if they had already heard of Anya Hindmarch. Ask them to read the statements, then to read the first part of the article. They work in pairs to put the statements in the correct order.

> d, f, b, e, c, a

Ex 3 Ss discuss the questions in pairs.

Optional activity: Ss work in pairs to roleplay a job interview with Anya Hindmarch. Student A is Anya and prepares interview questions. Student B is the job applicant, who should think of reasons why they would like to work for Anya.

Grammar: Past tenses

Ex 4 Ask Ss what tenses they can see in the article about Anya Hindmarch. Ss read the information in the table and complete the sentences.

> We form the past perfect using *had* + past participle of the main verb.
> 1 past simple
> 2 past continuous
> 3 past perfect
> 4 past perfect

The other examples of the past perfect in part one are:
She hadn't gone to business school.
… she had made her name with stylish evening bags and fun bags …

Optional suggestion: Refer Ss to pages 164 and 165 of the Grammar reference and go through the notes on past tenses. Allow time to discuss examples and any problems Ss have. Provide further examples if required.

Ex 5 Ask Ss to discuss their ideas in pairs and write them down so that they can check against the second part of the text.

Ex 6 Ask Ss to read the next part of the article quickly to check their ideas. Did anything surprise them?

Ex 7 Ask Ss to complete the text using the past simple, past continuous or past perfect. Tell Ss to write the answer in the text so that they can read it again.

1 had photocopied
2 was
3 weren't ordering/didn't order
4 had saved
5 offered
6 didn't have to
7 spent/were spending
8 extended
9 served
10 gave
11 were treating/treated
12 wanted

Optional activity: Read out the following questions and ask Ss to read the completed text to find the answers.

1 What did Anya give £50 to her employees for? (For thinking of money-saving ideas)

2 How did she get people to spend more time at work? (By offering a weekly manicure)

3 What was her connection with ice cream and cosmetics? (She offered ice cream and makeovers in store.)

Ask Ss to discuss the advantages and disadvantages of these ideas in groups, and to suggest two other imaginative ways of getting more customers.

Speaking: Success stories

Ex 8 Ss look at two different stories and retell the stories to each other. As they listen, they should note any similarities or differences.

Possible answers:
The Life of Ricky Cash
When Ricky was 16 years old, he started selling electronic goods in markets in London.
He had left school at 14, but by the age of 27 he had become the Managing Director of an electronics group.
One year later, he married his wife Christine, who he had known since he was 21.
By the age of 45, he had made a fortune of £830 million and had become Sir Ricky Cash.
Then at 50, he started appearing on a successful TV business show, *How to Make Money,* where the prize winner got the opportunity to manage one of Ricky's companies.
He once said in an interview that he owed his success to hard work and he had had a tough childhood growing up in London.

The Life of Penny Winner
Penny started working for a fast food chain when she was 17. She had left college at 16.
By the age of 18, she had married her husband Cliff, who she had met at work, and by the age of 24 she had had three children.
One day she won a short story competition. She won $500,000 so she didn't have to work any more.
But she got bored and missed her workmates, so she went back to the same job. She immediately got a promotion and started training new employees, which was something she had always wanted to do.
Penny continued to live a modest lifestyle, because she had spent most of the money on a new home and had donated the rest to charity.
She once said in an interview that she owed her success to good luck and her family who had always supported her decisions.

Ex 9 Ss discuss the similarities and differences in pairs.

Optional homework suggestion
Ss write an email to a friend telling them about the success stories they discussed in Ex 9. (120–150 words)

Writing: A story

Ex 10 Make sure that Ss understand that they must write a short article for a local newspaper. Suggest they write 120–150 words. If Ss can't think of a successful person or business to write about, they can write about one of the people they discussed in the speaking task.

Sample answer:

The Life of Ricky Cash
When Ricky Cash was only 16 years old, he started selling electronic goods in markets in London. He had left school at 14, but by the age of 27 he had become the Managing Director of an electronics group. He didn't have a degree in business and he hadn't been to business school.
When he was 28, Ricky married his wife Christine, who he had known since he was 21. By the age of 45, he had made a fortune of £830 million and had become Sir Ricky Cash. Then at 50 he started appearing on a successful TV business show, *How to Make Money,* where the prize winner got the opportunity to manage one of Ricky's companies.
Ricky Cash once said he owed his success as a result of hard work and because he had had a tough childhood while he was growing up in London.

TALKING POINT
This can be used to round off the lesson if it has not already been done.

Homework suggestions
• Ask Ss to do some research and find an innovative business person (like Anya Hindmarch) they would like to tell the other Ss about in the next lesson. Ss should make notes on their chosen businessperson and make a short presentation at the start of the lesson.
• Ask Ss to write an email to a friend telling them what they have found out about Anya Hindmarch and how they feel about her. (120–150 words)

C Humour

Aims and objectives

In this lesson Ss will:
- consider their own sense of humour by doing a quiz
- identify key topic vocabulary
- read a short article about a researcher into humour and jokes
- listen to the researcher talking about finding the world's funniest joke

Word focus: Humour

Ex 1 Discuss the questions with the whole class.

Ex 2 Ask Ss to do the quiz in pairs.

Ex 3 Ss report back to the class on their partner's answers and what they mean. Ss can agree or disagree with the findings.

Write the words *fun* and *funny* on the board and ask Ss to use each one in a sentence. Refer them to the **Watch out!** box and explain that these words are often confused. Get Ss to write a sentence for each to bring out the difference in meaning.

Ex 4 Do the first two examples with the class to give Ss the idea that the word can be 'odd' for different reasons: meaning, use, grammatical form, etc. Then let Ss continue in pairs.

Suggested answers:
1 a **comedian** is a person, the others are things that are funny
2 **fun** is an uncountable noun which means an activity that is enjoyable, the others are adjectives
3 **history** means all things that happened in the past, especially political, social and economic
4 a **clown** is a funny person with a red nose, e.g. in a circus, the others are types of humour
5 **frown** is a negative verb – it is a mark you get in your forehead, between your eyes, when you are angry, the other words are related to laughter
6 **say a joke** is an incorrect collocation, the others are correct, e.g. *tell a joke*
7 **serious** – the other adjectives are similar in meaning to *funny*
8 **no fun** has a negative meaning, the other expressions have a positive meaning

Listening: Humour across the globe

TALKING POINT
You could use the Talking point here to introduce the topic.

Background information

Humour

In 2001 Richard Wiseman and The British Association for the Advancement of Science started a project to answer important questions about the psychology of humour. The project involved people from different cultures and of different ages, rating how funny they found a random selection of jokes that had been submitted by others. During the year the site received over 40,000 jokes and 1.5 million ratings. (http://laughlab.co.uk/)

Ex 5 Tell Ss about the project. Ss read the title and predict what questions the researcher might have asked. Ss then read the text to check their ideas.

1 Do people from different countries laugh at the same jokes?
2 When is the best time of day to tell a joke?
3 When is the best time of the month to tell a joke?
4 Which animal do people find the funniest?

Ex 6 🔊 **2.1** Ask Ss to listen and find out what the answers to the research questions were.

1 No, for example people from Ireland, the UK, Australia and New Zealand like jokes involving a play on words. But Americans and Canadians prefer jokes which laugh at someone's sense of superiority: while other European countries like France, Belgium and Denmark enjoy surreal jokes.
2 Six in the evening.
3 In the middle of the month/the 15th.
4 The duck.

Track 2.1: 7C, Page 73, Exercise 6

P = Presenter, **A1 and A2** = Members of the audience

P: We asked everyone coming to the website to tell us which country they were from. Then we studied the data from the ten countries that rated the highest number of jokes.

There were some interesting differences between nations in terms of the jokes they found funny. For instance, people from The Republic of Ireland, the UK, Australia and New Zealand liked jokes involving a play on words – you know – where a word has two meanings. Americans and Canadians preferred jokes which make fun of someone's sense of superiority – so jokes where someone looked stupid, or was made to look stupid.

Many European countries, such as France, Denmark and Belgium, liked jokes that were a bit surreal. Do you know what I mean? European countries also enjoyed jokes about topics that often make us feel anxious, such as death, illness and marriage, like this one:

A woman told her friend, 'For eighteen years my husband and I were the happiest people in the world! Then we met.'

The other interesting thing about humour is that it's all about timing. … Our computers recorded the time that each person rated the jokes. We then looked at the data and examined how the way people found jokes funny changed over the course of the day. It seems people find the jokes funniest at six in the evening …

A1 and A2: Really? At six?

P: Yes, and they found a joke is least funny at half past one in the morning. People also found jokes funnier at different times during the month. They were the funniest on the fifteenth and less funny towards the end or start of the month. … So, if you want to make people laugh, tell a joke on the fifteenth of the month, at six in the evening!

And finally, many of the jokes people sent were about animals. We found that jokes about ducks are funnier than others. Why do you think that is?

A1: Perhaps it's because of their feet, and their funny walk.

A2: Or the funny sound they make?

P: That's right. Anyway, if you are going to tell a joke about an animal, make it a duck. *Quack, quack.*

Optional homework suggestion
Ask Ss to write an email to a friend telling them about the project and explaining what they think about it and what they think the project might tell people. (120–150 words)

Ex 7))) **2.2** Tell Ss they are going to hear the funniest joke in the world. Ask them if they know any funny jokes themselves. Then ask Ss to read the questions and listen to what was voted the funniest joke in the world. Discuss the questions with the whole class. The class could vote on whether they thought it was funny or not.

> 1 'Calm down. I can help. First, let's make sure he's dead.'
> 2 The hunter kills the other hunter, instead of just checking that he's not dead.

Track 2.2: 7C, Page 73, Exercise 7

A couple of hunters are out in the woods when one of them suddenly falls to the ground. He doesn't seem to be breathing and his eyes are rolled back in his head. So the other guy quickly takes out his cellphone and calls the emergency services. He shouts to the operator: 'My friend is dead! My friend is dead! What can I do?' The operator says: 'Calm down. I can help. First, let's make sure he's dead.' There is a silence, and then a shot is heard. Bang! The hunter's voice comes back on the line. The guy says: 'OK, now what?'

Ex 8 Ask Ss to look at the tenses in the jokes in the audio script. Point out the difference between telling jokes and telling stories. (Jokes often use past tenses but stories often use present tenses for dramatic effect.)

> **Possible answers:**
> We often use the present simple for telling jokes. We also use the present tense when talking about the plots of films and books.

Speaking: Find someone who

Ex 9 Tell Ss that they should use the words in brackets to form follow-up questions to ask other Ss. Ss complete the task in pairs or small groups, then share their findings with the rest of the class.

> **Suggested follow-up questions:**
> 1 Which TV sitcoms do you enjoy watching?
> 2 Did you (use to) like the same cartoons when you were a child? Which ones?
> 3 Have you laughed out loud recently? Why?
> 4 Have you sent a funny email recently? What was in the email?
> 5 Did you like playing practical jokes as a child? What did you do?
> 6 Do you think that there isn't a best time to tell a joke? Why?
> 7 What are your favourite comedy films? / Do you like (Woody Allen) films? etc.
> 8 Do you think that a sense of humour is the most important things in a relationship?
> 9 Do you think humour is important at work? Why?
> 10 Are you good at telling jokes and stories? Can you tell me one?

Ex 10 Ss could report back orally or they could write an email to their teacher explaining what they found out.

TALKING POINT

If not used to start the lesson, discuss these questions with the class.

Homework suggestions

● Ask Ss to prepare to tell a joke to the class at the start of the following lesson.
● Ask Ss to write an essay explaining why they think some jokes are often 'lost in translation' and discussing whether humour can actually cross cultures. Tell them to give reasons for their opinions. (150–180 words)

D Communication strategies
Storytelling

Aims and objectives

In this lesson, Ss will:
● listen to a story
● identify tenses and expressions used in the story
● study ways of asking about and responding to stories
● focus on the meaning and use of linkers

Culture and language
Storytelling

Telling stories and sharing life experiences, is an important part of socializing and building relationships in any culture. According to narrative research, it is thought that stories have a variety of uses: they may entertain, educate and inform. The research indicates that stories often symbolize the values, beliefs and attitudes of a group of people, as well as functioning as 'social glue'.

Storytelling is something that many learners find especially challenging, not only because they have to use past tenses, key vocabulary and various linking devices, but also because it involves an extended piece of communication that puts the storyteller 'on the spot'. It can also be very disconcerting for the storyteller if the listener doesn't show interest or respond appropriately at the right time, or doesn't respond at all. While listening to a story, English speakers will respond saying, *Really*, *That's so funny*, or *Oh no!* and ask questions to encourage the storyteller, *So, what did you do?*

Some languages such as Japanese have very formal conventions for storytelling when the listener is expected to ask frequent questions at the beginning and encourage the storyteller to continue. In English we can ask permission to start a story like this:
> A: *Did I tell you about the time …?*
> B: *No, what happened?*
> A: *Well, once I was travelling with some friends when…*

And, at the end of the story, the listener may respond in kind telling her own story starting with something like this, *Actually, that reminds me of the time …* (See pages 74 and 75 on *Storytelling* in Unit 7.)

Humour plays a significant role in telling stories and anecdotes, but different cultures may have a different sense of humour from our own. Americans will enjoy poking fun at authority, which could prove disastrous in an Asian culture, and British speakers are well-known for their self-deprecating humour and irony, which might easily be misinterpreted or lost on another culture.

7 Tell us a story

Use of humour in the workplace varies from culture to culture: English speakers might appreciate a joke in a presentation or meeting; French speakers may prefer just a witty comment in a work situation, whereas Spanish speakers often enjoy an extensive joke-telling session after dinner with colleagues. Having fun at work is seen to be acceptable in many Anglo-American companies. You may want to explore your students' views on appropriate use of humour and storytelling in working relationships in this unit.

Listening: A night bike ride

Ex 1 Ss discuss the questions in pairs. Take brief feedback, then tell Ss that the picture illustrates a story. What do they think the story will be about?

Ex 2 🔊 2.3 Before playing the recording, tell Ss that the story they are going to hear is in two parts. Ss listen to the first part of the story. Ss discuss in pairs what has happened so far.

Ben went on a bike ride but wasn't prepared for his trip because he had a girls' mountain bike and he was wearing an ordinary helmet, whereas the other cyclists were wearing protective clothing and had helmets with lights.

Track 2.3: 7D, Page 74, Exercises 2 and 4
Part one
B = Ben, G = Georgia

B: Mmm, did I tell you about the time I went on a bike ride at night?

G: No, what happened?

B: Well, I have a friend who's really into cycling and he once said, 'Come on, Ben! Go on a night ride with us.' My wife has a bike so I took it out that night. Three of his friends were there who were sort of super jocks.

G: Really athletic, huh?

B: Yeah, but they immediately started laughing. Apparently, I have a girl's mountain bike …

G: Really?

B: Yeah, I didn't know … Anyway, they started putting on elbow pads and all this protective clothing … and I was dressed in my shorts and T-shirt … and then they started putting on their helmets, like those helmets that have lights on them …

G: Like the ones you use for camping.

B: That's right. So, we started going along this road by the ocean and it was great. The moon was out … We'd gone three miles and I was getting kind of tired but I was enjoying it, …

G: So, what happened next?

Ex 3 🔊 2.4 What do Ss think will happen next? Ask Ss to write down their ideas to compare with the recording. Ss listen to check their ideas.

When they stopped at the top of the hill, the other cyclists took out some Powerbars (high energy snacks). Ben thought it was the end of the bike ride but it wasn't. The others were going fast downhill but Ben had fallen behind them. Then he crashed into a tree.
He thought they were shouting, 'No brunch!' but they were shouting, 'Low branch!'. He didn't see the tree branch because it was night and he didn't have a light on his helmet.

brunch (AmE): meal usually eaten late morning (cross between breakfast and lunch)
branch: part of a tree that grows out of the main part

Track 2.4: 7D, Page 74, Exercises 3 and 5
Part two
B = Ben, G = Georgia

B: After we'd gone five miles, we got to the top of this hill and everybody got off their bikes. I was thinking, 'Yes! We did it.' But then they started checking their bikes and gear and pulling out Powerbars, you know, those high energy cereal bars. And I said, 'What's going on?' and they said, 'Well, we're ready to start now.'

G: You mean, you'd just started!

B: Uhuh. And one guy, who's super-serious, just looked at me and said, 'Whatever happens, don't fight the mountain.'

G: Don't fight the mountain? You're kidding!

B: I had no idea what it meant but it scared me … And as they were going down the hill, I was falling behind.

G: They were too fast for you.

B: That's right, but I got this adrenaline rush and I was doing OK and I could hear them up ahead, shouting 'Come on, Ben!' and I suddenly heard one of them yell out, 'No brunch! No brunch!' And I think, this is some kind of biking term. I mean, we're going so well, we're not gonna stop to eat the Powerbars now. So I'm thinking, 'Yeah! No brunch! No brunch!' Then I look up and suddenly there is this great, big tree in front of me!

G: Oh no!

B: And you know they say when an accident happens everything slows down, you go in slow motion and you do whatever it takes to save yourself in that moment?

G: Yeah.

B: That didn't happen! So I slammed right into it … and as I came to, they were all looking at me saying, 'Ben, didn't you hear? We were shouting low branch!'

G: Oh, I see! Low *branch*, not *brunch*! … That's so funny … Actually, that reminds me of the time I went for a midnight swim with some friends …

Ex 4 🔊 Before playing part one again, ask Ss to read through the expressions. Ask Ss to listen and choose the expressions they hear.

1 b **2** a **3** b **4** a

Ex 5 🔊 Before playing part two again, ask Ss to read through the expressions. Ask Ss to listen and choose the expressions they hear.

1 a **2** b **3** b **4** a **5** b **6** a

She introduces her own story – *Actually, that reminds me of the time I went for a midnight swim with some friends …*

Ex 6 This exercise focuses Ss on tenses used in storytelling. Ss work in pairs and consider why Ben changed the tense he used and what the effect of this is on the listener.

Ben used past tenses: past simple, past perfect and past continuous.
Example: *So, we started going along this road by the ocean and it was great. The moon was out … We'd gone three miles and I was getting kind of tired but I was enjoying it, …*

He then changed to the present tense to make the story more interesting and exciting – the part when he crashed into the branch of the tree:
Example: *And I think, this is some kind of biking term. I mean, we're going so well, we're not gonna stop to eat the Powerbars now. So I'm thinking, 'Yeah! No brunch! No brunch!' Then I look up and suddenly there is this great, big tree in front of me!*

Ex 7 Ask Ss to read the phrases and all the notes in the table. Ss work in pairs to complete the notes. After checking answers, ask Ss to think about stories they have heard or read. What tenses were they in? What difference did it make to the dramatic effect of the story?

1 d **2** e **3** f **4** a **5** b **6** c

Word focus: Linkers

Ex 8 Asking Ss to think of a title focuses them on the gist of the story. Ask Ss to read the text. Tell them not to worry about the spaces. Then ask them to discuss a possible title with a partner. Ss could vote on the best suggestion.

Possible answers:
A scary moment / The scariest moment of my life

Ex 9 Explain that the missing words in the text are all linkers. Elicit some examples of linkers that they know. Ask Ss to read through the options in Ex 9 and work in pairs to complete the text. Encourage them to read the whole sentence beyond each gap before making their choice.

After checking answers, go through the information in the **Watch out!** box with Ss, as these words are often confused.

1 At the time **2** so **3** because **4** When **5** so **6** but
7 Anyway **8** In the end **9** Luckily **10** although

Ex 10 Ask Ss to work in pairs. Take feedback and check that Ss all understand the use of the linkers.

1 in the end **2** while **3** because **4** and **5** although
6 when **7** After that

Ex 11 Ss tell each other their stories. Encourage them to use a variety of tenses as well as the linkers they have just studied.

Optional homework suggestion
Ask Ss to write one of the stories they spoke about in Ex 11 in their own words.

Speaking: One-minute stories

Ex 12 Divide Ss into A and B and ask them to read the topics on the different pages and tell their partners their stories.

Ex 13 Ss change pairs to tell their new partner their stories.

Variation: Ss work in pairs; Pair A + Pair B. Ss discuss and prepare their stories together in Ex 12. Then regroup the students A + B, so that they can tell each other their favourite stories in Ex 13.

Photocopiable notes 7.2 (page 120)
Explaining to others (Prompt cards page 132)

Homework suggestions
● Ss write an email to a friend explaining what they learnt about communication strategies in this lesson. (120–150 words)
● Ask Ss to write a short story of their own using a range of tenses and linkers they have studied. If they have no ideas, they could start the story with the line: *I'll never forget the time I first met David.* (120–150 words)

E Interaction Presentations

Aims and objectives

In this lesson, Ss will:
● read a website about a new business concerned with office space
● listen to a presentation about the new business and analyse the presentation
● consider what techniques and language make a good presentation
● prepare and present a short presentation

Refer Ss to the Reminder box and draw attention to the language that the lesson will focus on. Check Ss can use this language by looking at pages 163, 164 and 165 of the Grammar reference and at previous lessons of the unit.

Listening: Elevator pitch

Ex 1 To start Ss thinking about the topic of working spaces and workplaces, ask Ss to discuss the questions in pairs.

Ex 2 Ss predict what the business is. Ask Ss if they think this is a good website. Point out the use of rhetorical questions to catch people's interest. Ask Ss if they think this could be a successful idea. Why?/Why not?

It's an online business that rents desk space.

Ex 3 🔊 2.5 Before playing the recording, tell Ss that they are going to listen to a presentation. It is divided into two parts. Ask Ss to listen to the first part of the presentation and decide what the presenter is doing.

He's introducing himself; selling himself.

Track 2.5: 7E, Page 76, Exercises 3 and 4
Sam Harris
Part one

Let me tell you a bit about myself. I have a problem: I can't stop setting up online businesses. I'm basically a serial e-commerce entrepreneur, which is my real passion. In 1998, I started one of the UK's first price comparison websites. Then I became a co-founder of a clothing online retailer.

But today I'd like to tell you about Instant Desks. We can make a desk appear like magic. It's our new business venture and it's already profitable. Well, we haven't lost any money … yet. Don't you think that's great? Most start-ups don't make any money in their first year.

Ex 4 🔊 Tell Ss to imagine that they are an investor and are listening to the first part of the presentation. Before playing the recording again, ask Ss to read the questions.

1 He's an e-commerce or online entrepreneur.
2 He mentions three online businesses: a price comparison website, a clothing online retailer, and his new venture, Instant Desks.
3 Yes, he says it's already profitable. But he makes a humorous comment, 'We haven't lost any money … yet.'

Ex 5)) **2.6** Tell Ss they are going to listen to the second part of the presentation. Before playing the recording, ask Ss to read the questions.

1 It's a website which brings together businesses with spare desks and people who want to rent desks.
2 'Deskers' are professionals like entrepreneurs, consultants, graphic designers or other kinds of freelancers.
3 If you're an advertiser, you fill in details of where your office is, how much you want to charge and information about printers, the type of people who work there, and any other services and facilities, e.g. tea and coffee.
4 It's free for 'deskers', but advertisers pay a small fee, according to the number of completed forms or phone calls a company receives from people who might become deskers or customers.

Track 2.6: 7E, Page 77, Exercise 5
Part two

At Instant Desks we bring together businesses with spare desks with people who want to rent desks. If your mum is an entrepreneur, consultant, graphic designer or any other kind of freelancer, and she would like to rent some desk space with similar kinds of people – then she should use our site. Professionals, who we call 'deskers', can move into an office with interesting colleagues, where they'll have access to not only a desk, but also a broadband connection, a meeting room and other facilities. We can also help companies who are hoping to make a bit of extra money and want to rent out some spare desks.

So, how does Instant Desks work? The site has a really simple search engine. Enter the city or postcode of the area where you need desk space and how far you want to travel. You'll then get descriptions of desk spaces that are available in that area, complete with photos and maps. And if you're an advertiser, you just need to fill in details of where your office is, how much you want to charge for the work space and add anything else like descriptions of printers, the type of people who work there, tea and coffee facilities, that kind of thing. Don't worry, it doesn't take long – the site is incredibly user-friendly.

Right. You're probably thinking, 'How much does it cost?' The great thing about Instant Desks is it's absolutely free. It will always be free for people looking for desk space. And there's only a small fee for advertisers. We charge according to the number of completed forms or phone calls a company receives from people who might become deskers or customers. Any questions?

Ex 6 Ask Ss to work in pairs and discuss the advantages and disadvantages of investing in the website. Do they think it is a viable business proposition?

Ex 7 Tell Ss that they are going to consider presentation techniques. Ask Ss to read the techniques and discuss those used by Sam in the recording they have heard. If necessary, play the recording again.

He uses techniques: a, b, e, f, g
Examples:
a *Extract 1:* I'm basically a serial e-commerce entrepreneur, which is my real passion.
b *Extract 1:* Let me tell you a bit about myself. But today I'd like to tell you about Instant Desks. Don't you think that's great?
Extract 2: If your mum is an entrepreneur, consultant, graphic designer or any other kind of freelancer, and she would like to rent some desk space with similar kinds of people – then she should use our site.
e *Extract 1:* Most start-ups don't make any money in their first year.
f *Extract 1:* my real passion
it's already profitable
Extract 2: The site has a really simple search engine. … the site is incredibly user-friendly.
The great thing about Instant Desks is it's absolutely free.
g *Extract 1:* Don't you think that's great?
Extract 2: So, how does Instant Desks work?
You're probably thinking, 'How much does it cost?'

He doesn't mention c) Telling a joke, although he makes a couple of humorous comments in Extract 1, e.g. *I have a problem: I can't stop setting up online businesses. … it's already profitable. Well, we haven't lost any money … yet.*

Ex 8 This exercise moves from techniques to language and the impact certain expressions can have when used in a presentation. Ask Ss to discuss each one in pairs and then check their ideas with the audio script on page 151.

1 b	2 a	3 b	4 b	5 a	6 a

Ex 9 Ask Ss to work in pairs to match the sentences. Monitor, then check answers with the class.

a Sounding enthusiastic
2a – I'm an e-commerce entrepreneur, which is my real passion.
b Connecting with the audience
1b – Let me tell you a bit about myself.
f Using positive language
3b – It's our new business venture and it's already profitable.
6a – The great thing about Instant Desks is it's absolutely free.
g Asking rhetorical questions
4b – So, how does Instant Desks work?
5a – You're probably thinking, 'How much does it cost?'

Homework suggestions
• Ss write a short report on the website saying why they are or are not impressed with it.
• Ss write a short report on Sam's presentation.

Speaking: A proud moment

Ex 10 Ss should write their presentations on their own, but then practise them with a partner. Encourage Ss to use the techniques they have studied.

Ex 11 Make sure Ss think about their listeners, and the purpose of their presentation, and plan their presentations carefully. Ss work in pairs and practise their presentations.

Variation: Divide Ss into A and B. Ss A prepare their roles together and Ss B prepare together. Regroup them into A + B and let them roleplay the situation. Ss then write a dialogue and read it to the rest of the class.

Ex 12 Ss present their pitch to the class. Make sure that the listening Ss write questions to ask the presenter.

Ex 13 Discuss these questions with the whole class.

Ex 14 Ask Ss to prepare and practise their anecdotes in pairs. When they tell their anecdotes, ask the listening Ss to give feedback on the presentation and provide constructive criticism. Monitor all the Ss and collect some general comments that you can give to the whole class.

Ex 15 The class could vote for the best anecdote.

Homework suggestions
* Ss write an email to a friend telling them about one of the presentations they have heard. (120–150 words)
* Ss write an email to a friend telling them about the place they work in and how they feel about it.
* Ask Ss to write an article for a magazine titled
A memorable moment in my working life. (120–150 words)

8

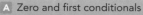
A Zero and first conditionals
B Products
C Second conditional
D **Communication strategies** Problem solving
E **Interaction** Planning a green office

Green chic

A Zero and first conditionals

Aims and objectives

In this lesson Ss will:
• listen to a radio programme about businesses that are aware of environmental issues
• study useful topic vocabulary
• study uses of the zero and first conditionals
• discuss ideas for making business more eco-friendly

Listening: Eco-revolution 1

Ex 1 Before looking at Ex 1, establish what you and Ss understand by 'green issues'. Are they the same in daily life and business? Do Ss think that a business can ever be truly 'green'?

Find out whether companies they know are taking any green initiatives. Write initiatives Ss suggest on the board. Do Ss know anything about the initiatives in the newspaper headlines?

Ex 2 This exercise establishes key collocations to help Ss with the listening. Ss work in pairs. Encourage Ss to think about the sentences they produce to make them relevant to the topic and to the situation in their own town/country, or to businesses they know about. Once they have written their sentences, Ss read them to the rest of the class.

1 d	**2** c	**3** a	**4** e	**5** b

Ex 3 ⟩⟩ 2.7 Tell Ss they will hear part of a radio programme about green businesses. Ask Ss to listen and tick the initiatives in Ex 2 that they hear. Add them to the list on the board. Do Ss think they are sensible initiatives?

The initiatives mentioned are:
reduce energy costs
replace light bulbs for low-energy ones
drive fuel-efficient cars
launch a recycling scheme

Other ideas:
• use less electricity
• buy energy efficient equipment
• buy part of the electricity supply from renewable sources (e.g. wind and solar power)

Track 2.7: 8A, Page 78, Exercises 3 and 4
Part one
P = Presenter, E = Erik

P: Has your organization gone green? If so, it is one of a few. According to a recent international survey, 80% of the world's businesses are still trying to work out what sustainability means to them. Earlier today I spoke to Erik Andersson, a consultant and expert on green business.

E: Now is the perfect time for businesses to go green. The typical first action to take is to work out how to use less electricity and reduce energy costs. If you replace your old light bulbs with low-energy ones, it can cut your electricity bills drastically and make the Finance Officer very happy.

Switch to more eco-friendly, fuel-efficient cars if you have a fleet of company vehicles. Many companies now buy energy efficient equipment as well.

Another typical move is to do something with all that stuff in the wastepaper bins. If you launch a recycling scheme, it probably won't save you money, but it will help to engage your employees and to win the all-important approval of your customers. Companies are also starting to buy part of their electricity supply from renewable sources, such as wind and solar power. Unless you have a lot of time and money, it makes sense to start with these simple initiatives.

Ex 4 ⟩⟩ Before playing the recording again, ask Ss to read the advice for companies. In pairs, Ss discuss what the eight errors might be. Ss listen and correct the advice.

1 If you ~~exchange~~ replace your old light bulbs with low-energy ones, it can ~~increase~~ cut your electricity bills.
2 Switch to ~~less~~ more fuel-efficient cars if you have a fleet of company ~~buses~~ vehicles.
3 If you ~~drive~~ launch a recycling scheme, it probably won't save you ~~time~~ money, but it will help to ~~replace~~ engage your employees.
4 Unless you have a lot of time and ~~energy~~/money, it makes sense to start with these ~~big~~ simple initiatives.

Grammar: Zero and first conditionals

Ex 5 Go through the information about the zero conditional. Ask Ss to complete the sentences as you go.

1 leaves, switches off	3 leaves, switches off
2 Switch off, leave	4 have, makes

Ex 6 Ask Ss to work in pairs to complete the sentences. Discuss each sentence with the class. Do Ss agree with them?

1 use	4 save, help
2 don't print	5 are, will clean
3 turn	6 pay

Ex 7 Go through the information about the first conditional. Ask Ss to complete the sentences as you go.

> 1 use, will be
> 2 will get, reduce
> 3 will save, turn

Optional suggestion: Refer Ss to pages 169 of the Grammar reference and go through the notes on zero and first conditional sentences. Allow time to discuss examples and any problems Ss have. Provide further examples if required.

Ex 8 Ask Ss to work in pairs to complete the sentences. Check each sentence with the class and make sure they understand why the answer is correct.

> 1 have, will take
> 2 will help, don't understand
> 3 don't turn down, will be
> 4 will go, don't implement
> 5 won't be, don't get
> 6 won't buy, reduce

Listening: Eco-revolution 2

Ex 9))) **2.8** Tell Ss they are going to listen to the second part of the radio programme about green businesses. Before playing the recording, ask Ss to read through the notes. Ss listen and fill in the gaps. Ask Ss to compare their answers with a partner.

> 1 Google
> 2 9,000
> 3 30
> 4 7½ years
> 5 ride their bikes, walk, skateboard
> 6 bus
> 7 use an eco-friendly version (drive fuel-saving hybrid cars)
> 8 digital printing
> 9 exercise bicycle
> 10 riding the bike

Track 2.8, 8A, Page 79, Exercise 9

Part two
P = Presenter, **R** = Robyn, **K** = Kevin

P: The experts agree that easy measures such as energy-efficient lighting or recycling schemes can only produce limited results. The search engine Google is one corporation that is taking green initiatives to the next level. Robyn Beavers leads the company's Green Business and Operations Strategy team in California. I spoke to her by phone.

R: We use a lot of electricity and it just seems like the responsible thing to do, to show that a corporation can make a positive impact on the environment, but also that we can do it in a way that makes sense for our business. For instance, our large solar installation was a major project. Nine thousand solar panels now cover the rooftops of our headquarters Googleplex. These produce renewable energy without greenhouse gas emissions and provide 30% of the power we need at peak times. It makes good business as well as environmental sense. We'll earn our investment back in seven and a half years, and after that, we'll have cheap power for decades.

P: The company finds ways to engage its staff, too. Google donates money to charity if employees ride their bikes, walk or skateboard to work. It manages shuttle buses to carry Googlers to and from work and provides benefits for those who car share or take the train. And if they must use a car, the company encourages them to use an eco-friendly version, offering a cash incentive to staff who drive fuel-saving hybrid cars.

And it's not just large corporations that are making the transition to sustainable business. PB Copy, a two-man digital printing operation in Surrey, Canada, has found an innovative way to go green. The owners, Kevin LaHay and Shane Fortune, have connected an exercise bicycle to a battery pack to generate power for their office equipment. I spoke to Kevin LaHay.

K: We put in a couple of hours a day on the bike in the winter months. On days with lots of sunshine, our solar panels are able to generate most of the power to charge the batteries. If you pedal for ten minutes, it'll power 100 copies on the digital printer. When the battery is full, it can power three to four hours of printing. We ask customers to participate by riding the bike for a few minutes while they're waiting for their copies. They usually think we're joking but most people agree when they see we're being serious.

P: Combining this with two solar panels means 90% of the company's print jobs now use renewable energy. LaHay believes this gives his company a competitive advantage.

Ex 10 Before Ss look at the audio script, ask if they can remember hearing any other conditional sentences. Ask Ss to work in pairs to find more conditional sentences in the audio script.

> 1 If you pedal for ten minutes, it'll power 100 copies on the digital printer.
> 2 When the battery is full, it can power three to four hours of printing.
> 3 … most people agree when they see we're being serious.

Speaking: Bright ideas

Ex 11 Ask Ss to work through the instructions in groups. Make sure that Ss justify their ideas in their proposals.

Optional activity: Ss prepare a formal presentation of their proposals to present to the class.

TALKING POINT
Discuss the question with the class, and get Ss to explain what measures have been taken in their workplace and/or any measures they would like to be taken.

Homework suggestions
- Ss write a short report on any green initiatives that are being taken in their own workplace. If none are being taken, ask Ss to recommend initiatives they would like to see put in place and why. They can take ideas from Ex 2 if necessary. (120–150 words)
- Ss write a short presentation giving three ways in which the place they study English could become more 'green'. Ss make their presentations to the class the following lesson. (100–130 words)

 **Products**

Aims and objectives

In this lesson Ss will:
- focus on key topic vocabulary and collocations
- consider their own lifestyles by doing a quiz

Word focus: Products

Ex 1 Ask Ss what they know about carbon footprints. Write suggestions on the board then compare Ss' ideas with the definition in Ex 1. Ask Ss to work in pairs to discuss each item and decide which two create the most carbon dioxide. Take feedback and see if there is class consensus.

> **Transport and Home energy**
> For example, transport accounts for 33% of CO_2 emissions and home energy use accounts for 21% of CO_2 emissions in the United States.
> (Source: http://science.howstuffworks.com/carbon footprint2.htm)

Optional homework suggestion
Ask Ss to do their own research on the internet to check their ideas and bring evidence to present at the start of next lesson.

Ex 2 Ask Ss to work in pairs and match the definitions to the words. Take feedback and do pronunciation practice on the words in the box.

> **1** reusable **2** organic **3** disposable **4** recycling
> **5** packaging **6** eco-friendly **7** pollute **8** appliance

Ex 3 Ss work in pairs and match the words with the pictures. Do pronunciation practice on the words.

> **a** fridge-freezer **b** fan **c** carton **d** cardboard box
> **e** cooker **f** glass bottle **g** washing machine **h** can

Ex 4 This exercise focuses on collocations. Ss could work in groups to share ideas. They can use dictionaries if necessary.

> **1** plastic **2** pollution **3** bicycle **4** electricity **5** paper
> **6** battery **7** computer **8** light bulbs

Ex 5 Ask Ss to work in pairs. This time Ss should not use dictionaries. Ss discuss the differences between the words before making their choice. Take feedback and then discuss which product Ss would buy with the whole class. Encourage Ss to use the words they have studied and to think about how the products might contribute to protecting the environment. Remind Ss of the work done in Lesson A.

> **1** reusable **2** recycled **3** energy-efficient
> **4** eco-friendly **5** biodegradable

Speaking: Your carbon footprints

Ex 6 Ask Ss to work in pairs to discuss the questions and analyze their answers.

Variations:

1 Ss complete the quiz for themselves and then compare their answers with their partner.

2 Ss complete the quiz for what they think their partner will say. Ss then compare their ideas.

TALKING POINT
Ask Ss to discuss the question in pairs or small groups and make a list of the differences that can be shared with the class.

Homework suggestions
- Ss write an email to a friend telling them what most people in the class already do to reduce their carbon footprints and what they might consider doing in future. (120–150 words)
- Ss research and bring two suggestions for reducing carbon dioxide emissions in one of the areas in Ex 1 to present to the class the following lesson.
- Ss choose Q 1, 2 or 3 from Ex 6 and write an email to a friend telling them what they do in one of those situations. (100–120 words)

C Second conditional

Aims and objectives

In this lesson Ss will:
- consider eco-friendly forms of transport
- read an article about electric cars
- study uses of the second conditional
- discuss ways of being responsible travellers

Reading: Electric cars

Ex 1 Ask Ss to discuss the forms of transport in small groups. Take class feedback and vote on the most eco-friendly form of transport.

TALKING POINT
Do the Talking point here to introduce the idea of green travel.

Ex 2 Ask Ss to work in pairs and write down any advantages and disadvantages of driving an electric car. Ss then read the article to check against their list. Take class feedback. Did Ss have any more ideas?

> **Advantages**
> It's very cheap. It emits no carbon dioxide or carbon monoxide. There is no noise as you accelerate.
>
> **Disadvantages**
> It takes a long time to charge it. Top speed is only 60 mph/97 kph. It only has a range of 70 miles/113 km before you need to charge it. It's difficult to charge the car if you don't have a garage. It has a very small boot. It's not suitable for more that two people.

Ex 3 Before asking Ss to read the text again, ask them to work in pairs, read the definitions and see if they can guess or remember any of the words. Then ask Ss to work in pairs to find the answers in the text.

> **1** fuel and petrol **2** engine **3** speed **4** accelerate
> **5** two-seater **6** boot **7** garage **8** commuting

Ex 4 Ss could discuss the questions in small groups.

Optional activity: Ss work in groups to prepare an advertisement or leaflet promoting electric cars. Groups present their advertisement/leaflets to the class, who then vote on the best or most persuasive.

Grammar: Second conditional

Ex 5 Go through the information in the table with the class. They complete the information and choose the correct option. Ask Ss to suggest their own sentences for each use of the second conditional.

> **1** past simple, would
>   if
> **3** could
> **4** likely
>   unlikely
>
> We can also substitute the modal *would* for *might* or *could*.

Optional suggestion: Refer Ss to pages 170 of the Grammar reference and go through the notes on second conditionals. Allow time to discuss examples and any problems Ss have. Provide further examples if required.

Ex 6 Explain the situation in the instructions and point out that the politician is not yet mayor, but is hoping to be elected in the future. The sentences are comments made by the candidate or by the local residents who might elect the candidate. Ask Ss to work in pairs to complete the sentences using first or second conditionals.

> **1** will introduce
> **2** was/were
> **3** am, will pass
> **4** would encourage
> **5** won't fine, am
> **6** would probably ban
> **7** wouldn't charge, would be
> **8** will definitely put up, will offer, stop

Ex 7 Ask Ss to read the questions and to look back at the sentences in Ex 6. Ss discuss each question with a partner. Check their answers and discuss any problems Ss may have had choosing the form of the conditional. Then ask Ss to read the sentences again for their meaning. What do Ss think of the ideas the candidate expresses? Would they be good ideas in an election campaign?

> **1** politician **2** local person **3** politician **4** local person
> **5** politician **6** local person **7** local person **8** politician

> **Photocopiable notes 8.1 (page 120)**
> **If … (Matching sentences page 133)**

Write the following words on the board: *trip, journey*. Ask Ss to explain the difference. Go through the information in the **Watch out!** box to make sure that they all understand.

Speaking: Eco-friendly travel

Ex 8 Go through the situation given and check that Ss know what to do. Ss then prepare the class survey in groups. Monitor them and give help if needed. Ask them to write their ten questions neatly and to check that they are correct.

Ex 9 Each group should ask other groups their questions. Take class feedback and see what the most popular ideas were.

Homework suggestions
- Ss write an email to a friend describing the survey and explaining what the most popular ideas were and why. (120–150 words)

- Ss write an email to a friend telling them about a long journey they went on, explaining what the journey was like and how they felt about it. (120–150 words)
- Ss write a short presentation explaining how they choose to commute and why, and how they would like to commute if they could. (about 100 words)

D Communication strategies
Problem solving

Aims and objectives

In this lesson Ss will:
- read an article about problem-solving techniques
- listen to people discussing their problems and possible solutions
- discuss situations and suggest possible solutions
- write PowerPoint slides presenting a problem, options and the best solution

> ### Culture and language
> **Problem solving**
>
> Problem-solving discussions often follow a similar path. People generally begin by identifying the problem and then they move on to generating possible solutions. Together they agree on the best course of action and then there is some kind of summing up at the end. So the task in hand shapes the structure of the conversation.
>
> The final summing up phase generally includes positive evaluations of the discussion itself such as, *That was useful. Thanks!* or *We haven't figured it out yet, but I think I know what to do now.* (See pages 84 and 85 on *Problem solving*.)
>
> Phrases like these can perform a valuable function in English. They not only signal the end of the discussion, but they also build rapport and solidarity.

Word focus: Talking about problems

Ex 1 Give Ss about a minute to think of a problem they feel comfortable discussing in class.

Ex 2 Ask Ss to read the article to see if the techniques suggested would be of any help with their problem. They can discuss this with other Ss if they feel comfortable.

Ex 3 This exercise focuses on the details of the article. Ask Ss to discuss the questions in pairs and find the answers to the questions in the article.

> **1** You should prioritize them so that you can deal with the most urgent ones first.
> **2** Come up with as many different solutions as you can and ask other people for suggestions. Don't reject any now. You can reject them later.
> **3** You can revise it.

Ex 4 Ask Ss to work in pairs. Ask them to read the definitions and match the phrasal verbs to them. Then get them to check their answers by finding the phrasal verbs in the article and checking how they are used.

8 Green chic

1 deal with
2 work out
3 come up with

Ex 5 Explain that Ss should work in pairs to find verbs that are associated with the three different options given.

a) problem(s): tackle, face, prioritize, deal with, look at
b) solution(s): come up with, suggest, find
c) option(s) and plan(s): reject, examine, implement, revise

Ex 6 Ss discuss the questions in pairs. Once Ss have identified another idea to add to the article, take class feedback and discuss all the new ideas. Ss could vote on the best idea.

Listening: Working together

Ex 7)) **2.9** Tell Ss they are going to hear a conversation between two people. Before playing the recording, ask Ss to read through the questions. After listening once, ask Ss to compare their answers. Play the recording again if necessary.

1 A manager and an assistant.
2 A problem with paper getting stuck in the photocopier.
3 Using normal paper rather than recycled paper.
4 Use normal paper in half the copiers and recycled paper in the others. And record any paper jams over the next month.
5 People might mix up the recycled and normal paper in the copiers so they don't get reliable data.

Track 2.9: 8D, Page 84, Exercises 7 and 8
Conversation 1
A = Andy, **B** = Beth

A: Can I have a word?

B: Sure, what's up?

A: We've got a little problem with the photocopiers. They keep jamming.

B: Oh no!

A: I think it might be the new recycled paper. It's a bit of a pain.

B: Perhaps we should go back to using normal paper. It's not very eco-friendly though.

A: I called the paper manufacturers and they say their paper isn't the problem.

B: But you think it is.

A: Don't know. Maybe.

B: Do we know how often the copiers jammed before we used the recycled paper?

A: Well, no, not really.

B: So, what if we do a little experiment. Er, we could use normal paper in, say, half the copiers and the recycled stuff in the others. And record any paper jams over the next month, say.

A: Um. Why's that?

B: Well, then we'll know if it's a problem with the copiers or the recycled stuff.

A: OK. I like that idea. It's a start.

B: That's right and we can see what happens.

A: Good. Well, we haven't figured it out yet, but I think I know what to do now.

B: Great!

A: That was useful. Thanks!

Ex 8)) Before playing the recording again, ask Ss to read the sentences and discuss if they can remember the missing expressions.

1	a word	7	stuff
2	up	8	start
3	little	9	see … happens
4	pain	10	figured
5	what	11	know
6	if	12	useful

Ex 9 Tell Ss they are going to listen to another conversation. Before playing the recording, ask Ss to discuss the questions.

Ex 10)) **2.10** Play the recording so that Ss can check their answers.

The correct order is: b, c, e, a, d

1 husband and wife
2 Unreliable car. Their car keeps breaking down.
3 Buy a second-hand car that is just a couple of years old and borrow some money from the bank against the house to pay for it.
4 The woman is going to call the bank tomorrow to ask for the loan.
5 The bank might refuse to lend them the money. They might not be able to pay back the loan. The car they buy might be equally unreliable.

Track 2.10: 8D, Page 84, Exercise 10
Conversation 2
S = Sophie, **B** = Bill

S: My car's broken down again.

B: What's the problem this time?

S: Oh, I don't know. It's a real headache.

B: It's so unreliable. You need a new one.

S: Have you seen the prices of new cars?

B: Yeah, I know. But you can't do your job without it.

S: Mmm.

B: If we buy one second-hand, it'll be cheaper.

S: What? Get one that's just a few years old?

B: Yes.

S: We'd still need a loan to pay for it. Interest rates are terrible.

B: Not if we borrowed against the house.

S: That's an idea! I'll call the bank tomorrow.

B: So we have a plan of action now.

S: Yeah, I'm glad you thought of that.

> Photocopiable notes 8.2 (page 120)
> What are you doing? (Card matching page 134)

Speaking: We can work it out

Ex 11 Tell Ss they are going to work in groups to discuss different problems and come up with solutions for each situation, which they will present to the class. Give Ss time to discuss all the possible scenarios and agree on a plan of action. If time is short, assign one scenario only to each group. Don't take class feedback at this stage, but monitor their discussions and help if necessary.

Writing: Presenting solutions

Ex 12 Ss write PowerPoint slides and present their solution to the class with reasons. The class can vote on the best presentation and solution.

Sample answer:

> **Office temperature**
> 1 The problem
>   • Hot and cold
>   • Staff disputes
>   • High energy bills
> 2 The options
>   a Staff control of temperature settings
>   b Manager controls settings
>   c Settings are not controlled by anyone
> 3 The consequences
>   a Disputes will continue and energy bills will increase
>   b Staff complaints to manager. Reduces conflict and helps save money.
>   c Takes control away from everyone. Best option for low energy costs
> 4 The best solution: manager controls setting
>   • Best placed to mediate between staff
>   • Able to keep energy costs under control
>   • Can adapt to individual staff needs, e.g. buy extra heaters, move people

Homework suggestions

• Ss write an email to a friend telling them about their problem identified in Ex 1 and what they think would be a good way of solving the problem. (120–150 words)
• Ss write a report on one of the classmate's presentations in Ex 12, giving their opinion of the ideas. (120–150 words).
• Ss research and see if they can find any other problem-solving techniques not mentioned in the lesson that they think might be useful. They should present the techniques to the class the following lesson and explain why they think they might be useful.

E Interaction Planning a green office

Aims and objectives

In this lesson Ss will:
• discuss what makes a good office space
• read about different types of office
• listen to a presentation about green office design
• discuss ways of making an office a greener place to work

Refer Ss to the Reminder box and draw attention to the language that the lesson will focus on. Check Ss can use this language by looking at pages 169 and 170 of the Grammar reference and at previous lessons of the unit.

Speaking: A new look

Ex 1 Ask Ss to think about different offices they have worked in. What did they like/dislike about them? Then ask Ss to discuss the questions in pairs. Which do Ss think is the most important factor in creating a pleasant workplace?

Possible answers:
Advantages
Communication between colleagues may improve; more access to fresh air; more access to natural light

Disadvantages
Lack of privacy; individual space is reduced; lots of noise and interruptions; no walls to reduce noise and prevent interruptions; no ability to control heating and lighting

Ex 2 Check Ss' pronunciation of the words. Ask Ss to work in pairs to complete the sentences.

> 1 renovate, refurbish   4 partition, screen
> 2 soundproof   5 cubicle
> 3 perimeter

Ex 3 Ask Ss to look at the two photos. Explain that they are going to read three descriptions of workplaces and they have to match two of them to the photos.

> A Meguro Office – Photo 2
> C Devalon Headquarters – Photo 1

Ex 4 Ask Ss to work in pairs and list their reasons for preferring one workplace over the other. Ss will need to use the words they have identified in Ex 2. Take feedback and see if the class agree on one choice.

Ex 5 Ss could work in groups to do this activity. Tell them that they are going to use the vocabulary and ideas from Exs 1–4 to discuss improving the office space in the photo. After the activity, each group should present their ideas to the rest of the class. The class then decides on the best ideas.

Possible answers:
• Buy bigger desks.
• Replace monitors with flat-screen computers.
• Get some plants.
• Put desks into groups to allow staff to see each other and communicate.
• Design smaller glass-walled offices.
• Have a meeting room space.
• Add more colour to the walls and furnishings.
• Buy some colourful paintings.
• Allow staff to have personal possessions on their desks.
• Put in brighter coloured flooring.

Optional homework suggestion
Ss write a short proposal for refurbishing the office, including the recommendations that the class decided were the best.

Listening: Sustainable offices

Ex 6))) 2.11 Tell Ss that they are going to listen to an architect giving a presentation on ways of designing green offices. Before playing the recording, ask Ss to discuss in pairs what they think the presenter might say without looking at points a–e. Explain that the presenter will cover five main points. Ask Ss to read the points a–e and explain that they are in the wrong order. Ss listen to decide on the order the points are mentioned.

> *Correct order is:* b, c, e, a, d

Track 2.11: 8E, Page 87, Exercises 6 and 7

Environmental considerations play an important part in office design today. And we're not just talking about new projects, but also existing buildings. So, what makes an office 'green'? Well, there are various things that can reduce the negative environmental impact of a building. And improve the well-being of its occupants.

Firstly, let's take the location of the building. It's important to ask the question 'Can staff easily walk, cycle or take public transport to the office?' A second consideration is the use of water and a commitment to saving water wherever possible. Thirdly, in order to help reduce the organization's carbon dioxide emissions, offices should be designed to use less energy, for instance, through the use of energy-efficient equipment.

A fourth factor is materials selection. Is it an office that's been built using recyclable materials and organic non-volatile paints? We now realize that chemical emissions from certain paints and materials aren't good for our health. Fortunately, there are organic products which offer healthier, eco-friendly alternatives.

The fifth area is indoor environmental quality; for instance the use of glass walls and doors to make the most of natural light. And also improved ventilation systems. The green office doesn't just look nicer, it makes people feel better, too. Better quality of air and access to natural light make a huge difference. Studies show that access to daylight improves worker productivity by between five to twenty-five per cent.

Organizations are naturally concerned about the cost of all this. But there is a strong business case for the green office. Many examples show that over time, it actually saves money because energy bills are lower and staff productivity is higher. One recent example in the US, is the case of the software maker Adobe Systems. The company spent $1.4 million on a green office project at its San Jose headquarters and earned that investment back in energy savings in under 10 months.

To conclude, I believe that the sustainable office is both good for the environment and good for business, too.

Ex 7 🔊 Tell Ss that they will focus on the detail of the presentation. Ask Ss to read though the notes and see if they can remember anything mentioned. Play the recording again, Ss fill in the missing information and compare their answers in pairs.

1	public transport	4	natural light
2	energy-efficient	5	energy bills
3	recyclable materials	6	1.4

Speaking: A greener place to work

Ex 8 Tell Ss that they are going to roleplay a situation involving the refurbishment of an office. Put Ss into groups of three and ask Ss read their own information. Check any vocabulary Ss might not be sure of before asking them to complete the table and check that they all know what to do.

In one-to-one classes, choose one of the files for the S to complete.

Ex 9 Ss work in their groups to come up with proposals. Make sure that Student A chairs the meeting and uses the *Points to consider* information to focus the discussion.

In one-to-one classes, discuss the S's proposal.

Ex 10 Ss prepare presentations of their proposals. Monitor them and give help when needed.

Optional activity: Each group presents their proposals to the class using their PowerPoint slides.

Homework suggestions
- Ss write up their proposals identified in Ex 10 as a formal proposal. (120–150 words)
- Ss write an email to a friend telling them about their own office (open plan or individual offices) and explaining the advantages and disadvantages of their own situation.
- Ss research and find an office situation that they would like to work in. Ss present their findings to the class at the start of the following lesson.

A Passive forms
B Active or passive
C Telephoning
D Communication strategies Making requests
E Interaction Remote manager

IT generation

A Passive forms

Aims and objectives

In this lesson Ss will:
- read an article about cellphone novels
- study uses of passive forms
- discuss information about mobile phones

Reading: The cellphone novel

Ex 1 Ask Ss to discuss the question in pairs.

Optional activity: Ask Ss to work in groups. Group A think of three advantages of reading a novel on a mobile phone and Group B think of three disadvantages. Put the groups together to debate and decide whether the advantages outweigh the disadvantages.

Ex 2 Ask Ss in pairs to read the sentences and discuss the possible answers. Take feedback and ask if Ss had any surprises. Were there any other advantages or disadvantages mentioned that Ss had not thought of?

1 half	**4**	100 million
2 three	**5**	210 yen ($2.10), 450 yen ($4.50)
3 $200 million	**6**	400

Ex 3 Ask Ss to work in pairs to answer the questions. Encourage Ss to write their answers so that they can check their ideas with the text.

1 While she was commuting to work.
2 In cafés, during breaks from work, and travelling to and from work.
3 Because she started to enjoy reading them.
4 Internet browsers, games and digital cameras
5 You can watch TV, go through train-ticket barriers and pay your bills.
6 Bigger screens and faster download times.

Optional activity: Ask Ss to write down any words they were not sure of in the text and exchange their list with a partner. Ss explain their partner's words if they can, or Ss look them up together.

Optional homework suggestion

Ss write an email to a friend explaining what they read in the article and explaining what they think about it. (120–150 words)

Grammar: Passive forms

Ex 4 Ask Ss to work in pairs to complete the example sentences from the article in the notes for 2 and 3. Ss can check their answers with the text. Tell them to underline the examples in the text so that they can find them again easily when they reread the article. Ss then complete the rules on passive forms in the notes for 1.

1 be, past participle, by
2 are used, has … been launched
3 are … being accessed, were … written

Optional suggestion: Refer Ss to page 170 of the Grammar reference and go through the notes on passive forms. Allow time to discuss examples and any problems Ss have. Provide further examples if required. Ask Ss where they often find passives and why. (Suggestions: newspaper headlines, guidebooks.)

Optional homework suggestion

Ss research on the internet and bring other examples of the passive to class for other Ss to explain why the passive is used.

Speaking: Mobile facts and figures

Ex 5 Tell Ss that they are going to read some information about mobile phones. (Student B's information is on page 140). Tell them some of the information is missing. They must ask their partner questions to complete the text. You could do an example first by doing Student A's first sentence with a S who has read the information in B's text. Then ask Ss to work in pairs. Monitor Ss during the activity and encourage them to ask extra questions for more details. After the activity, check the answers, then ask Ss to underline all examples of the passive in their texts.

1 When was the first call on a mobile phone made? – in April 1973
2 What was sent on Vodafone's network in December 1992? – the first SMS text message
3 How many text messages are sent worldwide each day? – around one billion
4 Where is chatting on your mobile forbidden? – in 'quiet' train carriages in the UK.
5 What are the train's windows covered with? – a high-tech material
6 Where was the world's most expensive mobile phone number sold? – at a charity auction in Quatar
7 Where was the ring tone first launched? – in Finland
8 What was introduced on mobile phones in 1999? – The first full internet service
9 Where were early mobile phones installed? – in vehicles as car phones

10 Who agreed on a standard charger for mobile phones? – the GSM Association

TALKING POINT
Discuss the questions with the class.

Homework suggestions
• Ss do any necessary research and write an email to a friend giving their answers to the questions in the Talking points. (120–150 words)
• Ss research an invention they would like to talk about and present it to the class next lesson.

β Active or passive

Aims and objectives
In this lesson Ss will:
• read an article about the advantages and disadvantages of social networking sites
• study when active or passive forms should be used
• roleplay a union meeting about allowing internet access at work

Reading: Online social networking

TALKING POINT
The Talking point could be used to start the lesson.

Ex 1 Ask Ss to discuss each web technology in turn and decide which are the most important in daily life. Write Ss' suggestions on the board. Check pronunciation of these key words.

Ex 2 Ask Ss to read the title of the text. What do they think it will be about? Ss discuss the questions in pairs, read the text and compare their ideas. During feedback, ask Ss how they react to the text. Do they agree/disagree with it? Why?

> **Possible answers:**
> **Advantages**
> Social networking websites are more interactive. New technology means employees can access employee blogs, customer forums, multimedia, wikis, etc.
>
> **Disadvantages**
> Privacy: there is a danger of private information or photos being used without permission.
> Cost for employers: employees spend more time networking (*more than 39% of people are typically accessing such a site for more than an hour a day*) so they are less productive; and employees use the company's network for personal use such as social networking.

Grammar: Active or passive

Ex 3 Ask Ss to work with a partner and underline uses of the passive in the text and explain why they are used.

> There are eleven examples of the passive form in the text.
> **1** Paragraph 1: … which <u>have been made</u> as interactive as possible. (*present perfect passive*)
> **2** Paragraph 2: … this technology <u>is being adopted</u> by many companies. (*present continuous passive*)
> **3** Paragraph 2: Employees <u>are encouraged</u> to access employee blogs, (*present simple passive*)

> **4** Paragraph 3: These Web technologies <u>can be accessed</u> at work. (*passive form of modal*)
> **5** Paragraph 3: … not only personal emails <u>are being sent</u>. (*present continuous passive*)
> **6** Paragraph 3: These days photos, music files and videos <u>can</u> also <u>be shared</u> (*passive form of modal*)
> **7** Paragraph 4: … privacy <u>is threatened</u>. (*present simple passive*)
> **8** Paragraph 4: Professional information <u>can be stolen</u> on the web. (*passive form of modal*)
> **9** Paragraph 4: … private information <u>could be used</u> without permission. (*passive form of modal*)
> **10** Paragraph 4: … employee productivity <u>has been decreased</u>. (*present perfect passive*)
> **11** Paragraph 5: Use of social networking technologies <u>needs to be controlled</u> at work (*passive form of modal*)

Ex 4 Ss choose the correct options to complete the information.

> **1** writing, passive, active
> **2** passive
> **3** formal, less formal
> **4** active, less formal, formal

Optional suggestion: Refer Ss to page 170 of the Grammar reference and go through the notes on active and passive forms. Allow time to discuss examples and any problems Ss have. Provide further examples if required.

Ex 5 Ask Ss to work in pairs. Ss should read the sentences aloud to each other and explain why they think the active or passive sounds best in each case.

> **1** a and b – Both possible
> **2** b – Passive
> **3** a – Active
> **4** b – Passive because we don't want to say who was responsible
> **5** b – Passive because we don't know who did it
> **6** b – Passive because we don't know who did it
> **7** a and b – Both possible

Ex 6 Encourage Ss to explain their ideas and to make any other suggestions.

> **1** an article from a newspaper or science magazine
> **2** a newspaper article
> **3** a recipe
> **4** an email or report
> **5** a newspaper article
> **6** a company website
> **7** instructions, a technical manual, an experiment

Speaking: A union meeting

Ex 7 Explain that Ss are going to do a roleplay between management and employees about internet access at work. Encourage Ss to share their own experiences in groups.

Ex 8 Ss work in the same groups. Allocate 'A' or 'B' to each group and ask them to discuss the situation. Ss should make notes on their ideas so that they can use them at a union meeting.

In one-to-one classes, ask the S to prepare one of the situations on their own to discuss with you at the meeting.

Ex 9 Ss roleplay the meeting. After the activity, take class feedback. Encourage Ss to share their ideas and experiences.

Writing: Notes on a meeting

Ex 10 Before they do the writing, remind Ss that the email should clarify the situation and that bullet points would be appropriate. As it is an official email, the style should be impersonal. Suggest that Ss use 150–180 words.

Sample answer:

> To: …
>
> Cc: …
>
> From: …
>
> **Subject:** Report: Use of the internet
>
> Dear employee
> I'm sending you a summary of our meeting with management on 9th April concerning the use of the Internet at work.
>
> **Summary report: Use of the internet at work**
> **Main concerns:**
> • A lot of work time is being spent on personal use of the internet.
> • Productivity is being lost.
> • Staff can write personal emails and go online at any time.
> • Inappropriate websites might be accessed.
>
> **Points to consider:**
> • Recent research has shown that staff who take a break to surf are more productive.
> • Employees should be encouraged to use web skills.
> • Staff must be allowed some personal freedom.
>
> **Action to be taken:**
> • Staff have to be given set times for internet use.
> • Employees need to be disciplined when they misuse the internet.
> • Web use at work cannot be banned because this will be counter-productive.
>
> Management will be sending you a list of set times for internet use shortly and further details regarding any disciplinary action that may be taken. In the meantime, please do not hesitate to contact me if you have any questions, or if anything is not clear.
>
> Best wishes
>
> Bill Woods
>
> Trade Union representative

TALKING POINT
Discuss the questions with the class if you have not done so at the beginning of the lesson.

Homework suggestions
• Tell Ss that they are planning to write to a new penfriend in another country they have met on Facebook. Ss should write an email to their new friend telling them about social network sites in their country, explaining how popular they are and why. (120–150 words)
• Ask Ss to write an essay discussing the statement: *Technology causes more problems than it solves.* (120–150 words)
• Ss write an email to a friend telling them about the meeting your union and management had about using the internet at work, what happened and what the final outcome was. (120–150 words)

C Telephoning

Aims and objectives
In this lesson Ss will:
• study phrasal verbs connected to telephoning
• listen to different telephone conversations
• roleplay telephone conversations

Word focus: Telephoning phrasal verbs

TALKING POINT
The Talking point could be used here to introduce the lesson. Discuss the questions with the class.

Ex 1 Ask Ss to discuss the questions in pairs. Take class feedback. Ask Ss about any differences between phoning in English and in their own language.

Ex 2 2.12 Tell Ss that they are going to listen to people giving tips on dealing with phone calls in English. Before you play the recording, ask Ss to discuss four key tips they would give someone in that situation and write down their ideas. Take feedback and compile a class list on the board. Play the recording and ask Ss to listen and compare with their own ideas. Add any news ideas to the list on the board. Ask Ss which they think is the best tip.

> **Speaker 1**
> Prepare what you are going to say or write it down, e.g. *Hello, it's Martine here. I'm phoning about the email you sent me. I have a few questions about …*
> **Speaker 2**
> Take a deep breath before you phone someone up, or when you hear the phone ringing.
> Use phrases to give yourself time like, *Hold on a minute, please. I'll just check that for you.*
> End the call positively, *Thanks for calling. It's good doing business with you. I'll look into that and get back to you.*
> **Speaker 3**
> Ask a colleague to make an excuse (*I'm in a meeting or out of the office*) and take a message.
> **Speaker 4**
> Take any phone calls in English in a quiet place, like a meeting room.
> Put the speaker phone on and ask a colleague to listen to the call with you.
> If you don't understand, put the caller on hold and check with your colleague.
>
> **Suggestions for other tips:**
> Practise important phone conversations with a colleague before you call.
> Ask questions and confirm or clarify what you have understood.
> Confirm in an email.

Track 2.12: 9C, Page 92, Exercises 2 and 3
1

I always prepare what I'm going to say before I make a phone call in English. I write down something like, 'Hello, it's Martine here. I'm phoning about the email you sent me. I have a few questions about …', and so on. If you know what you're going to say before you pick up the phone, it makes it easier.

9 IT generation

2

I'm a trainer in communication skills. I often tell people, take a deep breath before you phone someone up or when you hear the phone ringing. Breathing really helps because the caller can hear it in your voice – they can tell if you're prepared or not. You can also use neat little phrases like, 'Hold on a minute, please. I'll just check that for you.' You can use the time to check the information, or think about what you're going to say next. It's also good to end the call on a positive note saying, 'Thanks for calling. It's good doing business with you,' or, 'I'll look into it and I'll get back to you.'

3

Well, I work in sales and I'm on the phone all day, but I avoid making calls in English. If someone rings up, I ask a colleague to make an excuse and say I'm in a meeting or out of the office. Most people don't phone back. Once, I didn't understand anything a guy was saying. He had a funny accent and spoke too fast and I kept saying, 'Could you repeat that, please?' But in the end I hung up because I didn't understand a word.

4

We work in a busy open-plan office, but I prefer to take my phone calls in English in a quiet place, so I always ask the receptionist to put the caller through to a meeting room. And I usually ask my colleague to come with me. She's good at listening, so we put the speaker phone on and we can both listen at the same time. And if I don't understand something, I put the caller on hold and check with my colleague. But you can't do that very often.

Ex 3 🔊 Tell Ss that phrasal verbs are often found in speech in general and that there are several found in telephone language. Explain that a phrasal verb is a verb + preposition/adverbial particle and ask Ss to suggest some examples. Can Ss remember any they heard in the tips? Ask Ss to read through the tips and fill in any they can remember or guess. Play the recording again for Ss to check their ideas and complete the tips. Encourage Ss to check their answers with a partner.

1	pick up	6	rings up
2	phone … up	7	phone back
3	Hold on	8	hung up
4	get back	9	put … through
5	'm on	10	put … on hold

Optional activity: Ss choose two verbs and write two-line dialogues in pairs. Ss read their dialogues to the class.

Photocopiable notes 9.1 (page 120)
Phrasal verbs (Pelmonism page 135)

Ex 4 Ss work in pairs. Ss read the sentences and decide which phrasal verb best completes the sentences. They can use dictionaries if necessary.

1 phone back
2 pick it up
3 get back to
4 hung up
5 put you through
6 ring up, put me on hold
7 am on
8 Hold on

The speakers are talking on the phone in sentences 1, 3 (automated voice mail), 5, 7 and 8.

Optional activity: Ss work together to check the meaning of the phrasal verbs they did not use in the sentences in Ex 4 and write their own sentences to demonstrate their meaning. Ss read their sentences to the class to compare their ideas.

Ex 5 Encourage Ss to share their experiences with the class, especially if they are amusing!

Optional homework suggestion
Ss write an email to a friend who is going to live and work in an office in England, suggesting some tips for dealing with telephone calls in English. (120–150 words)

Listening: Improving your phone manner

Ex 6 🔊 2.13 Tell Ss that they are going to listen to four phone calls and that they should not try to listen for detail but for the purpose of each phone call. Before you play the recording, ask Ss to read the four possibilities.

a	call three	**c**	call four
b	call one	**d**	call two

Track 2.13: 9C, Page 93, Exercise 6
Call 1

Could you erm … we're not available right now, sorry. Could you please leave a message after the tone … oh, and our hours of operation are nine to five, that's Monday to Friday, but not Saturday. Bye.

Call 2

Hello, it's Amrit here from Nano-tech Systems in Delhi. I'd like to speak to the laboratory manager, Isabel Fernandez. It's about some equipment we ordered from you last month. I sent you a couple of emails last week, Isabel. Could you call me back as soon as you can? Thank you.

Call 3
S = Steve, C = Chloe

S: Hi.

C: Oh, uh, hello. Is that the IT department?

S: Yep. … How can I help you?

C: Oh, I'd like to speak to Steve, please.

S: That's me.

C: Right, well, this is Chloe Jones from Hydra Energies. I'm phoning about the software you installed for us recently. I'm afraid we're still having a few problems with it.

S: Oh, you want to speak to Danny about that.

C: Danny?

S: Yep, he's the boss.

C: The thing is, it's a bit urgent and I was wondering if you could …

S: Yeah, sorry. It's his day off. He'll be in tomorrow. I'll tell him you called. Bye.

Call 4
D = Danny, C = Chloe

D: OK, Chloe, so one of our engineers will come round on Thursday morning to reinstall the programme.

C: The thing is, we're working on a big project at the moment.

D: Yes, I understand. I'm sure we'll be able to fix it on Thursday. And I'm really sorry again about not calling you sooner but, you know, I only got the message this morning. Was there anything else, Chloe?

C: Yes, just one thing. What's the name of the engineer who's coming?

D: Er, let's see … Greg.

C: Oh, fine. Not Steve then?

D: No, it's Greg. He's our software specialist.

C: Great. I'll see Greg on Thursday at eight then.

D: Yes, Thursday at eight a.m. And if there's anything else, Chloe, just call me on my mobile, OK?

C: Thanks a lot, Danny.

D: Thanks for calling. It's good doing business with you. Bye.

C: Bye.

Ex 7 Ss discuss the effectiveness of each call briefly in pairs, giving their reasons. Take class feedback. Make sure Ss justify their answers and clarify why the calls are or are not effective. Point out that it's not always just the language used but also the manner and the actions, e.g. hanging up before the end of the conversation.

> **Possible answers:**
> Calls two and four are the most effective and calls one and three the least effective.
> In call 1 the person sounds unprofessional as if she hasn't prepared what she was going to say in the voicemail.
> In call three the person who answers the phone (Steve) is unhelpful and sounds rude. He hangs up quickly at the end before she's finished speaking.

Ex 8))) **2.14** Play the recording of the voicemail (call one) again. Ask Ss to work in pairs to improve the voicemail.

Track 2.14: 9C, Page 93, Exercise 8
Call 1

Could you erm … we're not available right now, sorry. Could you please leave a message after the tone … oh, and our hours of operation are nine to five, that's Monday to Friday, but not Saturday. Bye.

Ask Ss to work in pairs, A and B. Ss prepare a voicemail on their own, then read them to each other.

Variation: Ss read their voicemails to the class for other Ss to comment.

Ex 9 Ss compare their scripts with the ones in File 40, page 140.

Optional activity: Ss could record their voicemails using their mobile phones and then listen to themselves. Comment on their manner and language.

Ex 10))) **2.15** Before playing the recording, ask Ss to read the calls and see how much they can remember of what was said. Play the recording for Ss to write the missing words. Can Ss suggest any other ways of ending a call?

> **Call two**
> 1 Hello, it's, here from
> 2 It's about some
>
> **Call three**
> 3 like to speak to
> 4 This is, from
> 5 I'm phoning about

Track 2.15: 9C, Page 93, Exercise 10
Call 2

Hello, it's Amrit here from Nano-tech Systems in Delhi. I'd like to speak to the laboratory manager, Isabel Fernandez. It's about some equipment we ordered from you last month. I sent you a couple of emails last week, Isabel. Could you call me back as soon as you can? Thank you.

Call 3
S = Steve, C = Chloe

S: Hi.

C: Oh, uh, hello. Is that the IT department?

S: Yep. … How can I help you?

C: Oh, I'd like to speak to Steve, please.

S: That's me.

C: Right, well, this is Chloe Jones from Hydra Energies. I'm phoning about the software you installed for us recently. I'm afraid we're still having a few problems with it.

S: Oh, you want to speak to Danny about that.

C: Danny?

S: Yep, he's the boss.

C: The thing is, it's a bit urgent and I was wondering if you could …

S: Yeah, sorry. It's his day off. He'll be in tomorrow. I'll tell him you called. Bye.

Ex 11))) **2.16** Before playing the recording, ask Ss to read the text message and check that they understand the abbreviations. After Ss have listened to the call, Ss work in pairs to correct the message.

> Hi Greg. Can u ~~ring~~ visit Chloe Jones @ Hydra Energies ~~Tues @ 8.30~~ Thursday @ 8.00? Probs with new ~~PC~~ software/programme. ~~Not~~ Urgent. Danny
>
> Ending the call: Chloe and Danny confirmed the arrangements and Danny thanked her for calling saying, 'It's good doing business with you' before saying goodbye.

Track 2.16: 9C, Page 93, Exercise 11
Call 4
D = Danny, C = Chloe

D: OK, Chloe, so one of our engineers will come round on Thursday morning to reinstall the programme.

C: The thing is, we're working on a big project at the moment.

D: Yes, I understand. I'm sure we'll be able to fix it on Thursday. And I'm really sorry again about not calling you sooner but, you know, I only got the message this morning. Was there anything else, Chloe?

C: Yes, just one thing. What's the name of the engineer who's coming?

D: Er, let's see … Greg.

C: Oh, fine. Not Steve then?

D: No, it's Greg. He's our software specialist.

C: Great. I'll see Greg on Thursday at eight then.

D: Yes, Thursday at eight a.m. And if there's anything else, Chloe, just call me on my mobile, OK?

C: Thanks a lot, Danny.

D: Thanks for calling. It's good doing business with you. Bye.

C: Bye.

Ex 12 This exercise helps Ss prepare for the roleplay in Ex 14. Ask Ss to work in pairs to complete the table by matching the expressions to their headings. Encourage Ss to add their own ideas.

> **1** c **2** d **3** f **4** a **5** e **6** b **7** g
>
> *Other similar expressions:*
> Voicemail: I'm sorry but I can't come to the phone right now.
> Asking for someone: Could I speak to Steve, please?
> Taking a message: How can I help you? I'll ask him/her to call you back.
> Ending a call: Is that everything? Speak to you soon. (It's been) good talking to you.

Optional activity: Ss phone one another and leave a message on their mobile phone. Ss listen to the message, write it down and check with the S who left the message.

Ex 13 Ss work in pairs to check that they can remember the expressions. Encourage Ss to check not only the words but also the pronunciation and the intonation so that Ss sound polite and interested.

Speaking: Ring ring

Ex 14 Ss work in pairs to rewrite the conversation between Chloe and Steve (call three). Tell Ss to think about what went wrong with the first phone call and to think of ways to improve it. Ss then sit back-to-back and act out their conversations in front of the class. Other Ss listen and comment.

Ex 15 Ss work in pairs and read information. They then roleplay the telephone conversations using the information they have been given. Monitor the Ss and give feedback on their conversations.

TALKING POINT

Ss discuss the questions in pairs, then feedback to the whole class.

Homework suggestions

- Ss write an email to a friend describing a misunderstanding they had in a phone call and what happened. (120–150 words)
- Ask Ss to call each other before the following lesson and speak to each other in English. During the phone call Ss should give one another a message that they should bring to the following lesson, when they should discuss any problems they had with the message or the phone call.

D Communication strategies
Making requests

Aims and objectives

In this lesson Ss will:
- discuss what to say in different situations
- listen to people talking in different situations and discuss problems
- consider ways of making and responding to requests
- consider indirect requests and how to respond to them

Culture and language
Making requests

To get someone to do something, English speakers generally say things like *Can you do it?* or *Could you possibly do it?* instead of a simple *Do it*. So we use question forms where an imperative would be used in other languages. These request forms don't translate simply into other languages. Failure to use them appropriately can create a negative impression.

The size of the request (how much we are asking for) influences the form we choose. We tend to use more basic forms such as *Can I / you …?* for smaller or routine requests. We tend to use longer request forms such as *Do you mind / Could you possibly …?* with requests that involve a larger imposition (asking people to do more).

People's perceptions of the size of a request can vary across cultures. For example, in a culture where phone calls are cheap or free, it may be easy to ask to use someone's phone. In a culture where phone calls are expensive, it would be a larger imposition. Related to this is what right we feel we have to make a request. We may find it easy to ask a waiter in a restaurant to bring us a glass of water if we are a customer. If we're asking our boss for the same favour, it could be more difficult.

When we are asking people we don't know well to do things, we often use basic, short request forms. Similarly, with people we are very close to socially, shorter forms are also common. This means that *Can you take me to the station?* could work equally well for your spouse or an unknown taxi driver.

For the vast majority of relationships that fall between 'socially close' and 'socially distant', requests need handling with care. Before we make larger requests, we often apologize or give an explanation:
Sorry, do you have a moment? Do you think you could go over that again? I'm not sure if I understand you.

Sometimes English speakers avoid asking for something directly. They may hint and the other person might offer to help:
A: Oh dear, my computer's crashed again.
B: Here, let me help you.
(See pages 94 and 95 on *Making requests.*) Be ready to explore different perceptions of 'request size' and 'rights' as you work through the situations such as the ones in Ex 9 in this lesson.

Listening: Spoken requests

Ex 1 Ask Ss to discuss the questions in pairs.

Ex 2))) 2.17 Tell Ss they are going to hear three conversations where there is a problem. Before you play the recording, ask Ss to read the questions. Make sure that Ss understand Q 1a – 'too direct' (saying things too plainly and without thinking about being polite). Ss then listen to the recording and identify the answers to the questions. They then discuss their answers in pairs.

> **1** a **2** b **3** b

Track 2.17: 9D, Page 94, Exercise 2

Conversation 1

A = Alex, **R** = Receptionist

A: Hi.

R: Hello. Can I help you?

A: Yes, tell me how to get to the IT department.

R: … The IT department?

A: Yes.

R: It's that way.

A: Thanks.

Conversation 2

W = Waitress, **H** = Horst

W Can I help you?

H: Would you be so kind as to give me a chicken sandwich and an orange juice, please?

W: Excuse me?

H: Would you be so kind as to give me a chicken sandwich and an orange juice, please?

W: Yeah, OK. I heard you the first time.

Conversation 3

T = Teacher, **P** = Pieter

T: OK, so we'll go by train. Pieter, do you think you could check the train times on the internet tonight?

P: No, I can't tonight. Sorry.

T: Oh, OK … Ana, would you mind checking the times?

Background information

Requests

Making a direct request is perfectly usual and acceptable in some languages. But in English, using a straight imperative to ask for something can be inappropriate and may even sound authoritarian. It's better to form a request using a modal verb like *can* or *could*. Horst has probably learnt that it is polite in English to use more indirect structures when making requests. However, you can be too indirect and this level of 'politeness' could make the British waitress think he's being sarcastic or funny. The teacher's request may be inconvenient for Pieter. It's good that he says *sorry*, but he hasn't made it clear if it is a big problem by explaining why he can't check the bus times. It would be usual to make that clear. You can sound unhelpful if you don't explain why you can't do something.

Ex 3 Ss work in pairs to read the audio scripts and improve the dialogues. Each pair reads out their suggestions to the class or acts out the dialogue.

Possible answers:

1

Alex: Can/Could you tell me how to get to the IT department? / Do you think you could tell me how to get to the IT department?

Employee: Sure. It's that way.

2

Horst: A chicken sandwich and an orange juice, please./ Can/Could I have a chicken sandwich and an orange juice, please?

Waitress: Sure. Do you want any mayo (mayonnaise) with that? Is that a small or large orange juice?

3

Teacher: Pieter, do you think you could check the train times on the internet tonight?

Pieter: No, I'm sorry I can't today. You see/The thing is I've got football practice this evening. / Actually, I've got football practice this evening.

Teacher: Never mind. Ana, would you mind checking the times?

Ex 4 🔊 **2.18** Tell Ss they are going to listen to four situations in which people make requests. Before you play the recording, ask Ss to read the situations and listen for which request they hear first in each case. If necessary, play the recording again so that Ss can hear the language used in each situation.

Situation 1: a then b	Situation 3: a then b
Situation 2: b then a	Situation 4: b then a

Track 2.18, 9D, Page 94, Exercises 4 and 5

Situation 1

1

W = Woman, **Wa** = Waiter

W: A caffè latte, please.

Wa: One latte, coming up.

2

A: Do you mind if I help myself to coffee?

B: Sure. Go ahead. The kitchen is the first door on the right.

Situation 2

1

A: Would it be OK to use the Canon projector for my presentation?

B: I'm afraid not. The thing is, it's being repaired at the moment.

A: Oh, OK. I'll just use my laptop then.

2

A: I'd like to speak to somebody in technical support, please.

B: Press *one* for technical assistance. Press two for all other services.

Situation 3

1

A: Do you mind leaving at four?

B: Actually, four is a bit early. I thought we could leave at about four thirty if that's all right with you.

A: Of course. That'll be fine.

2

A: Let's leave around four, OK?

B: Is that four o'clock real time or your time?

A: Four my time, of course. Cheeky!

Situation 4

1

A: Do you think you could send me those pdf files?

B: Certainly. I'll do that right away.

2

A: Oh no, my computer's crashed. Can I use yours?

B: Actually, I have to send an urgent email. Sorry. Try Liz.

Ex 5 🔊 Tell Ss they are going to focus on the language used in making requests in different situations. Before you play the recording again, ask Ss to read through the requests in the box and discuss what the missing words might be. Play the recording and Ss complete the information. Encourage Ss to compare their answers with a partner before taking feedback.

People we know well and strangers	People in the middle ground
1 please	5 Do you mind if
2 Press	6 Would it be
3 Let's	7 mind leaving
4 Can I	8 Do you think you

Ex 6 Ask Ss to work in pairs and underline the responses in the table that were used for the different requests in Ex 5. Explain that there is no response for 2 as this is an instruction rather than a request, and in 3 the man responds with a joke.

1 Coming up.
4 Actually, …
5 Sure. Go ahead.
6 I'm afraid + clause. The thing is …
7 Actually, …
8 Certainly.

Ex 7 Ask Ss to work in pairs to match the requests and responses. Take feedback by asking one S to read a request and nominate another S to read the response.

1 f **2** g **3** h **4** e **5** d **6** a **7** b **8** c

Speaking: Making requests

Ex 8 Tell Ss that people often ask for something indirectly. Go through the information and point out the importance of using *I'm sorry* when responding politely. Ask Ss to work in pairs to make and respond to requests.

Ex 9 Ask Ss to prepare to roleplay the different situations. Tell half the Ss they are A and should look at the information below, and the other half are B and should look at the information in File 12 on page 134. Give Ss three to four minutes to read their information by themselves and think about what they would say in each situation. Then put the students into pairs A + B and ask them to roleplay each situation. Monitor and help if necessary. Then discuss the situations with the whole class. Which situation was easiest/ most difficult? Why?

Variation: Put the students into pairs and tell each pair that they are either pair A or pair B. They read the information and think about the different situations and possible responses together. Regroup the students into pairs with one A and one B to roleplay the situations. Monitor and help if necessary. Then discuss the situations with the whole class. Which situation was easiest/most difficult? Why?

Ex 10 Ask Ss to work in pairs to prepare the roleplay. Ss act out their roleplays in front of the class.

Homework suggestions

- Ss read the audio scripts again and think about the language that was direct and polite. Ss make a record of useful expressions for making and responding to requests.
- Ask Ss to write a short dialogue involving a request that they can read to the class the following lesson.
- Ss write an email to a friend about one of the situations in Ex 9, describing the situation, explaining what happened and how they felt about it. (120–150 words)

E Interaction Remote manager

Aims and objectives

In this lesson Ss will:
- read interviews from a college magazine about old students
- read a report about managing remote teams
- listen to people talking about the challenges of remote working
- listen to and roleplay phone calls

Refer Ss to the Reminder box and draw attention to the language that the lesson will focus on. Check Ss can use this language by looking at page 170 of the Grammar reference and at previous lessons of the unit.

Reading: Remote workers

Background information
Remote working

Remote or tele-working has many potential benefits for employee and employer. The work can be done in any location and is especially useful for people who spend a lot of time commuting to meetings or who live a long way from the office. It can also give a better work–life balance. By cutting travelling time, people can focus on important aspects of the job more effectively, which helps to reduce stress. There are benefits for the environment such as reducing congestion and carbon emissions, and companies can benefit from a greener image.

Different types of tele-working include:

• home/flexible working: work hours are adjustable and/or people work from home a few days each week

• working from a tele-centre: working in an office base that is not the employee's usual work location

• virtual meetings: using technology like video-conferencing for meetings

Ex 1 Discuss the question with the class briefly.

A remote manager is a manager who you only communicate with via email, videoconference, phone, etc.

Ex 2 Ask Ss to read the text quickly and note the answers to the questions.

1 Tanya Wang is an artist based in Hong Kong.
2 Lauren West works for Google Street View in a small town in Canada.
3 Lidia Popescu is a software developer and works for a telephone company in Oslo.

Ex 3 Ask Ss to work in groups to explain the work that the alumni do and how they choose to communicate in their jobs. Monitor the discussion and help if necessary. If Ss have a problem understanding the detail or vocabulary in the text, ask them to help each other or use a dictionary.

Possible answers:
1 Tanya Wang has to communicate with 50 artists around the world for her project. She also has to arrange shipment of the artwork – 50 freight containers. She communicates virtually using email, Skype, video and teleconference.

2 Lauren West's job is to change the photos that are taken for Google Street View, e.g. individuals' faces and car licence plates have to be obscured and then the photos can be uploaded. She mostly communicates on the intranet.
3 Lidia Popescu communicates with her boss, who's based in India, using email, Instant Messenger and the phone. Team meetings are held via videoconference.

Ex 4 Ask Ss to discuss the advantages and disadvantages of remote working in pairs or small groups. Take feedback by asking one S from each pair/group to write their ideas on the board under the headings of 'Pros' and 'Cons'.

Possible answers:
Pros
1 more autonomy/independence/freedom
2 fewer face-to-face meetings – saving time
3 reduced business travel – saving time and money
4 improved communication – more effective and shorter meetings; more written communication so verbal agreements are confirmed
5 more flexible hours – if it involves tele-working/ working from home
6 less regular contact with your manager because he/ she trusts you to do the work (this can also be a disadvantage)
7 reduced 'office politics'

Cons
1 It's unsociable – face-to-face meetings are more sociable and more human
2 The 'Superman syndrome' – the worry of having to do everything yourself
3 Time differences if team members are in different locations
4 Cultural differences
5 Difficulty of knowing how much to communicate and when
6 Having to confirm everything in writing – misunderstandings on the phone can be a problem
7 Time pressure and need for constant connectivity
8 (Remote managers) Managing a team in different locations
9 Finding a balance between control and independence

Listening: Working virtually

Ex 5 Tell Ss they are going to read a report about managing remote teams, but the headings are missing. Ss read the report and add in the headings.

1 Management style
2 Using technology
3 Building teams

Ex 6))) **2.19** Explain that Ss are going to listen to the interviewees from Ex 2 talking about the challenges of remote working. Ss should underline ideas that are mentioned. Before playing the recording, ask Ss to read the report again.

1 A high degree of trust is needed between the remote manager and the employee.
Lauren: … she trusts me to get on with the job.
• staff should be given regular and positive feedback
Lauren: She's also really good at giving me regular positive feedback …

• remote teams need regular communication and team meetings
Lauren: … she always replies within 24 hours. But we usually meet up face-to-face with the team once a month …
and **Lidia:** … but I think the team should meet more often face-to-face.
• phone calls should include personal/social content and not purely business.
Lidia: We usually start talking about work straightaway and there's no time to make small talk.
• remote workers are in danger of developing the 'Superman' syndrome
Tanya: I think I'm developing a bit of a 'Superwoman' syndrome. You know, you think you can do everything yourself and it's difficult to know when to stop …
3 Too much use of technology can isolate people from their colleagues and business partners.
Lidia: The thing I find challenging is that I feel quite isolated.
– Steps need to be taken to ensure teams meet together.
Lidia: I think the team should meet more often face-to-face.
– face-to-face meetings can be sociable
Lauren: But we usually meet up face-to-face with the team once a month, which is good fun. I think it's important to have that social contact.

Track 2.19: 9E, Page 97, Exercise 6
Tanya

I spend a lot of time writing emails and using Skype and I sometimes organize teleconferences. But they're difficult to set up because of the time differences. And then I have to confirm everything and put any verbal agreements in writing. I think I'm developing a bit of a 'Superwoman' syndrome. You know, you think you can do everything yourself and it's difficult to know when to stop, but I'm really excited about the project!

Lauren

My supervisor is busy all the time, so I don't get to speak to her on the phone that much. But she trusts me to get on with the job. She's also really good at giving me regular positive feedback and she always replies within 24 hours. But we usually meet up face-to-face with the team once a month, which is good fun. I think it's important to have that social contact. The downside is I've got to be connected to the intranet most of the time and sometimes at weekends, but I enjoy the autonomy. That's cool.

Lidia

The thing I find challenging is that I feel quite isolated. The time differences are a problem, too. We usually start talking about work straightaway and there's no time to make small talk. I think remote managers have a difficult time managing people in different locations. I know travel budgets are being cut these days, but I think the team should meet more often face-to-face.

Ex 7 Discuss the question and see if the whole class agrees. Encourage Ss to give reasons for their ideas.

Tanya and Lauren seem to enjoy working remotely more than Lidia, who feels more isolated.

9 IT generation

Speaking: Do me a favour

Ex 8))) **2.20** Before playing the recording, describe the situation to Ss and ask them to read the list. After listening Ss should compare their ideas with a partner.

> 1 Check Erik got the updated user manual ✓
> 2 I won't have all proposals ready until Friday. ✓
> 3 Suggest face-to-face meeting with team. (She tried to but he didn't listen.)
> 4 Confirm when Erik's back in Oslo. ✗

Track 2.20: 9E, Page 97, Exercises 8 and 9

E = Erik, **L** = Lidia

E: Hi, Lidia.

L: Hello, Erik.

E: What's up?

L: I'm just phoning to check if you got the user manual for the new software because it's been updated …

E: Listen, Lidia, I'm between meetings, so this will have to be quick. Before I forget, can you send me those pdf files with the new project proposals? It's urgent.

L: The thing is, I haven't received all the proposals yet. There are two missing …

E: … I'm sorry, this line's bad. It would be great if you could email them to me today.

L: Today? I'm really sorry, Erik. Do you mind if I send them on Friday? For the weekend …

E: The weekend? No, no, that's too late.

L: The thing is, all the project managers have been very busy with this new software.

E: I know. I know. But I've got meetings all day today and tomorrow. Look, can you do me a favour?

L: Sure. What is it?

E: Do you think you could phone the project managers?

L: Uh, OK. I'll do that straightaway. Actually, Erik, I think the team should meet to, er …

E: No problem. It's already been set up.

L: Er, I don't mean another videoconference. I mean a face-to-face …

E: Lidia, is it OK if I call you this evening? About nine?

L: Is that Oslo time?

E: … Sorry, got to go now, Lidia.

L: I'll speak to you later then.

E: Oh, by the way, I'm having trouble using this new software.

L: I've already sent you the manual, Erik.

E: Thanks. Bye.

L: Bye.

Ex 9))) Tell Ss they are going to listen again, this time for what Lidia is asked to do. Ask Ss to read the list. After listening to the recording, Ss should compare their answers and identify the problem with the conversation.

> 1 Send me project proposals today! ✓
> 2 Phone project managers ✓
> 5 Send me new user manual (Erik doesn't directly ask her to send her the user manual. He wants Lidia to help him to use the new software.)

Problems:
Erik is too busy to listen and there were technical problems with the line. But maybe Lidia often phones him for help and doesn't work well unsupervised.

Ex 10 Ss prepare their roles in pairs, then act out the conversation. Encourage them to think about what was wrong with the original conversation and to improve it by using better expressions and strategies.

Ex 11 Ss act out their phone calls. Monitor as they work and note any good examples of language use. Take feedback from the whole class and collect any useful expressions.

> Photocopiable notes 9.2 (page 121)
> Telephoning situations (Roleplay page 136)

Homework suggestions
- Ss write a report on their last telephone roleplay for their own manager. (120–150 words)
- Ss write an email to a friend who is thinking about taking a job involving remote working. Ss should point out the advantages and disadvantages of this kind of work. (120–150 words)
- Ss write a report for their own company setting out the advantages of introducing flexible and remote working. (120–150 words)

The Review checks work covered in the previous three units, including grammar, vocabulary, communication strategies, collocations and pronunciation. It can be approached in a number of different ways, depending on classroom size and situation and time available, for example:

- as a whole-class activity
- with Ss in pairs or groups, followed by class feedback
- as a test to be marked
- as homework

1
1 was talking **2** noticed **3** were taking **4** couldn't
5 discovered **6** had escaped **7** (had) got **8** went
9 was driving **10** heard **11** had happened
12 didn't catch **13** got **14** saw **15** didn't panic
16 was looking **17** came **18** had found **19** had to
20 was

2
1 d **2** h **3** f **4** a **5** c **6** g **7** e **8** b

3
1 Call me if you ~~will~~ need anything.
2 You won't get good results ~~unless~~ if you work hard.
3 If the weather is ~~be~~ good this weekend, I might go away.
4 We won't have a holiday unless we ~~don't~~ save some money.
5 Where are you going to stay when you ~~will~~ go to London?
6 Life always feels better when ~~unless~~ you get a good night's sleep.

4
1 inherited, 'd buy
2 would you change, were
3 could, 'd love
4 'd do, had
5 'd buy, didn't have to
6 were, wouldn't worry

5
1 be kept **2** has been improved **3** are being made
4 are paid **5** can be left **6** were asked

6
1 carton **2** disposable **3** battery **4** bulb **5** pollute
6 charge

7
1 e<u>mi</u>ssions /ɪ/. All the others have the sound /aɪ/
2 s<u>ur</u>vey /ɜ:/. All the others have the sound /ʌ/
3 sh<u>a</u>re /æ/. All the others have the sound /ɑ/
4 br<u>ow</u>ser /aʊ/. All the others have the sound /ɒ/
5 b<u>u</u>lb /ʌ/. All the others have the sound /u/
6 spr<u>ea</u>d /e/. All the others have the sound /i:/

8

					¹B	R	O	W	²S	E	R
			³N						P		
⁴F	I	L	E						R		⁵F
			T		⁶U				E		E
⁷P			W		P				A		A
A		⁸D	O	W	N	L	O	A	D		T
S			R		O				S		U
S			K		A						R
W			I		⁹D	E	L	E	T	E	
O			N								S
¹⁰R	I	N	G	T	O	N	E				
D											

9
1 c **2** f **3** b **4** a **5** h **6** g **7** e **8** d

10
1 fun **2** joke **3** told **4** so **5** work out **6** deal with
7 come up with

11
1 told **2** happened **3** time **4** so **5** Anyway **6** when
7 believe **8** Then **9** that **10** Really **11** end
12 funny

10

A Third conditional
B *should have*
C Collocations
D **Communication strategies** Saying sorry
E **Interaction** Doing the right thing

Right and wrong

A Third conditional

Aims and objectives

In this lesson Ss will:
- consider what should be included on a CV (resume)
- study uses of the third conditional
- listen and practise pronunciation
- discuss a hypothetical situation using the third conditional

Reading: Daily dilemmas

TALKING POINT
Use the Talking point to start the lesson. Discuss the questions with the whole class.

Ex 1 Ask Ss think about their CVs and discuss the questions. Encourage Ss to think about why they might have different versions and the importance of adapting CVs for each job application.

Ex 2 Tell Ss they are going to read an article about a man who lied on his CV. Ask Ss to work in pairs to answer the questions.

Lee McQueen was a contestant on the reality show, *The Apprentice.* He lied on his CV about his education.

Ex 3 Ask Ss to discuss their reactions to what they have read. Take feedback on Ss suggestions on acceptable reasons for lying on a CV (if any).

Optional activity: Ss read the text in more detail and summarize the argument against lying on a CV.

Optional homework suggestion

Ss write an essay discussing the statement: *It is never acceptable to tell a lie.*

Ex 4 Tell Ss that people have responded to the article by posting messages on the newspaper's message board. Ask Ss to read both messages and discuss each one in pairs. Take feedback to see if all the class agree.

Ex 5 Ask Ss to read the messages again and answer the questions in pairs.

Karl's message talks about real past events. Rowan's message imagines a different past event.

Grammar: Third conditional

Ex 6 Ask Ss to read the information in the table and the examples given. In pairs, Ss underline four examples of the third conditional in the messages in Ex 4.

- If the interviewers had been good at their job, they wouldn't have given you the position.
- Imagine if they had asked a couple of in-depth technical questions, they would have discovered the truth.
- Or a quick test would have shown that you weren't as good as you claimed.
- You would have lost all credibility.

Optional suggestion: Refer Ss to page 170 of the Grammar reference and go through the notes on the third conditional. Allow time to discuss examples and any problems Ss have. Provide further examples if required.

Ex 7 Ss work in pairs. Tell Ss to read the messages through before thinking about the missing conditionals so that they concentrate on the meaning of the messages.

1 had been
2 would have done
3 had known
4 would have had
5 wouldn't have got
6 hadn't claimed
7 would … have fired
8 hadn't been

Optional activity: Dictate the following sentence beginnings to Ss. Ask Ss to complete the sentences and then share their ideas with a partner.
If I had known the truth, I …
If I had wanted the job, I …
If I had been Lee, I …

Ex 8))) **2.21** Point out that in natural speech the auxiliary verbs in third conditional structures are often contracted, which can make them difficult to hear. Write an example on the board. Show how the sounds link together:
If I'd done that, I'd've got the job.

Tell Ss that they are going to practise contracting these forms to help them identify the structures when they hear them. Ask Ss to work in pairs to read the conditional sentences in Ex 7 to each other. Take feedback, then play each sentence in turn and ask Ss to repeat them. Ask Ss to compare what they hear with their own ideas at the start of the exercise. Play the recordings as often as necessary.

Track 2.21: 10A, Page 101, Exercise 8

1
If I'd been in Karl's position, I'd've done the same.

2
If he'd known nothing about the software, he'd've had problems doing his job.

3

My sister wouldn't've got her first job in radio if she hadn't claimed that she already had some experience.

4

Would the company've fired him if he hadn't been the boss?

Speaking: What would you have done?

Ex 9 Ss read the anecdote. Check that there are no problems with vocabulary, then discuss the questions with the whole class.

Variation: Put Ss in groups of four and allocate a role to each S. Ask Ss to discuss what they would have done from each person's point of view. Make sure Ss use the full form of the third conditional.

> **Possible answers:**
> a) If I'd known what was going to happen I wouldn't have lied on my CV. (Vanessa)
> b) I wouldn't have asked Vanessa to lie for me, if I'd applied for a job. (Saskia)
> c) If I'd known from Vanessa's CV that she didn't have a degree, I wouldn't have given her the job. (HR manager)
> d) I'd have sacked Vanessa if I hadn't been happy with her work. (her boss)

Ex 10))) **2.22** Ask Ss to discuss what they think happened to Vanessa in groups. Elicit their ideas and write them on the board. Play the recording so that Ss can check their ideas.

> Vanessa didn't lose her job because her boss was happy with her work, but she learnt her lesson and never lied on a CV again.

Track 2.22: 10A, Page 101, Exercise 10

Then I went into my new boss's office and told her that she'd be getting a call from Human Resources in a moment. I explained exactly what I'd done. She thanked me for my honesty and told me that there was more on my resume that recommended me besides my degree. She said that I seemed to be doing OK – although I'd only been working there for two weeks or so. And she let me stay on. I did very well there, but I learnt my lesson and I've never lied on my resume since.

Homework suggestions
- Ss write an email to a friend telling them about Vanessa, what she did, what happened to her and how they feel about her. (120–150 words)
- Ss write a report written by the HR manager after Vanessa told them the truth, saying what happened, how they feel about it and what they intend to do. (120–150 words)
- Ss prepare to tell the class about a situation in which they did something that they wish they had not done. Ss should prepare a short talk using the third conditional.

β should have

Aims and objectives

In this lesson Ss will:
- read a story about money and friendship
- listen to friends discussing a situation
- study uses of *should have* and *shouldn't have* for criticism and regret
- roleplay the situation

In this lesson all the activities are based around a central situation

Word focus: Money

TALKING POINT
You could start with the Talking point to introduce the topic.

Ex 1 Ask Ss to work in groups to ask and answer questions about the topic.

Ex 2 Tell Ss they are going to read about a man (Dan) who wants to borrow money from an old friend (Kumar). Ask Ss to read the title. What effect do they think the request for money might have on their relationship? Ask Ss to read the article to see if they were right. Ask Ss to discuss whether they would have lent money to Dan.

Ex 3 Ask Ss to work in pairs and identify the odd word out. Take feedback and make sure that Ss justify their answers. If necessary, ask Ss to check the meanings in a dictionary.

> **Possible answers:**
> 1 saving up – the others involve spending money
> 2 return – because it's the opposite of *borrow* and *take*
> 3 interest – because *mortgage* and *debt* refer to money you owe or have to pay back
> 4 lend – because it's the opposite of *repay* and *pay back*, i.e. you give the money to someone
> 5 credit card – because *notes* and *cash* refer to physical money
> 6 loan – because it's something you borrow but *down payment* and *deposit* refer to money you pay
> 7 can't afford – because it means you don't have enough money to buy something
> 8 finance – because *bank* and *lender* refer to financial institutions

Ex 4 Ask Ss to work in pairs to complete the questions. Check answers, then ask Ss to read and discuss the questions.

> 1 borrowed   4 down payment
> 2 can't afford 5 cash/money
> 3 pay … back   6 saving up

Listening: Different points of view

Ex 5))) **2.23** Tell Ss that they are going to listen to Dan explaining his point of view to another friend. Before playing the recording, ask Ss to read the questions. Then ask Ss to work in pairs to compare their answers.

> 2 ✓ 3 ✓ 5 ✓
> Dan hasn't paid back the money yet. Kumar asked him to pay it back by the end of the year.

Track 2.23: 10B, Page 103, Exercises 5 and 6
Dan

It was a dream house. Just what I'd always wanted – in a quiet suburb, perfect for writing. I've been a good friend to Kumar. I've helped him move and I've also lent him my car. I didn't want to ask him for the money, but, hey, house prices are so high these days. … Yeah, I guess I should have waited another year.

… Sure, if Kumar had had financial difficulties, I would've done the same for him. I mean, we've known each other since we were at college. Anyway, he agreed, I paid the down payment and moved in and spent loads of time writing on weekends and during my vacation. The thing is, I couldn't find a publisher for the book. It was really frustrating. So, after six months of this, I explained the situation to Kumar, saying that I was really sorry but I didn't have enough money to pay him back. Actually, I was a bit surprised when he looked annoyed and asked me to pay it back by the end of the year. He knows I have the mortgage to pay and that I don't earn much money at the bookstore. And he earns much more than me.

… Yeah, of course I plan to pay back two thousand dollars by the New Year.

I'm going to save up and if it doesn't work out, I suppose I'll get some extra work in the evenings. … I dunno, as a waiter, or something.

… No, I can't ask my mom for the money. No way.

She can't afford it on her pension. I just think Kumar could've been a bit more understanding about my financial situation. After all, that's what friends are for, right?

Ex 6))) Tell Ss they are going to listen to the recording again and this time they must think about the questions Dan's friend asks him.

> **Possible answers:**
> • Why didn't you wait another year?
> • Would you have done the same for Kumar?
> • Are you going to pay him back?
> • What are you going to do? What kind of work?
> • Why don't you ask your mother for the money?

Ex 7))) **2.24** Tell Ss they are going to listen to Kumar's point of view as he talks to the same friend. Play the recording and ask Ss to compare their ideas in pairs.

> **Possible answer:**
> Kumar lent Dan the money because they were good friends. Dan told him he didn't want to ask his mother for the money because she was retired and he promised to pay it back. But Dan couldn't find a publisher for his book and couldn't pay back the money, so Kumar asked him to pay it back by the end of the year. Dan doesn't answer Kumar's phone calls now. Kumar thinks Dan should ask for a bank loan and that the money has affected their friendship.

Track 2.24: 10B, Page 103, Exercises 7 and 8

Kumar

Dan and me used to get on really well until this business with the money. We'd been to college together and I'd always been able to talk to him about everything. But we'd never discussed personal finances. I mean, I knew he earned less than me, but he'd never asked me for money before. … Sure, when he asked for five thousand dollars for the down payment for the house, I was surprised.

It was a lot of money. But I thought, hey, he's a great guy, so I gave it to him.

… Yeah, I felt a bit uncomfortable about the situation 'cos I wasn't sure how he planned to repay it.

He said he didn't wanna ask his mom because she was retired and all that. What was I supposed to do? I couldn't say no, could I? Dan promised to pay me back and I believed him, although my other friends say I shouldn't have lent him the money.

Anyway, six months later, he *still* hadn't paid me back. We'd never agreed on an exact date or anything. He hadn't been able to find a publisher for his book and I thought, well, that's not my problem. So I just asked him to pay it back by the end

of the year. I wasn't charging interest, was I? And he looked kind of offended, but I thought, five thousand dollars is five thousand dollars. I mean, we've always been close but he's not family, or anything.

… No, I don't see much of him these days.

It seems as if he's avoiding me. He's not answering my calls – stuff like that. If he doesn't have enough money to pay me back, he should ask for a bank loan. But the worst thing is the money has changed things between us. It shouldn't have affected our friendship.

Ex 8))) Tell Ss they are going to listen to the recording again and this time they must think about the questions Kumar's friend asks him.

> **Possible answers:**
> • Were you surprised when he asked you for the money?
> • Didn't you feel uncomfortable about the situation?
> • Do you see him very much these days?

Grammar: *should have/shouldn't have*

Ex 9 Ask Ss to read the information in the table and complete the sentences.

> **1** should have waited
> **2** shouldn't have lent

Optional suggestion: Refer Ss to pages 170 of the Grammar reference and go through the notes on *should have/shouldn't have*. Allow time to discuss examples and any problems Ss have. Provide further examples if required.

Ex 10 Ask Ss to work in pairs to complete the sentences. After checking answers, ask Ss to read the sentences again and in pairs discuss whether they agree with them. Take feedback from the whole class and see if everyone agrees.

> **1** shouldn't have lent
> **2** should have borrowed
> **3** shouldn't have asked
> **4** shouldn't have bought
> **5** should have agreed
> **6** should have asked

Optional activity: Ask Ss to work in pairs and write two more sentences criticising Dan or Kumar.

> Photocopiable notes 10.1 (page 121)
> Giving advice (Discussion cards page 137)

Speaking: Asking for a friend's advice

Ex 11 Ask Ss to discuss the questions in pairs or small groups. This discussion will help Ss with the roleplay in Ex 12.

Ex 12 Ss prepare the roleplay in pairs.

Variation: All the As prepare together and all the Bs prepare together. Then re-pair them in to one A + one B for the roleplay.

Ex 13 Ss do the roleplays. Monitor and give feedback.

Writing: Explaining your view

Ex 14 Ss write the email. Then ask them to work in pairs to check and edit each other's email. Remind Ss to use *should have* and *shouldn't have* and suggest they write 150–180 words. Note: This could also be set for homework.

Variation: Divide the Ss into A and B pairs. S A writes to Dan and S B writes to Kumar. They then compare their emails and discuss their different approaches and ideas.

Sample answer:

> **To:** …
>
> **From:** …
>
> **Subject:** Kumar
>
> Dear Dan
>
> I'm writing to you about Kumar. I have spoken to both you and Kumar and I understand your different points of view, but maybe you shouldn't have asked for so much money from a friend, or perhaps you should have borrowed the money from someone else. I guess Kumar shouldn't have lent you the money in the first place because it has ruined your friendship. Remember, he could have asked for interest on the loan but he didn't.
>
> I know you are working hard to pay your mortgage but I think you should try to pay him back as soon as you can. Maybe you could get a job at the weekends or something. I think it would be a good idea to talk to him again and apologize to him. You and Kumar have been very good friends for a long time and it would be a shame if you stopped being friends because of the money. I'm sure he'd like to hear from you.
>
> Phone me if you'd like to talk about it.
>
> Best wishes
>
> …

Homework suggestions
- Ss write an essay discussing the statement: *It is never a good thing to lend money to a friend.* (120–150 words)
- Ss write a short story about two friends whose friendship was spoilt by money. (120–150 words)
- A friend has emailed asking for advice on whether he/she should ask a friend for money. Reply to his/her email. (120–150 words)

C Collocations

Aims and objectives

In this lesson Ss will:
- study easily confused words
- study common verb + expression collocations
- play a game involving assigning blame and making excuses

Word focus: *blame* and *fault*

TALKING POINT
Start with the Talking point to introduce the topic. Ask Ss to discuss their ideas in pairs or small groups.

Ex 1 Tell Ss they are going to focus on different uses of the words *blame* and *fault*. Ask Ss to work in pairs to complete the text.

1	fault	5	fault
2	blame	6	blame
3	blame	7	blame
4	fault	8	blaming

Optional activity: Ask Ss to underline the words surrounding each answer. Explain that these are collocations – words commonly used together.

1 It's your fault
2 get the blame for something
3 put the blame on other people
4 at fault
5 It's not my fault
6 be to blame
7 Taking the blame
8 blaming someone else

Ex 2 This exercise focuses on collocations. Tell Ss that collocations are a useful way of learning new language and that making a mistake with a collocation may not cause misunderstanding but it will certainly sound strange. Ask Ss to work in pairs to identify the collocations that are not possible.

1	something wrong	4	a serious mistake
2	fault	5	your own fault
3	my fault	6	responsible

Optional activity: Ss use a dictionary to find collocations for the words that are not possible. Ss write sentences using the collocations they have identified.

Ex 3 Ask Ss to work in pairs or small groups. Ask them to identify the problem, then discuss who is to blame in each case. After the activity, get feedback from the class.

Variation: Divide the class into four groups or pairs and allocate one topic only to each group. After discussing their topic, they present their ideas to the class, who can ask them questions and decide whether they agree with the group's opinions.

Optional homework suggestion
Ask Ss to look again at the news items in Ex 3 and write an email to a friend telling them about the news item and explaining who they think is to blame and why. (120–150 words)

Word focus: *make* and *do*

Ex 4 Ask Ss to work in pairs to complete the diagrams.

make	do
a mistake	something wrong
a complaint	some work
a mess	a good job
a decision	some housework
a suggestion	business with someone
a noise	the shopping
a lot of money	the best you can
an excuse	your duty

Ex 5 Ask Ss to work in pairs and tell them that all the expression are in the diagrams in Ex 4. Point out that the verb in the collocation may follow the noun or expression rather than precede it, as in number 1.

1	do	5	made
2	made, done	6	do
3	make	7	do, doing
4	made	8	makes

Optional homework suggestion

Ss look again at the questions in Ex 5. Ask them to choose one and write a short paragraph in answer to the question and giving more details.

Speaking: The Blame Game

Ex 6 Practise pronunciation of expressions for blaming and making excuses with the whole class. Explain the rules of the game and ask Ss to play it in groups of three. Monitor the Ss and after the activity discuss with Ss how easy it was to make good excuses. Ask Ss what the best excuses were in each group and tell the class. Ss could then vote on the best excuse.

In one-to-one classes, the S could practise making excuses with any or all of the cards.

Homework suggestion

Ss write an email to a friend telling them about one of the situations in *The Blame Game* (Ex 6) and what the best excuse was. (100–130 words)

D Communication strategies
Saying sorry

Aims and objectives

In this lesson, Ss will:
● read a public apology from a company
● listen to a podcast about two companies that made public apologies
● listen to people apologizing in different situations
● do an activity making and responding to apologies

Culture and language
Saying sorry

Many languages have words and expressions like *Sorry*, *Excuse me*, and *Please forgive me*. People use them in the same way we use these expressions in English in many situations, but sometimes they may use them differently. For example, English speakers often apologize before they do something like squeeze round someone or cross in front of them. In other cultures, people might apologize after the event. Also things that require an apology in one culture may require no mention in another. For example, English speakers might say *sorry* if they touch someone in a crowded place like an elevator. This wouldn't be necessary in Romania.

Students may also have expressions in their own language that don't translate into English. For example, *I am ashamed* could serve as an apology in Farsi. In Bulgarian it could be polite to say *Don't get angry with me* to apologize and get someone's attention in some situations. So be aware that some phrases can't be translated into English and customs for apologizing may vary across cultures.

Sorry vs. *Excuse me*

Be ready to explain the difference between *Sorry* and *Excuse me* if asked. British English (BrE) and American English (AmE) speakers commonly use *Excuse me* to gain someone's attention:

Excuse me, is this seat free?
AmE speakers also use *Excuse me* to signal they haven't heard something and ask someone to repeat.
It's eight oh four.
Excuse me?
Eight oh four.
BrE speakers would generally say *Sorry?* in this context.
I beg your pardon is a rather an old-fashioned expression. If your students ask, explain that it's generally used to apologize for doing something embarrassing or for correcting a mistake in what we have said, e.g. *There are sixty five ... I beg your pardon ... fifty six boxes.*
In Ex 6 draw students' attention to the intensifier in conversation 1: *I'm **really** sorry.*
Really makes the apology sound more sincere. If the speaker just said *I'm sorry* or *I'm very sorry* here, it wouldn't sound so genuine. *I'm very sorry* is often something we say as a matter of etiquette. *I'm really sorry* is something we say when we're feeling regret. (See pages 106 and 107 on *Saying sorry*.)

Background information
Apologizing strategies

Pragmatic research seems to show that native English speakers typically express regret when apologizing, e.g. *I'm sorry, but ...* In other cultures such as in Spain, Italy, Arabic-speaking countries, Japan, China, and so on, asking for forgiveness is frequently used in apologies. The perceived level of offence varies across cultures, e.g. in some societies being a little late or accepting interruptions during meetings may not be seen as causing any offence, and therefore an apology may not be offered.

Listening: When sorry isn't enough

Ex 1 Ss could discuss the questions in small groups.

Ex 2 Tell Ss they are going to read a public apology from a new company on its website. Ask Ss to discuss the questions in pairs. Take class feedback. Does the class agree on whether customers will respond well to the apology? Why?/Why not? Take suggestions on what makes a good public apology.

> The company was apologizing for problems customers were experiencing ordering goods both on their website and by phone. They explained that the problems were due to changes they were making to the website and at their call centre.
> Customers may respond well to this apology but probably only if the problems are solved quickly, and possibly if they are offered some sort of compensation.

Optional homework suggestion

Tell Ss that their company has made a mistake with information on their website, and has put an apology on the site. Ss should write the apology, using Ex 2 as a model.

Ex 3 🔊 **2.25** Before playing the recording, tell Ss they are going to listen to a podcast about two companies who made public apologies and that they should make notes. Ask Ss to read the chart and identify what they must make notes on. Play the recording and encourage Ss to compare their answers.

Name of company	British Airways	Mattel (US toy company)
Apologized for	delays and lost luggage the day that Heathrow Airport terminal 5 opened	recall of faulty toys made in China
Apologized to	(thousands of) passengers affected	Chinese manufacturers, political officials, Chinese people and customers

Track 2.25: 10D, Page 106, Exercise 3

Companies often resort to the public apology when things go wrong. Take the disastrous opening of Heathrow Airport's terminal 5. The day the terminal went into full operation in 2008, thousands of passengers suffered long delays and lost their luggage. British Airways quickly apologized and promised immediate action. The company even organized four hundred volunteers to help sort out the mess and reunite passengers with their luggage.

In another famous example in 2007, US toy company Mattel apologized publicly to Chinese manufacturers and political officials for the recall of nearly 20 million toys made in China. Executive Vice President Thomas Debrowski said at the time, 'Mattel takes full responsibility for these recalls and apologizes personally to you, the Chinese people, and all of our customers who received the toys.'

Mr Debrowski added that a majority of the problems were associated with design problems, not Chinese manufacturers. Experts said this public apology by Mattel in China was important to maintain good relationships with suppliers there. It was all about saving face and a private apology wouldn't have done that for China.

Ex 4 Discuss Ss reactions to the apologies with the whole class. Link their ideas back to their suggestions about what makes an effective apology in Ex 2.

Ex 5 Ask Ss to discuss each situation in groups. Then take class feedback. Which situation did Ss find it easiest/most difficult to apologize in?

Ex 6 2.26 Tell Ss they are going to listen to four conversations and match them to the situations they have discussed in Ex 5. Ask Ss to compare their ideas. Were the apologies they heard similar to the ones they thought about in Ex 5?

> **Conversation 1** d
> **Conversation 2** a
> **Conversation 3** c
> **Conversation 4** b

Track 2.26: 10D, Page 106, Exercises 6 and 7

Conversation 1
E = Employee, **A** = Alicia

E: I'm really sorry, Alicia. You know that progress report you wanted today? I'm afraid I haven't had time to finish it. There's just been so much to do and a few people are off sick. I'll get on to it first thing tomorrow.

A: Well, thanks for letting me know. Don't worry about it. Tomorrow will be fine.

Conversation 2
A: I'm sorry. I didn't see you there. Are you all right?
B: Yes, yes. Fine thanks.

Conversation 3
J = Jin, **W** = Werner

J: I'm sorry, Werner. I did something silly and accidentally deleted that match you were recording.
W: What?
J: I feel really bad about it. I know you love your tennis.
W: Jin! It was the Shanghai Open final. I really wanted to watch that later.
J: I know, I know. I'm sorry. Look, I'll make us something special for dinner.
W: Oh, go on then.

Conversation 4
A: Next, please.
B: Yes. Can I have …?
C: Excuse me, I was here before you.
B: Oh, so sorry. I didn't mean to push in.
C: That's OK

Ex 7 Before playing the recording, ask Ss to read the conversations. Tell Ss that they should listen and correct what was said.

> **Conversation 1**
> ~~Please forgive me~~, I'm really sorry, Alicia. You know that progress report you wanted today? I'm afraid I haven't had time to finish it. ~~It isn't my fault;~~ There's just been so much to do and a few people are off sick. I'll get on to it first thing tomorrow.
>
> **Conversation 2**
> I'm sorry. I didn't ~~mean to do that~~ see you there. Are you all right?
>
> **Conversation 3**
> **Jin:** ~~I'm such an idiot,~~ I'm sorry, Werner. I did something silly and ~~wiped~~ accidently deleted that match you were recording.
> **Werner:** What?
> **Jin:** ~~You're right to be angry.~~ I feel really bad about it. I know you love your tennis.
> **Werner:** Jin! It was the Shanghai Open final. I really wanted to watch that later.
> **Jin:** I know, I know. I'm sorry. Look, I'll ~~pay for the damage~~ make us something special for dinner.
>
> **Conversation 4**
> **Customer 1:** ~~Pardon me.~~ Excuse me, I was here before you.
> **Customer 2:** Oh, so sorry. I ~~feel awful about pushing in~~ didn't mean to push in.

Ex 8 Ask Ss to read the conversations through again and discuss the questions.

Ex 9 Point out to Ss that there are different strategies used when making apologies, and that these can depend on the situation or the culture. Ask Ss to read through the information in the box and think about the strategy being used. Which strategies did they use in Ex 5? Ask Ss to work in pairs and complete the information in the box using examples from the conversation in Ex 7.

Conversation 1: expressing regret, giving an explanation and offering to put things right
Conversation 2: expressing regret, giving an explanation and showing concern for the other person
Conversation 3: expressing regret, taking responsibility and offering to put things right
Conversation 4: expressing regret and not taking responsibility

Possible answers:
1 *Expressing regret:* I'm really sorry, I'm afraid … , I feel really bad about it … , so sorry
3 *Giving an explanation:* There's just been so much to do … , I didn't see you there.
4 *Taking, or not take, responsibility:* I did something silly …
5 *Not taking responsibility:* There's been so much to do and a few people are off sick, I didn't mean to push in
6 *Showing concern for the other person:* Are you all right? I know.
7 *Offering repair:* I'll get on to it first thing tomorrow, Look, I'll make us something special for dinner.

Ex 10 Ss work in pairs and match parts 1–6 to a–f to make apologies. Take feedback by asking Ss to read the whole apology. Discuss why the strategies are used in each case.

1 d 2 e 3 a 4 f 5 c 6 b

Strategies:
1 expressing regret, giving explanation and showing concern
2 expressing regret and offering to put things right
3 expressing regret and giving explanation
4 expressing regret and not taking responsibility
5 expressing regret and giving explanation
6 expressing regret and giving explanation

Speaking: I'm so sorry

Ex 11 Ask Ss to work in pairs. They read the situations and then roleplay the situations. Monitor and help if necessary. Then take feedback from the class.

Variation: Ss work in groups of three. Two Ss do the roleplay and the third S listens and monitors the strategies being used. The group can discuss the success of the strategies after the roleplay, using the questions in Ex 12.

Ex 12 Ss discuss the questions in pairs.

Photocopiable notes 10.2 (page 121)
Apologizing and responding to apologies (Roleplay page 138)

Homework suggestions
• Ss choose one of the situations in Ex 5 and write a short dialogue to read to the class next lesson.
• Ss choose one of the situations in Ex 11 and write an email to a friend telling them about it. (120–150 words)

€ Interaction Doing the right thing

Aims and objectives

In this lesson Ss will:
• focus on vocabulary describing personal characteristics
• listen to a boy telling his parents about a situation
• read emails about a difficult situation at work
• listen to and discuss different dilemmas

Refer Ss to the Reminder box and draw attention to the language that the lesson will focus on. Check Ss can use this language by looking at page 170 of the Grammar reference and at previous lessons of the unit.

Word focus: Personal characteristics

Ex 1 Do pronunciation work on the adjectives. Ask Ss to work in pairs to do the matching exercise. Check the answers, then ask Ss to find the opposites and the nouns of the words in the box. Ss can use dictionaries if necessary. Check the pronunciation of all of the words.

1 honest – dishonest – honesty
2 consistent – inconsistent – consistency
3 open-minded – narrow-minded – open-mindedness
4 thoughtful and kind – thoughtless and unkind – thoughtfulness and kindness
5 sensitive – insensitive – sensitivity
6 rational – irrational – rationality
7 brave – cowardly – bravery
8 wise – unwise – wisdom

Optional homework suggestion
Ss write a short character reference for an imaginary friend, using vocabulary from Ex 1.

Ex 2 Ask Ss to discuss the question in pairs.

Variation: Divide the class into groups of three and allocate each group a friend, a partner and a boss. The groups choose the three characteristics for their person, justifying their reasons. Regroup the class so that there is a member of each group in the new groups. Ss share their ideas and see if they agree on the most important characteristics.

Ex 3 Ss discuss the questions in pairs.

Listening: Telling right from wrong

Ex 4 🔊 **2.27** Tell Ss they are going to listen to a family talking at dinner. Before playing the recording, tell Ss to listen for what Tom tells his parents about his day. Check answers.

Tom's friend Raul found a cellphone in the park and kept it for himself.

Track 2.27: 10E, Page 108, Exercise 4

S = Susan, **T** = Tom

S: How was your day, Tom?

T: Not bad, not bad, nothing special.

S: How's that friend of yours, Raul?

T: Hey, he found a fantastic cellphone in the park on the way home from school.

S: Yeah? What did he do with it?

T: He's gonna keep it. It's much better than his old phone. He threw away the chip and put in his.

S: Oh!

Ex 5 Discuss the questions with the class. Take suggestions as to what Raul and Tom should have done.

Optional activity: Ss roleplay the continuation of the conversation between Tom and his parents before they listen to what was actually said.

Ex 6))) **2.28** Tell Ss that they are going to listen to Tom's parents' reactions. Ss listen to compare with their own ideas.

Track 2.28: 10E, Page 108, Exercise 6

T = Tom, **S** = Susan, **J** = John

T: He's going to keep it. It's much better than his old phone. He threw away the chip and put in his.

S: Oh! Do you think he should've done that, Tom? Kept the phone?

T: Well, no. I guess not.

J: Why not?

T: Well, it's not exactly stealing, but it's kind of dishonest.

J: What did you say to him?

T: I said he was lucky. I'd really like a cellphone like that.

S: You know, you could've told him to use the phone to call the owner or given it to a teacher to find the owner.

T: Yeah, I know. I'm really sorry. But, hey, you found twenty dollars the other day and kept it.

S: That's not the same!

Reading: Challenges at work

Ex 7 Ss read the email and discuss the questions in pairs.

Possible answers:
Susan is hardworking, thoughtful and kind.

Dilemmas she faced last week:
Her friend Anton is also her business partner. He is planning a two-week holiday in the middle of a major project and he's leaving Susan to do all the work. She doesn't know what to say to him.
Last week Susan needed to find someone to do Karen's job while she's on maternity leave. Karen's friend Paula wanted to do it. Susan wanted to employ someone else who was more qualified than her. However, she was worried about how Karen would react if she rejected her friend, so she gave her the job.

Ex 8 Ss read the email and discuss the questions. Take class feedback on the advice and how Ss feel about it.

Speaking: More dilemmas

Ex 9 Put Ss in pairs. Tell them to read their information and roleplay the conversation. After the activity, ask Ss to compare how their conversations developed.

Ex 10))) **2.29** Tell Ss they are going to listen to John and Susan who are shopping. Before playing the recording, ask Ss to look at the pictures and discuss what might have happened. Play the recording and ask Ss to put the pictures in order.

The correct order is: b, d, a, c

Track 2.29: 10E, Page 109, Exercises 10 and 11

S = Susan, **J** = John, **D** = Driver

S: Well, we've finished all the shopping.

J: What'll we have for dinner?

S: I don't know. How about pizza? It's nice and quick.

J: OK, sounds good to me. Hey, isn't that Michelle's new boyfriend over there? Who's he with?

S: I don't know. Look! They're holding hands!

J: I knew there was something I didn't like about him.

S: So, are you going to tell Michelle?

J: Tell her? Would that be a good idea?

S: And if she finds out you knew something, but didn't tell her?

J: Oh! But what if she hates me for telling her? Why don't you talk to her?

S: She's your sister. I think it's better if you do it.

J: I'll have to think about it. Hey, I wanna go to the bookstore. Let's cross here.

S: Wait for the light! …

D: Get out of the road!

J: Watch where you're going!

D: Are you blind? The light was red!

J: The light was changing! I had the right of way.

S: Come on, John, let's go.

Ex 11))) Ask Ss to read the questions before you play the recording again. Tell Ss to compare their answers before you take class feedback.

1 Michelle's (John sister's) new boyfriend.
2 Should he tell his sister that he saw her boyfriend with another woman?
3 He wants to go to the bookstore.
4 Because the driver says that John was crossing the road when the pedestrian lights were red, but John says the lights were changing and therefore he had priority.

Ex 12 Ask Ss to discuss their ideas about the situations in pairs. Then ask some of the pairs for their advice.

Ex 13 Ss read the email and identify the dilemmas. Ask them which one had an unexpected ending.

The dilemma about her business partner – Susan became ill because she was overworked. This dilemma is not resolved.
The dilemma about John's sister – she isn't seeing that boyfriend anymore, which was unexpected and the dilemma has been resolved.

Homework suggestions
• Ss write a dilemma to bring to class next lesson for the class to discuss.
• Tell Ss to imagine that they are going to write a letter to a help column of a magazine explaining the dilemma in Ex 13 and asking for advice. Ss can look again at the problems in the lesson for ideas.

11

A Relative pronouns
B Writing emails 2
C Present perfect continuous
D **Communication strategies** Networking
E **Interaction** Team-building

Working together

A Relative pronouns

Aims and objectives

In this lesson Ss will:
- read an article about a charitable organization
- study uses of relative pronouns
- roleplay a situation organizing a fund-raising event

Reading: Aid

TALKING POINT
You could start the lesson with the Talking point as it introduces the idea of working for nothing and charity work. Discuss the question with the whole class.

Ex 1 Ask Ss what they know about NGOs and NPOs. Take feedback then ask Ss to match each term to its definition. Ss might also mention the word *aid* (n), which is help such as money or food given by an organization or government to people who are in a difficult situation.

> 1 a non-profit organization (NPO)
> 2 a charity
> 3 a non-governmental organization (NGO)

Background information
Charities, NGOs and NPOs

A charity (or charitable organization) is a non-profit organization (NPO) but it focuses on activities and goals that are in the public interest or do good.The legal definition of charity varies across jurisdictions.

A non-governmental organization (NGO). Even when NGOs are partly or totally funded by governments, they still have non-governmental status and government representatives cannot be members of the organization.

A nonprofit/not-for-profit organization (NPO) does not share surplus funds or profits with owners or shareholders, but uses them to further its aims. Examples of NPOs include charitable organizations, trade unions and public arts organizations.

Ex 2 Ask Ss to suggest more examples of the three types of organization.

Ex 3 Tell Ss they are going to read an article about an NGO. Ask them to read the title and discuss what the article might be about. Take their ideas and write them on the board.

Ex 4 Before they read the article, ask Ss to read the options in Ex 4. Ss then read the article quickly to decide what the organization does. Compare their answer with their suggestions in Ex 3.

> c It performs for people who have experienced difficult situations.

Grammar: Relative pronouns

Ex 5 Refer Ss to the information in the table and ask them to work in pairs to choose the correct options. Monitor and take class feedback.

> 1 things   2 people   3 where, when   4 that
> - There are now Clowns Without Borders teams <u>that</u> are based in …
> - … to bring smiles to the faces of those <u>who</u> need it most.

Optional suggestion: Refer Ss to page 173 of the Grammar reference and go through the notes on relative pronouns. Allow time to discuss examples and any problems Ss have. Provide further examples if required.

Optional activity: Ss read the text again in detail. Then, in groups, discuss what they think of the idea of Clowns Without Borders.

Ex 6 Ss work in pairs to choose the best relative pronoun for the definition. Ss then read the text again to find the words in the article that match the definitions.

> 1 who/that – clown
> 2 who/that – volunteer
> 3 which/that – non-profit organization/NGO
> 4 when – performance
> 5 who/that – refugee
> 6 where – refugee camp
> 7 who/that – disadvantaged child
> 8 when – natural disaster

Optional homework suggestion
Ss choose one of the sentences from Ex 6 and expand it into a short paragraph to add more details.

Ex 7 Remind Ss of the difference between defining and non-defining clauses. If necessary, write the following sentences on the board:

My friend, who studied with me in London, works for an NGO.

A friend who studied with me in London works for an NGO.

Point out that the first sentence gives extra information about my friend, but it is not necessary to understand the main information 'My friend works for an NGO'. It is non-defining. The second sentence, which explains which friend it is, is necessary to understand the whole sentence. It is defining.

Ask Ss to work in pairs to match the two halves of the sentences and decide whether they are defining or non-defining.

1 e – which was affected by floods. Defining.
2 g – who's a nurse. Extra information.
3 a – whose aim is to make children smile. Extra information.
4 c – whose real name is Jaume Mateu Bullich. Extra information.
5 d – that he does while balancing chairs on his nose. Defining.
6 b – where I saw him perform. Defining.
7 f – which exploit animals. Defining.

Photocopiable notes 11.1 (page 121)
who, which, where, when, while, whose or *that?* (Card activity page 139)

Speaking: A fund-raising event

Ex 8 Explain the situation to the class. Tell S A to look at the information on the page 137 and Ss B and C to turn to their pages. Make sure they understand what to do, then ask Ss to prepare to act out the roleplay in groups of three. Monitor the discussions, then take feedback from the whole class.

In one-to-one classes, ask the S to read through all three file cards and then discuss the points.

Optional activity: Tell Ss they are going to ask their partner about people and things. Write the points below on the board.

• A charity/NGO you would like to work for
• A person who makes you laugh
• The best performer you have ever seen
• A charity/NGO you would give money to if you were rich
• A person who helped you in difficult times
• Any volunteer work you did recently
• A performance you have seen recently

Ask Ss to choose one point at random and their partner asks them questions to find out more details about their ideas or opinions. Then their partner chooses a topic. Tell Ss they should be polite in their questions and begin with *Could you tell me about … ?*

TALKING POINT
Discuss the question with the whole class if it was not used to start the lesson.

Homework suggestions
• Ss write a report on their proposed fund-raising event. (120–150 words)
• Ss write an essay discussing the statement: *All companies should raise money for charity.* (120–150 words)

β Writing emails 2

Aims and objectives

In this lesson Ss will:
• discuss different kinds of emails Ss receive
• identify and match formal and informal expressions
• read emails and identify formality
• write an email

Reading: A TV charity marathon

Ex 1 Ask Ss to work in groups and discuss the kind of emails they normally send and receive and how they feel about them. What do the people ask Ss to do in their emails?

Ex 2 Tell Ss they are going to read some emails sent to and by Brenda, a television employee who is organizing a marathon in aid of a children's charity. Tell Ss they are going to identify the main point of each email by identifying a suitable subject. Ask Ss to work in pairs. Take feedback and write their suggestions on the board.

Ex 3 Ss match the subject headings to the emails. Were their ideas similar?

1 b – Charity marathon celebrities
2 c – Donations for Kanga's Kids
3 a – Availability for TV charity marathon

Ex 4 Ask Ss to work in pairs to underline the requests in the emails.

There are eight requests in total: three in email 1, three in email 2 and two in email 3.

Email 1
Can you please send me …
Could you also let me know their availability …
It would be great if you could send me this information …

Email 2
… please tell all your family and friends about the marathon.
Tell them to text us or phone …
Remember to switch on at 7 p.m. on Friday …

Email 3
We would really appreciate it if you could …
Could you please confirm your availability …

Writing: Formal and less form expressions

Ex 5 Explain that it is important to use the correct register in writing (formal or informal) so that you don't give a bad impression. Ask Ss to work in pairs to identify the formal and less formal expression and complete the notes. After the activity, ask Ss to compare their answers with other pairs.

1 Hi Brenda/ Hello everyone!
2 *This is just to confirm*
3 Can you please send me … / please tell all your family / Tell them to text us / Remember to switch on at 7 p.m.
4 It would be great if you could …
5 if you have any questions, please let me know.
6 Thanks.
7 Looking forward to seeing you.
8 *Best wishes / See you soon. / Take care*

TALKING POINT
The Talking point could be discussed here.

Speaking: Formality in emails

Ex 6 Ask Ss to discuss the questions in groups.

Ex 7 Ask Ss to read the email to Steve and discuss whether it is too formal or informal. Ss should justify their ideas. Take class feedback, then make the points below.

> Brenda's email is too formal for an email to her boss when she only needs him to confirm Linda's appearance time on the TV show. The formal expressions used are:
>
> * Dear Mr Taylor,
> * I am writing to confirm …
> * I was wondering if it would be at all possible for you to …
> * Please do not hesitate to contact me should you …
> * I look forward to seeing you soon.
>
> Steve may think she's exaggerating or being ironic so it could have a negative impact when he reads it.

Ex 8 Ask Ss to work in pairs. Point out that there may be several possible answers and that Ss should justify their ideas.

Possible answer:

> **To:** Steve Taylor
>
> **From:** Brenda Rivers
>
> **Subject:** Linda McDonald's appearance
>
> Hi Steve
>
> Just to confirm that Linda McDonald is available for the charity marathon. Can you confirm her appearance time / time slot because she has a very busy schedule that week. Thanks.
>
> See you soon.
>
> Best wishes
>
> Brenda

Writing: Making requests

Ex 9 Ask Ss to write the email. Then ask them to work in pairs to check each other's work for formality and accuracy, and make sure that the email includes all four points in the exercise.

Sample answer:

> **To:** Linda McDonald's
>
> **cc:** Steve Taylor
>
> **From:** Brenda Rivers
>
> **Subject:** TV charity marathon
>
> Dear Ms McDonald
>
> I am writing to confirm your appearance times in our TV charity marathon in aid of Kanga's Kids. These will be at 7 p.m., 7.45 p.m., 8.45 p.m. and finally at 9.45 p.m.
>
> We would like you to do two performances during the marathon if possible, for example: dance a tango with a professional dancer and sing a song with some of the children from Kanga's Kids.

> We would also really appreciate it if you could attend three or four rehearsals before the show. Could you please confirm your availability for these?
>
> Finally, it would be great if you could donate some of your designer clothes, which will be auctioned in aid of Kanga's Kids.
>
> Please do not hesitate to contact me should you have any questions. Many thanks for your cooperation.
>
> I look forward to hearing from you soon.
>
> Regards
>
> Brenda Rivers
>
> Fund-raising coordinator

TALKING POINT
Discuss the question with the whole class.

Homework suggestions
* Read your partner's email from Ex 9. Imagine that you are Linda and write a reply. Agree to some things but refuse two of the requests. (120–150 words)
* Write a formal email to your boss, requesting time off to compete in a fund-raising event. (120–150 words)
* Write an essay discussing the advantages and disadvantages of asking people to do something for you face-to-face rather than on the phone. (120–150 words)

C Present perfect continuous

Aims and objectives

In this lesson Ss will:
* listen to people discussing articles for a hospital newsletter
* study uses of the present perfect continuous and present perfect simple
* discuss special occasions
* write an article about a colleague

Listening: The newsletter

Ex 1 Ss discuss the questions in groups.

Ex 2 2.30 Tell Ss they are going to listen to the editorial team talking about the Hospital's newsletter. Before playing the recording, ask Ss to read through the topics of the articles. As they listen, Ss put the articles into the order they are mentioned. Ss compare their answers and any notes they have made.

> *The correct order is:* c, b, a, d
>
> **Possible answers:**
> 1 Employee of the month – dental nurse Sandra Harzog. She's Australian. Two years at the hospital. No photo yet – Daniel will get one today.
> 2 Letter from the chief executive – Alan Murray's annual message about future plans, to put on page two. They want to keep the front page a bit light and fun.
> 3 Community news – New public park. Hospital staff have been helping to raise funds. Mayor to attend official opening.
> 4 Upcoming events – the Lunar New Year. They did an article on it last year as well, but there's a big Chinese community locally. So it will be OK.

Track 2.30: 11C, Page 114, Exercise 2

J = Jasmine, **D** = Daniel

J: So, what have we got lined up for next month, Daniel?

D: Well, there's an interview with dental nurse Sandra Harzog for our *Spotlight On* column. I spoke to her last week. She's Australian, you know. She's been working at the hospital for two years now. And we haven't done an article about anyone from that department recently.

J: Have we got a photo to go with the article about her?

D: Not yet, she's going to email one.

J: OK. And Alan Murray has sent his annual message about future plans for the hospital. We'll have to include that somewhere.

D: Do you think we could put that on page two, Jasmine, and keep the front page a bit light and fun for the staff?

J: Yes, he's a good sort. I don't think he'll mind.

D: And I've got a nice little piece about the new public park. Hospital staff have been helping to raise funds for improvements to the park and they've collected £5,000 already. The mayor has agreed to attend the official opening.

J: Yes, that sounds great.

D: Now what about something on a big public event? What's on the calendar for next month?

J: Not much. January and February is kind of a quiet time. Ah! There is the Lunar New Year, but we did something on that last year.

D: It doesn't matter. Nobody will mind. Anyway, there's a big Chinese community locally and it's colourful. We can include images of the Chinese horoscope as well. It'll look good on the page.

J: OK, I'll go along with that.

Grammar: Present perfect continuous

Ex 3 🔊 **2.31** Tell Ss they are going to listen to an interview with the employee of the month. Before playing the recording, ask Ss to read through the questions and answers. As Ss listen, they complete the missing words.

1	been working	4	been living
2	been working	5	been working
3	been living	6	been learning

Track 2.31: 11C, Page 114, Exercise 3

D = Daniel, **S** = Sandra

D: So, how long have you been working at the hospital, Sandra?

S: I've been working at Barkington for almost two years now.

D: Is that an Australian accent I hear?

S: Yes, that's right. I'm originally from Melbourne.

D: Have you been living in the UK long?

S: Not very. I've only been living here since 2007. I miss the sun but I love it here.

D: Tell us about the project you're working on.

S: I've been working on the new digital records scheme for six months. It's making a huge difference to the way we work.

D: What do you like doing in your free time?

S: Well, I never learnt to play a musical instrument when I was young and I've always wanted to. My partner surprised me and bought me a piano for my birthday in September. And I've been learning to play since then. But I'm terrible at it!

Ex 4 Ss work in pairs to read and complete the table, and discuss the use of the present perfect continuous in Ex 3.

> has/have + been + present participle.
>
> The sentences in exercise 3 are examples of the first use of the present perfect continuous – with *for* and *since*.

Optional suggestion: Refer Ss to page 162 of the Grammar reference and go through the notes on the present perfect continuous. Allow time to discuss examples and any problems Ss have. Provide further examples if required.

Ex 5 Ss work in pairs to complete the sentences and discuss what use of the present perfect continuous is shown in the examples.

> 1 've/have been reorganizing
> 2 **A:** have … been doing?
>   **B:** 've/have been planting
> 3 've/have been lifting … carrying
> 4 've/have been writing
> 5 've/have been looking for
>
> The sentences in exercise 5 are examples of the third use of the present perfect continuous – unfinished activities.

Ex 6 Ss work in pairs to complete the interview. When they have finished, ask them to compare their answers and to read the whole text through.

> 1 have been planning (unfinished)
> 2 've/have been telling (recent activity) *or* 've/have told (completed action)
> 3 has been getting (recent activity)
> 4 hasn't been sleeping (recent activity)
> 5 haven't had (state verb)
> 6 haven't decided (present perfect simple with *still*, *yet* and *already*)
> 7 has been talking (recent activity) *or* has talked (completed action)
> 8 haven't seen (state verb)

Optional activity: Ss write short questions about the text for their partner to answer.

Speaking: Special occasions

TALKING POINT
You could use the Talking point to introduce this section. Ss discuss the questions in groups.

Ex 7 Ss work in pairs to match the words to the special occasions. Take class feedback on their answers and on their extra words or expressions.

1	f – having a baby	4	a – promotion
2	e – public holiday	5	c – wedding
3	d – moving house	6	b – retirement

Ex 8 Ss could discuss the questions in groups

Variation: Write the first question on the board (or dictate it to the groups). Give Ss five minutes to discuss it. Call 'Time!' and move one student from each group on to the next group. Write the next question on the board or dictate it, and repeat the procedure.

Optional homework suggestion

Ss choose one of the questions from Ex 8 and write an email to a friend telling them about the situation. (120–150 words)

Ex 9 Ss work in pairs to write the questions and to add some more of their own. Check that they are correct before moving on to the interview stage. Tell Ss that they are going to write an article based on their interview so they should make notes.

> 1 How long have you been learning English?
> 2 How long have you worked/been working at (company, organization, etc.)?
> 3 What have you been doing at work recently?
> 4 Have you had any celebrations at work or at home lately?
> 5 What do you do in your free time? How long have you been interested in (hobby/sport)?
> 6 Are you a member of a social group or gym? How long have you been a member?

Writing: Newspaper article

Ex 10 Ss write the article based on their interview in Ex 9, using 120–150 words.

Sample answer:

> **Spotlight on Jorge Alvarez**
>
> *How long have you been learning English, Jorge?*
> Since 2009. I studied French at school. I've been doing English classes at the company for two years.
>
> *How long have you been working for this company?*
> All my working life. I came here straight from school when I was just 17.
>
> *What have you been doing at work recently?*
> I've been training my colleagues in the department on how to use some new machinery.
>
> *Have you had any celebrations at work or at home recently?*
> Yes, my wife had our second daughter, Maria, a month ago. We're so happy. I've been spending a lot more time with our eldest daughter, Carla, while my wife looks after the baby.
>
> *What do you do in your free time?*
> What free time? With two daughters under the age of three we don't get much time to ourselves.

TALKING POINT

If the Talking point has not already been used, Ss discuss the questions in pairs or small groups.

Homework suggestions

• Ss write an email to a friend telling them about a memorable occasion in their life and how they celebrated it. (120–150 words)
• Ss write an article for a local paper reporting on a local special occasion, saying why it was special, what happened and how successful it was. (120–150 words)

D Communication strategies
Networking

Aims and objectives

In this lesson, Ss will:
• discuss the impact of networking on people's careers
• read about different types of networking
• listen to conversations at a company social event
• roleplay different networking and socializing situations

> ## Culture and language
> ### Networking
>
> How people convey interest and engagement in social conversation varies across cultures. In some cultures, such as Finland, verbal responses may be minimal and a comfortable silence can last a long time. Japanese speakers, on the other hand, may make very frequent interjections along the lines of *Yes., Really?, Is that so?* English speakers fall somewhere in between, but probably closer to Japan than Finland. We expect frequent interjections, along with questions to develop the conversation.
>
> This lesson focuses on short questions and comments English speakers make which demonstrate they are actively listening. It provides practice with pairs of remarks and units of conversation, where one person says something that almost requires the other to respond in a certain kind of way. So, for example, if someone says *Hi, how are you?* we can almost predict the response will be along the lines of *Fine thanks and you?* Similarly, if someone says *I've just become head of special projects*, a response like *Have you? Congratulations!* would probably be appropriate while *I'm sorry to hear that* probably wouldn't be. (See pages 116 and 117 on *Networking* in unit 8)

Reading: Career success

Ex 1 Ss could work in groups to discuss their attitude to networking. Take feedback from the class to see if everyone agrees.

Ex 2 Ask Ss to debate the question in groups. Ss should give reasons for their opinions and personal experiences if appropriate.

Ex 3 Ask Ss to read the article about networking quickly to see if they were right about the impact of networking on men's and women's careers.

> The research found that two types of networking behaviour work well for men's careers but not women's careers.

Ex 4 Ask Ss to read the article again quickly and identify five types of networking. In their groups, Ss discuss which ones they engage in.

Ex 5 Ask Ss to work in the same groups. After reading the question and reply, Ss discuss what reasons the writer gives for socializing at work and how they feel about those reasons. Ss should also think of their own reasons. Take feedback from the groups and write their ideas on the board.

Possible answer:
- It's a good interpersonal skill to have.
- It builds useful relations with other departments, customers, co-workers, etc.
- It helps when problem-solving to know what's happening in other parts of the company.
- It's entertaining to hear gossip.
- It's useful to know what's going on inside the organization.

Other possible reasons: It helps if you manage staff. It helps motivate staff, improves the work environment and staff morale, boosts productivity and promotes a team spirit. It also useful for networking, i.e. sharing information and supporting each other.

Ex 6 Ss work in the same groups and read the message. What advice would they give the writer? After the discussion, ask Ss to share their ideas with the class.

Optional homework suggestion
Tell Ss that a friend is joining a new organization and wants some tips on ways of networking. Ss write an email to their friend offering advice and useful tips. (120–150 words)

Listening: Making connections

Ex 7))) **2.32** Tell Ss they are going to listen to a conversation at a company social event and that they must find out information about the people speaking. Before playing the recording, ask Ss to read the questions. They can make notes as they listen, but should compare their answers with a partner before you check with the class.

1 No, they're meeting for the first time
2 Dev works in PR. He's the Assistant to the Events Coordinator. Michaela works in IT. She's Head of Special Projects.
3 Dev's boss Amrita is pregnant with twins and she's going on maternity leave next month. Then Dev is taking over her job. Michaela has recently become Head of the Special Projects team and a colleague of hers left his job in mysterious circumstances.
4 She doesn't want to talk about why her colleague left the company.
5 Yes, they do. Dev asks Michaela for help with the PR department's database. Michaela wants help to organize some team-building events – Dev can't help with this, but he has a good contact for Michaela.

Tracks 2.32–2.34: 11D, Page 117, Exercises 7, 9 and 10

M = Michaela, **D** = Dev

M: Hi, I don't think we've met before. I'm Michaela Perry.

D: Nice to meet you, Michaela. I'm Dev Sharma.

M: So, tell me about yourself, Dev. Which department are you in?

D: PR. I'm the Assistant to the Events Coordinator, Amrita Krishen.

M: Really? That's cool! How's it going?

D: Things are pretty quiet at the moment. It's going to be hectic next month though. And Amrita's going to be away.

M: Oh yes, I hear she's expecting.

D: That's right. Twins!

M: Oh terrific. So who will be in charge when she goes on maternity leave?

D: Me, I'm taking over from her next month.

M: Are you? Congratulations!

...

D: So, how about you, Michaela? What do you do?

M: Well, I work in IT. I've just become Head of Special Projects, and I'm still finding my feet.

D: Wow! Sounds interesting! Doesn't Massimo work in your department?

M: Well, yes, he did. Actually, he left under a cloud.

D: No! I'm sorry to hear that.

M: It's probably best not to talk about it.

D: I see. So, Michaela, perhaps you could help me sort out a new database for the PR department.

M: I'd be very happy to. Hey! Maybe at the same time you could give me some ideas for some team-building activities for my new staff.

D: Um. It's not my area, I'm afraid, but I know just the man to help you. Let me introduce you to Stefan. He's just over there.

Ex 8 Ask Ss to work in pairs to order the conversation they have just heard.

The correct order is: 11, 1, 10, 2, 9, 7, 4, 5, 3, 6, 8

Ex 9))) **2.33** Ask Ss to read the completed dialogue in pairs before they check their answers with the first part of the recording. This will help to focus on the meaning.

Ex 10))) **2.34** Tell Ss that they are going to work with the second part of the conversation. Before playing the recording, ask Ss to read the conversation and try to complete it with their partner. They then listen to the second part of the recording again to check their answers.

1 What do you do?
2 I've just become
3 feet
4 interesting
5 he left under a cloud
6 sorry
7 perhaps you could help me
8 I'd be very happy to.
9 Maybe
10 I'm afraid
11 Let me introduce you to

Ex 11 Ask Ss to work in pairs, but check the answers by asking the pairs to read the news and the response aloud to the class.

1 d 2 e 3 a 4 f 5 c 6 b

Ex 12 Ss work in groups to answer the question and to add more expressions.

These expressions help people to build alliances in a number of ways: a) by finding out about the work other people do and seeing if there are ways they can help each other and work together, b) by exchanging information, news and gossip, and c) by putting people in touch with useful contacts.

Possible answers:
- So, how about you, Michaela. What do you do?
- So who will be in charge when she goes on maternity leave?
- So tell me about yourself.
- Which department are you in?

Photocopiable notes 11.2 (page 122)
Networking: responding to others (Matching activity page 140)

Speaking: Network your way to success

Ex 13 Explain the situation to Ss before asking them to work in pairs. Make sure that they focus on the four points in Ex 13 in their dialogues and think about useful types of gossip they could include.

Ex 14 Ss act out their dialogues for another pair to listen to and comment on. The listening pair should comment on the dialogue as well as saying what news was useful for them.

Ex 15 Tell Ss they are going to work in groups of four and that they are going to roleplay networking at a conference. Ask each S to read their information and prepare the roleplay. Ss then act out the situation.

Variation: Ask Ss to do Ex 15 in groups of four. Three Ss roleplay the situation and the fourth student listens and provides feedback.

In one-to-one classes, use File 9 and File 17 first, then use File 18 and File 36.

Ex 16 Discuss these questions with the whole class. Encourage Ss to also think about things that went wrong and suggest ways of improving their networking skills.

Homework suggestions
* Ss research networking gurus on the internet and bring in five ideas/suggestions/hints for the class to discuss next lesson.
* Ss write an email to a friend describing the situation at the conference and saying what they did to network and how successful they think it was. (120–150 words)

E Interaction Team-building

Aims and objectives

In this lesson Ss will:
* read about team-building events
* study key topic vocabulary
* listen to conversations about planning a team-building event
* discuss the best team-building event for a company

Refer Ss to the Reminder box and draw attention to the language that the lesson will focus on. Check Ss can use this language by looking at pages 173 and 162 of the Grammar reference and at previous lessons of the unit.

Reading: Special events

Ex 1 Ss discuss the questions in pairs. Ask Ss to share any experiences they have had of team-building events. What do Ss think might be the advantages and disadvantages of such events?

Ex 2 Explain that Ss are going to read advertisements for team-building events and match the events to the statements. There may be more than one event for some statements. Ask Ss to do the reading on their own, but to check their answers in pairs.

1 A	4 D
2 A and B	5 C
3 B	6 A and C

Ex 3 Tell Ss they are going to focus on vocabulary. Ask Ss to work in pairs to match the expressions from the adverts to their definitions. Check answers with the whole class.

Group 1
1 bond
2 challenges
3 customized (text A) / custom-made (text C)
4 trust
5 let off steam

Group 2
6 incentives
7 away days
8 stretch (their) legs
9 clear (their) minds
10 new perspective

Ex 4 Take feedback by regrouping the Ss so that they work with a partner from the other group. Ss explain their answers to each other.

Ex 5 Ask Ss to work in groups to discuss the events. After the activity, Ss could present their ideas to the class.

Ex 6 Discuss this with the whole class after discussing their choices in Ex 5.

Speaking: Planning an event

Ex 7 2.35 Tell Ss they are going to listen to a conversation between a boss and his assistant about a company event. Before playing the recording, tell Ss they must focus on two things only: what is proposed and what the assistant suggests. Ask Ss to compare their ideas before checking their answers.

Aidan wants to cancel the annual barbeque for staff and their families because he wants to do something more active. Marama suggests they consult staff about this to find out what interests them.

Track 2.35: 11E, Page 119, Exercise 7

A = Aidan, M = Marama

A: Marama, I've been thinking about the annual barbecue.

M: Yeah. I've been thinking about that myself. Summer's fast approaching, so we'll have to start working on it.

A: Well, I was wondering if we should do something different this year.

M: What did you have in mind?

A: Well, I get bored sitting around all day eating. I'd like to do something more active for a change. How about we cancel the barbecue with the staff and their families? I've been reading up on team-building events. We could organize one of these instead.

M: Would we invite the partners and the kids to it?

A: No, I'd like it to be more of a work event this year, but we'd have fun, of course. What do you think?

M: It could work. I mean, if you've involved staff in planning the activities, it will motivate them more. You know, find out what they enjoy doing and learning.

A: Good point. Can you ask around then?

M: OK, will do.

Ex 8))) **2.36** Tell Ss that at the end of the conversation the boss asked Marama to ask the staff for their opinions. Ss are now going to hear some of the staff's ideas. Before playing the recording, ask Ss to make notes on what they hear. After playing the recording, ask Ss to compare their notes and ask them how many of the staff like the idea of the barbeque.

Possible answers:
Speaker 1 suggests that a change would be good. The family barbeque isn't that interesting for younger members of staff as there are no sports activities.

Speaker 2 doesn't like team-building events. The winners go away happy, and the losers don't. There are lots of sporty types in the company, but he thinks it's a waste of time.

Speaker 3 suggests volunteering (e.g. tree-planting) as an alternative to the normal team-building events.

Speaker 4 says her husband and kiddies love the barbeque and most people at the firm have young families. She'll feel guilty if they can't come.

Speaker 5 mentions organizing team shows as a fun and non-competitive event.

Track 2.36: 11E, Page 119, Exercise 8

1

Yeah, we've been having a summer barbecue for years now. I think it's time for a change. I'm only 25, so it isn't of much interest to young people like me in the company. It would be different if they organized some team sports or something on the day, for those who want to do something more active.

2

To tell you the truth, I'm really not keen on team-building events. It seems like it's just for the sporty types and I don't see how being competitive helps to develop a team spirit. The winners go away happy and the losers feel miserable. I know there are a lot of sporty types among the engineers, but I think team-building events are a waste of time.

3

I've got a suggestion. I think it would be good if we do some volunteer work as a team-building exercise for the day. You know, we could plant some trees somewhere or do something more useful than hang off ropes. Let's make the event something that brings the team together and is worthwhile at the same time.

4

Most of us have young families in the company. And my husband and kiddies love coming to the barbecue every year. They'll miss it if we don't do it this year and I'm going to feel guilty if I have to go off somewhere without them.

5

A friend of mine told me about a great event she attended. She said that each group had to plan and put on a show together. She said it was fun and non-competitive and everyone was able to draw on their creativity. They discovered all sorts of hidden talents. At the end of the day, it was entertaining to see the shows.

Ex 9 Ask Ss to work in groups and use their notes to discuss the questions.

Ex 10 After the groups have made their decisions, ask them to summarize their ideas. Tell Ss that it is important for them to justify their ideas.

Variation: They could make PowerPoint slides. Each group should present their ideas to the whole class.

Ex 11 Ss work in their groups again to discuss what they have heard and to decide whether they want to adapt their plans.

Homework suggestions
• Ss write up their proposal with recommendations and reasons. Remind Ss of the format of a proposal and that bullet points are appropriate. (120–150 words)
• Ss think of a good team-building event and write an advert for it.
• Ss choose the event they think was most appropriate for one of the groups of people in Ex 5. Tell them to write a short paragraph explaining what their choice was and to give their reasons.

12

A Reported speech
B Embedded questions
C Consumer vocabulary
D Communication strategies Dealing with complaints
E Interaction Online entrepreneurs

Trial and error

A Reported speech

Aims and objectives

In this lesson Ss will:
- read an article about attitudes towards making mistakes
- study uses of reported speech
- discuss situations in which mistakes were made

Reading: Views on mistakes

TALKING POINT
You could use the Talking point here to start the lesson, as it allows Ss to think about their own situation before extending the topic. Discuss the question with the whole class so that Ss can compare their own experiences.

Ex 1 Ask Ss to discuss each person and think about the kind of mistakes they could make. This is a big topic area, so Ss could work in groups and be allocated just two people to discuss. The class could then share ideas. Ask Ss which person would make the most serious mistakes.

Ex 2 Tell Ss that they are going to read an article about different attitudes towards making mistakes at work. Ask Ss to read through the ideas, then read the article to decide whether they are true, false or not mentioned. Ss work alone, then compare their answers with a partner. After checking answers, ask Ss if there are any words they don't understand.

> 1 True.
> 2 Not mentioned. The writer says Drucker was a management guru/expert. Drucker said he would never promote a man who made mistakes, so it's likely he was also a manager/director but we don't know for sure.
> 3 True.
> 4 False. Drucker changed his mind in the 1960s, or later.
> 5 True.

Ex 3 Discuss Ss' reactions to the text with the whole class.

Optional homework suggestions
- Ss write a short paragraph about their job explaining what they do and whether it is important to take risks or not. (100–120 words)
- Ss write an essay discussing the statement *It is important to learn from mistakes in life*. (120–150 words)

Grammar: Reported speech

Ex 4 Go through the table and fill in the gaps with the whole class.

1	Past simple	4	Past perfect
2	Past continuous	5	her
3	Past perfect		

Optional suggestion: Refer Ss to page 174 of the Grammar reference and go through the notes on reported speech. Allow time to discuss examples and any problems Ss have. Provide further examples if required.

Ex 5 Point out the information in the **Watch out!** box. Then ask Ss to work in pairs to change the sentences into reported speech. Check answers and discuss any problems.

> 1 Our CEO tells us/says it is important to celebrate failure as well as success.
> OR, Our CEO told us/said it was important to celebrate failure as well as success.
> 2 My colleague says she's made a mistake and she (has) sent me the wrong file again.
> OR, My colleague told me/said she'd made a mistake and she (had) sent me the wrong file again.
> 3 Our supplier says the technician will come tomorrow.
> OR, Our supplier told me/said the technician would come the next day.
> 4 The football manager says they've just lost the match but they'll win next time.
> OR, The football manager said they had just lost the match but they'd win next time.
> 5 My friend says he's/she's sorry but he/she thought I said Tuesday. He/She can't come on Thursday.
> OR, My friend said he/she was sorry but he/she thought I had said Tuesday. He/She couldn't come on Thursday.
> 6 The designer says there are lots of faults in the design so they're going to start again.
> OR, The designer told me/said there were lots of faults in the design so they were going to start again.

Optional activity: Ask Ss to whisper something to a partner so that the rest of the class can't hear. Their partner has to tell the class what the S said. The S can correct the reported speech or accept it.

Speaking: Embarrassing mistakes

Ex 6 Ask Ss to work in pairs to discuss the mistakes.

Ex 7 Change the pairs so that Ss are working with a different partner. Ss tell each other what their previous partner said about the different situations.

TALKING POINT

Discuss the question with the class. Ss could compare their jobs and decide which is the most/least risky for different reasons.

Homework suggestion

Ss choose one situation they have discussed in Ex 6 and write an email to a friend explaining the situation and what their partner said. (120–150 words)

β Embedded questions

Aims and objectives

In this lesson Ss will:
- discuss different celebrities and things that have happened to them
- listen to a news interview with a celebrity
- study uses of embedded questions
- roleplay interviews using embedded questions

Listening: Celebrity gossip

TALKING POINT

You could use the Talking point here to start the lesson as it leads into Ex 1.

Ex 1 Ask Ss to work in pairs to discuss the questions. Why do Ss think people are generally fascinated with celebrities nowadays? Are Ss in the class interested in celebrities? Why?/Why not?

Ex 2 Tell Ss they are going to read some headlines about different celebrities. Ss match the names to the options.

a	Paul and Kate Morgan	d	Angie Cole
b	Stella Delaine	e	Richard Watson
c	Jake Cruz		

Ex 3 Ss work in pairs to identify the words in the headlines to match the definitions.

1	to split	3	to sue
2	collapses	4	quits

Ex 4))) **2.37** Tell Ss they are going to listen to an interview about one of the celebrities. Before playing the recording, ask Ss to check what they know about the celebrities from the headlines. Then ask them to identify which celebrity the interview is about.

Stella Delaine

Track 2.37: 12B, Page 122, Exercises 4 and 5

P = Presenter, **T** = Tim

P: So now we're going over to South London to speak to Tim Gordon, our correspondent there. Good morning, Tim.

T: Good morning.

P: Could you tell us how she is this morning?

T: Well, I heard from the hospital just half an hour ago. It seems she's a little better this morning. She's had breakfast and was talking to the hospital staff.

P: Do you know why she was taken ill like this?

T: The hospital hasn't made any official statement. It's possible that it was mainly stress. People are saying that the latest tour was a mistake so soon after her recent operation, and of course there's been her divorce as well.

P: But it was very dramatic, the way it suddenly happened during the interval of the concert. There has been speculation in the press that this was a heart attack. Is that still a possibility?

T: Well, like I said, the hospital hasn't confirmed anything.

P: Have you spoken to her daughter yet?

T: No, but she's staying nearby. We're expecting her to visit later this morning.

P: So we can't rule out the possibility that this was a heart attack?

T: No. It could have been.

Ex 5))) Ask Ss to read the questions before you play the recording again and see if they can remember any of the questions. Encourage Ss to check their answers with a partner.

1	how she is	4	Have you spoken
2	why she was taken ill	5	we can't rule out
3	Is that		

Grammar: Embedded questions

Ex 6 Do this with the whole class. Point out that embedded questions can appear to be more polite and less direct and are a good way of starting an interview with a person you don't know well. If necessary, do extra practice on embedded questions by asking a direct question and asking a student to embed it.

Direct questions
Question word(s) + auxiliary + subject + verb
Why did he quit the show?
Embedded questions
Expression + question word(s) + subject + verb
Could you tell me why he quit the show?
Direct questions (*Yes/No* question)
Auxiliary + subject + verb
Are they planning to get married?
Embedded questions
Expression + *if* + subject + verb
Do you know if they're planning to get married?

Ex 7 Ss work in pairs to answer the questions.

1 At the beginning.
2 So we can't rule out the possibility that this was a heart attack? – No, it doesn't contain a question form.

Ex 8 Ss work in pairs. They read the questions and change them to embedded ones.

Could you tell me … / Do you know …
1 if Richard's career will survive?
2 what time they left the club?
3 which law firm Angie is consulting?
4 if they've found a new presenter yet?
5 if they're living apart now?
6 what sort of financial settlement Kate wants?
7 if we've received a statement from the *Post*?
8 which direction their taxi went?

Speaking: Celebrity interviews

Ex 9 Ss work in pairs. Ask each S to choose a headline. Tell them that they are going to be interviewed in their chosen role and to tell their partner which celebrity they have chosen.

Ex 10 Ss work alone to prepare their roles. Remind Ss that they should be ready to talk about the topic given in the headlines and to answer the questions about the topic.

Ex 11 Monitor the roleplays and Ss' use of embedded questions.

Ex 12 Ss share their experiences with the class. Give general feedback on the use of embedded questions.

TALKING POINT
If the Talking point was not used at the start of the lesson, discuss the question with the class here. Would everyone ask the same type of question? Why?/Why not?

Homework suggestions
• Ss write an article on their interview (120–150 words). Ss should include a headline in their article.
• Tell Ss to imagine that they met their favourite celebrity in their local supermarket. Ss write an email to a friend telling them about the meeting, what happened, what they asked them and what the celebrity said. (120–150 words)
• Ss write an essay discussing the statement *Celebrities are too important nowadays.* (120–150 words)

C Consumer vocabulary

Aims and objectives

In this lesson Ss will:
• listen to podcasts about consumers and what happened to them
• study topic vocabulary
• tell each other stories
• discuss good and bad consumer experiences

Listening: Consumer stories

Ex 1 2.38 Before playing the recording, ask Ss to read the four topics. Ask Ss to listen and match the podcasts to their descriptions. Ss discuss why they made their choices.

a podcast 2		**c** postcast 3	
b podcast 4		**d** podcast 1	

Tracks 2.38–2.41: 12C, Page 124, Exercises 1, 2, 3 and 4

1

Well, I've often paid for flights and holidays on the internet and felt safe about giving my credit card details. But this one time I was nearly ripped off. You see, I hired a car through this cheap online car hire company, but when my credit card bill arrived, they'd overcharged me by 500 euros. So, you know, I email the company and they say the 500 euros is just being held as a deposit and they'd refund my money within 15 days. Well, it didn't happen, and so I keep phoning and emailing but I just get an answerphone message or no reply at all. It was really frustrating. Anyway, in the end, I reported them to the trading standards people. They were absolutely great.

They found out this car hire company was still operating, got the address and wrote to them. And, you know, I got my money back. Needless to say, I've learnt my lesson. I'll only give my details online to well-known, reputable companies now. I mean, there are a lot of internet scams about these days.

2

Results from a survey reveal that 60% of UK homeowners prefer cash-in-hand builders. The survey commissioned by the National Federation of Builders claims that over half of Britons would risk hiring a cowboy builder to carry out work on their home.

Sixty-one per cent of the 2,000 UK adults surveyed are tempted by a tax-free deal on their building work because of the high costs.

Many people are victim to cowboy tradesmen in order to save money, but then find they have no legal protection when things go wrong. There are over 100,000 complaints made about rogue tradesmen each year, according to figures from the Trading Standards.

3

So, yesterday I was at work – I work in a chemist's – this guy comes up and we were really busy for a Monday. And, so anyway, he drops off a prescription and I told him that it'd be about half an hour, because we were, you know, really busy. And so anyway, I passed his prescription to the pharmacist and continued to serve the other customers in the shop. Well, he comes back about forty minutes later. In the meantime, the pharmacist had given the prescription back to me 'cos we didn't have any in stock. Well, he got really angry about it at all. He started screaming and yelling, 'Ah, this service is terrible! Blah, blah, blah. Let me talk to your manager.' I mean this guy was really shouting. And, so, you know, my manager comes over and she tries to talk to him and, you know, he keeps shouting and insulting her. I mean, just, we didn't do anything wrong, we didn't make any mistakes. I didn't know we wouldn't have any of that medicine when I told him to come back in half an hour. Well, as you can imagine, we're not going to serve that man again.

4

Overcharged bills! Low quality goods! Poor customer service! Just when bad business thought it was safe to rip people off, there's a new consumer site that's hit the internet: www.iripoff.com. A site designed by consumers for consumers. By filling out an anonymous complaint, it's like putting up your very own website. Users can upload images and attach voice audio to their complaints. Complaints which are then visible to millions worldwide on www.iripoff.com.

Ex 2 2.39 Before playing the first recording again, ask Ss to read the notes. Ss listen, fill in the information and compare their answers with a partner.

1 car hire	**2** credit card	**3** 500	**4** 15	**5** address

Ex 3 2.40 Tell Ss they are going to listen to the second story again. Ask Ss to read the notes and see if they can spot five errors. Play the recording for Ss to identify the mistakes and compare their answers with a partner.

1 A survey reveals that ~~16~~ 60% of UK homeowners …
2 ~~20,000~~ 2,000 adults were interviewed for the survey …
3 … commissioned by the National Federation of ~~Architects~~ Builders.
4 … Trading Standards figures show that over ~~10,000~~ 100,000 complaints …

5 … unprofessional builders and tradesmen each ~~month~~ year.

Ex 4 🔊 **2.41** Tell Ss they are going to listen to the third story. Ss read through the story before they listen. Ask them to compare their answers after they have heard the recording.

1 chemist's **2** busy **3** 30 **4** in stock **5** manager

Word focus: Consumer vocabulary

Ex 5 Ss work in pairs. Suggest that they don't use a dictionary, but try to use the context to guess the meaning. Ask them to identify any words phrases that are informal.

1 *ripped off* – c (informal)
2 overcharged – c (formal)
3 refund – f
4 reported – a
5 reputable – g
6 scams – b
7 cash-in-hand – d
8 cowboy – e (informal)
9 rogue tradespeople – e (formal)

Ex 6 This gives Ss vocabulary for the Speaking section. You could call out the job and ask Ss to call out the tradesperson.

1 b **2** g **3** e **4** a **5** d **6** h **7** c **8** f

Suggested ways to choose a tradesperson:
personal recommendation, professional associations, adverts in press, phone directory, go to a local trades person's shop

Optional activity: Discuss the best ways to find a tradesperson and some of the problems that can occur.

Ex 7 Discuss the question with the whole class. Encourage Ss to give details and other Ss to ask questions about the experience.

Possible answers:
a plumber – install a new sink or bathroom suite
b electrician – fix plugs, install air conditioning
c mechanic – change the oil, test the brakes
d gas engineer – check for gas leaks, maintenance of boilers and radiators
e gardener – plant flowers/trees, mow the lawn, put up fences
f carpenter – put up some shelves, build a wardrobe
g decorator – hang/strip wallpaper
h builder – build walls

Photocopiable notes 12.1 (page 122)
Easily confused words (Card activity page 141)

Speaking: This is what happened

Ex 8 Put Ss into groups of three. Refer Ss to the pictures and explain that they are going to tell the others about the story behind one the pictures, using some of the expressions from Ex 5. Ss turn to their files, read their information and try to memorize it. Ss then tell their story to the group explaining what they learnt from the experience. The other Ss ask questions. Monitor and then discuss the experience with the class.

In one-to-one classes, ask the S to read through the three cards, and to choose one to memorize. They then tell you the story.

Ex 9 Ss discuss how they felt about each situation and decide which was the worst and why.

TALKING POINT
Discuss the questions with the class.

Homework suggestions
• Ss write an email to a friend about a difficult experience (they can use one of the examples from Ex 8 if they prefer) saying what happened, how they felt and what they learnt from the experience. (120–150 words)
• Ss write a report on one of the situations in Ex 8 to send in as part of a complaints procedure. (120–150 words)
• Ss write a letter of complaint to a customer services department about a situation where they needed help or didn't get good service. In the letter Ss should say what they want to be done about the situation. (120–150 words)

D Communication strategies
Dealing with complaints

Aims and objectives

In this lesson Ss will:
• listen to two customers complaining on the telephone
• discuss ways of responding to complaints
• roleplay different situations making and responding to complaints
• read and write an email

Culture and language
Dealing with complaints

Saying sorry might mean we accept responsibility for something we've done wrong, or it might not. It could just mean that we are sympathetic to someone else's misfortune. So if we tell someone we have a headache and they say *Oh, I'm sorry*, it probably doesn't mean they think they caused it.

How far 'sorry' implies accepting responsibility can be important in business dealings because it can result in financial penalties. To try to avoid this problem, some English-speaking customer service representatives have been trained to apologize to customers with a specific *I am sorry to hear that* rather than an unspecific *I'm sorry*. Some students may feel this lacks the quality of a full apology. (See pages 106–107 on *Saying sorry* in unit 10.)

We may also avoid saying who's to blame or admitting to a mistake by using the passive form, *There seems to have been a mistake*, rather than saying *We've/You've made a mistake*. (See pages 126 and 127 on *Dealing with complaints* in unit 12.) You may want to explore your students' views on what constitutes good customer service.

Speaking: Common complaints

Optional activity: Ask Ss to look at the photographs. How do they think the people are feeling? Ask Ss to brainstorm as many words as they can for each picture. Which one do Ss think shows the most extreme feelings? Which photo best shows how they feel when they want to complain about something?

Ex 1 Ss work in groups and discuss what they might complain about in these situations.

Possible situations:
- something missing from a product, e.g. a button from a shirt, or parts of a furniture kit that you need to assemble
- food in restaurants
- toys and other goods that come in packaging that doesn't include batteries
- colleagues who talk too loudly when you're trying to work
- people who push in in queues

Ex 2 Ask Ss to discuss the questions in groups. Ss should give reasons for their opinions and personal experiences if appropriate.

Ex 3 Ss relate their own stories and say how they felt at the time.

Listening: A customer complaint

Ex 4 🔊 **2.42** It is important for Ss to predict their ideas before they listen to the recording to identify the types of complaint, as this will make it easier for them to listen to the conversation. Explain the situation and ask Ss in pairs to discuss the kind of complaints Claire might receive. Take feedback and put Ss' suggestions on the board. Play the recording and ask Ss to identify the two complaints. Compare with the ideas on the board. Did Ss predict them correctly?

Call 1: a customer complains he has been overcharged for delivery of an online order.

Call 2: a customer complains she has received an incorrect delivery: she wanted a brown top, not a blue one.

Track 2.42: 12D, Page 126, Exercise 4
Call 1, Part 1
N = Neil, **R** = Recorded message, **C** = Customer Service rep

N: Hello, I'd like to speak to customer services, please.

R: If you would like to place an order, press 1.

N: Here we go again.

R: … If you wish to talk to one of our customer service representatives, press 2.

N: Two. …

C: Ritchie's Customer Services. How may I help you?

N: Hello, I'd like to make a complaint about the delivery charges on my last order.

C: Could I have your name, please, sir?

N: Yes, it's Neil Jackson, that's N-E-I-L Jackson.

C: And your order number?

N: Let me see … Um, it starts with a hash sign, then five, two, eight, oh sorry, that's five, eight, two, slash, one, O, seven, hyphen nine, four, O, three, six.

C: So that's hash, 582, slash, 107, hyphen, 94036.

N: That's right.

Call 2
C = Customer Service rep, **T** = Tara

C: Ritchie's.

T: Hello, is that customer services?

C: Yes, how can I help you?

T: I'm phoning about a delivery you sent me.

C: I see. Can you give me your name, please?

T: Tara Jackson.

C: Is that T-A-R-A?

T: Yeah. The thing is, you've sent me the wrong stuff. I didn't order a blue top. I ordered a brown one. Blue's not my colour …

C: Just one moment. Can I have the order number, please, Ms Jackson?

T: What? Oh yeah, it's somewhere here. … Dad, have you seen the piece of paper with the order number? … On the table? Wait a minute, it's here somewhere. … Got it. It's, er … one of those funny signs.

C: You mean a hash?

T: Yeah, hash, then five, eight, two, slash, four, one, two, hyphen, eight, seven … oh sorry, that's a nine, seven, double two, seven.

C: Can I read that back to you? Hash, 582, slash, 412, hyphen, 97227. And you say that you've received the wrong colour top?

T: Yeah, I've already told you. I wanted brown, not blue.

Ex 5 Ss work in pairs. Give Ss time to read their information and think about what they will say before they do the roleplay. They then take turns to be the customer and the customer service representative.

Ex 6 🔊 **2.43** Ss listen to the rest of the phone call so that they can compare the conversation with their own roleplay. Discuss the questions with the whole class.

Track 2.43: 12D, Page 126, Exercises 6 and 7
Call 1, Part 2
C = Customer Service rep, **N** = Neil

C: And what seems to be the problem, Mr Jackson?

N: The thing is, on your website it says all deliveries are free but I see from my bill that I have been charged for delivery.

C: Just one moment … I see your order came to 48 Euros, Mr Jackson. But the offer only applies to deliveries of over 50 Euros, not for orders of less than 50 Euros.

N: Well, I think your promotion is misleading because it doesn't say that.

C: If you look at our website, sir …

N: Hold on a minute. … Right, I have it here on my screen.

C: … and scroll right down to our terms and conditions, you will see that they refer to deliveries over 50 Euros only. It's the last part.

N: Oh, I didn't see that. The terms and conditions are at the bottom of the screen.

C: I'm afraid your bill is correct, sir. Do you require any more assistance?

N: No, but I don't think that's right.

C: I'm sorry to hear that, but you have been charged correctly. Would you like another service, Mr Jackson?

N: No. It's just that your website is confusing. If I'd known, I would have bought another item because my order only came to 48 Euros.

C: I understand, sir. That must be annoying for you. I'll pass on your complaint and you could also complete our online customer service questionnaire.

N: Oh, all right then. Where's that?

Ex 7 Ask Ss to read through the form so they know what they are listening for. When they have completed the form, encourage Ss to compare answers and discuss if they think the customer was satisfied.

> 1 (promotional) online offer
> 2 overcharged
> 3 over €50
> 5 customer service questionnaire
> 6 misleading/confusing
> 7 terms and conditions

Ex 8 This moves the language from making complaints to responding to complaints. Ask Ss to work in groups and think about the politeness and formality of the expressions.

> **Asking about the complaint**
> What seems to be the problem?
>
> **Showing sympathy**
> Oh dear, I'm sorry to hear that.
> Yes, I see/understand.
> That must be very annoying.
>
> **Apologizing**
> We're really very sorry about this.
> I do apologize.
> I'm afraid we've had some trouble with the system.
>
> **Correcting and explaining**
> If you look at our website, I think you'll find …
> There seems to have been a mistake.
>
> **Putting things right**
> You could complete our questionnaire.
> You'll need to complete this form.
> I'll see what I can do.
> I'll pass on your complaint.
> Thanks for letting us know.
>
> The other examples sound impolite or too forceful, or don't sound professional, e.g.
> *Impolite:* What's your problem? No, you're wrong. You've made a mistake.
> *Patronising:* Don't worry, my dear.
> *Forceful:* You must complete this form.
> *Not professional/admitting fault:* I know what you mean. Oops, sorry. The system doesn't work properly.

> **Photocopiable notes 12.2 (page 122)**
> **Making complaints (Card matching page 142)**

Speaking: Putting things right

Ex 9 Ss work in pairs. Ask Ss to choose some of the situations from Ex 1 to roleplay. Encourage Ss to experiment with using different language for making the complaint and for responding in different ways.

Variation: Ask Ss to do Ex 9 in groups of three. Two Ss roleplay the situation and the third S listens and provides feedback on language used and how well Ss complained and responded.

Ex 10 Ss could discuss the difference between complaining in writing and complaining on the phone. Which method do Ss think is the most effective? Ss could underline set phrases for making written complaints, e.g. *I am writing to complain about …*

> Amy's order was delivered to her neighbour's address and left in the garden without a delivery note in the rain. Some of the items were damaged.

Writing: Replying to a complaint

Ex 11 Students work on their own and write their emails. Tell them to check for politeness, spelling and grammar, and if they have included of all five points when they have finished.

Sample answer:

> **To:** Amy Henderson
>
> **From:** Ritchie's Customer Services
>
> **Subject:** Unsatisfactory delivery
>
> Dear Ms Henderson
>
> Thanks for your email about your order number # 5821/304-973478. We are very sorry to hear about the unsatisfactory delivery of your items.
>
> I can see that your parcel was sent by your local mail service. I am afraid we are not responsible for delivery using this service. We will, however, offer you a free replacement or refund for the damaged items.
>
> We take all feedback seriously at Ritchie's and we will add €5 of credit to your account on your next order. Please let us know if you have any further questions.
>
> We would like to thank you for your patience and we apologize again for any inconvenience caused.
>
> Regards
>
> *(Name)*
>
> Ritchie's Customer Services

Ex 12 Ss check each other's work. Ask them to check for grammar, spelling and also for the content of the email. Is it well-written and using appropriate language? Would the customer who complained be satisfied with the answer?

Homework suggestions

- Ss choose one of the situations from Ex 1 and write an email of complaint. (120–150 words)
- Ss write a short dialogue between a customer service manager and an angry customer. Ss read their dialogue to the class the following lesson.
- Ss research some shopping websites and see if there are any complaints on the site. Ss make notes about the most interesting or surprising complaints to present to the class the following lesson.

Interaction Online entrepreneurs

Aims and objectives

In this lesson Ss will:
- read about a young entrepreneur using online social networks for marketing
- read an interview with a fashion entrepreneur
- play a board game about things that happen while running a business

Refer Ss to the Reminder box and draw attention to the language that the lesson will focus on. Check Ss can use this language by looking at page 175 of the Grammar reference and at previous lessons of the unit.

Reading: Starting up

Optional activity: Ask Ss to discuss the following questions.

- *Would they like to run their own business? Why?/Why not?*

- *What kind of business would they like to run? Why? How would they start up?*

- *What do they think is the business model of the future?*

Ex 1 Ss discuss the questions in pairs. Ask Ss to share any experiences they have had of working from home or working for themselves. What are the advantages and disadvantages of working for yourself and/or working from home?

Ex 2 Explain that Ss are going to read an article about a young entrepreneur. Ask Ss to read it quickly to find the answers to the questions.

> Lauren Luke sells make-up/beauty products. panacea81 has become successful through online social networks such as MySpace and YouTube. But as social networking becomes more popular, it will be difficult for online businesses to stand out and be noticed.

Ex 3 Ask Ss to speculate about the questions. Have Ss ever bought or sold anything on eBay or other similar sites?

Background information
Stitsh.com

Stitsh.com started in early 2008 as a way of inspiring people to find a new look by documenting the latest styles on the streets of major cities around the world.

Ex 4 Tell Ss they are going to read about a successful entrepreneur. The article is written in paragraphs and each one was introduced by a question. Ask Ss to read the article and then work in pairs to note down what the questions were.

> **Possible questions:**
> 1 What kind of a business is Stitsh?
> 2 Could you explain your business to me? / What do you do exactly?
> 3 How does the site make money?
> 4 What are you working on at the moment?
> 5 What's your background?
> 6 Who do you go to for advice? / Who do you ask for advice?

> 7 Do you enjoy your work? / Do you find it difficult to stop thinking about work?
> 8 Where do you hope to be in five years' time?

Ex 5 Ask Ss to discuss their reactions to Dominic Fendius's interview. Would Ss like to work for this company? What other three questions would Ss like to ask him? Then ask Ss to work in pairs and roleplay the interview.

> **Possible questions:**
> - Who are your key customers?
> - Who are your main competitors?
> - What is in fashion at the moment?
> - How many people do you employ?
> - What do you see as your biggest challenge?
> - How easy is it for you to get a bank loan?

Homework suggestions

- Ss research a successful entrepreneur. Ss work in pairs to roleplay an interview with their chosen businessperson.
- Ss research a successful entrepreneur and write an email to a friend telling them about this person and why they are interested in them. (120–150 words)
- Ss research a successful entrepreneur. Ss write a list of questions they would like to ask this person, and decide which questions should be embedded and which could be direct and why.

Board game: Online business

Ex 6 Read out the situation and the rules to Ss. Make sure that everyone understands what they have to do. Then play the game.

After the activity, discuss with Ss which situations were easy/difficult to deal with. Why? How do Ss think they have benefited from playing the game?

Review 10–12

The Review checks work covered in the previous three units, including grammar, vocabulary, communication strategies, collocations and pronunciation. It can be approached in a number of different ways, depending on classroom size and situation and time available, for example:

• as a whole-class activity
• with Ss in pairs or groups, followed by class feedback
• as a test to be marked
• as homework

1
1 gossip 2 stolen 3 cash 4 credit 5 upset
6 had given 7 bought 8 save 9 fault 10 blame
11 camera 12 tell

2
1 wouldn't have happened, 'd had
2 hadn't been, wouldn't have stolen
3 had been, wouldn't have put
4 wouldn't have been, had had
5 shouldn't have left
6 should have noticed
7 should have caught
8 wouldn't have seen, had been

3

		B			D			F		
	L			M	I	S	T	A	K	E	S
	A			I			U				
	M	A	D	E			L		C		
	E			M			T		O		
		A	D	M	I	T			W		
				A		A			B		
		C				K			O		
	H	O	N	E	S	T	Y			L	
	E									I	
	A	P	O	L	O	G	I	Z	E		
	T										

4

Banking	Special occasions	Trades people	Complaints	Adjectives of personality
mortgage	wedding	electrician	apology	wise
loan	retirement	builder	overcharge	thoughtful
borrow	promotion	plumber	refund	sensitive
down payment	public holiday	mechanic	replacement	dishonest
pay back	anniversary	decorator	damaged goods	irrational

5
1 whose – **defining**
2 which – **extra information**
3 who/that – **defining**
4 where – **defining**
5 which – **extra information**
6 that/who – **defining**
7 that/who – **defining**
8 whose – **extra information**

6
1 e 2 f 3 c 4 b 5 g 6 a 7 h 8 d

7
1 you've been running (*embedded question*)
2 you've opened (*embedded question*)
3 have you had
4 have you been doing (have you done)
5 Have you found
6 Have you been getting
7 Have you been celebrating/Have you celebrated
8 have you won

8
1 c 2 h 3 a 4 e 5 b 6 d 7 g 8 f

9
1 g 2 h 3 b 4 e 5 a 6 f 7 d 8 c

Photocopiable activity 1.1 (p. 123)

Unit 1 Lesson A

Group interviews: How organized are you?

Aims: to practise asking and answering personal questions using different tenses
Time: 15 minutes
Grouping: Ideally groups of 3, although other groupings and 1:1s with the teacher are possible.
Preparation: Copy and cut up a set of cards for each group.

Procedure

- Explain to Ss they are going to interview each other about their lives.
- Put Ss into groups and give each member a different card.
- Ss work in pairs to ask the questions and any follow-up questions in turn and note down the answers in the columns provided. Encourage Ss to find out as much information as they can by asking follow-up questions.
- After the interviews, put Ss into new groups to discuss what they have found out about each other.
- After the activity you could finish with a class vote for the most organized student.

Homework or extension option

Ss write an email to a friend telling them about a person they interviewed.

Photocopiable activity 1.2 (p. 124)

Unit 1 Lesson E

Roleplay: Meeting with lifestyle coach

Aims: to practise giving and receiving advice sensitively and appropriately
Time: 20 minutes
Grouping: Ideally pairs, although other groupings and 1:1s with the teacher are possible.
Preparation: Copy and cut out a Student A card and a Student B card for each pair and two copies of the Written follow-up card.

Procedure

- Explain to Ss they are going to roleplay a situation in pairs. One will be a lifestyle coach (someone who provides advice for people who feel that they need help with their work–life balance) and the other will be his or her client.
- Put Ss into pairs and give each one a different role card (A or B). Tell them not to look at each other's card.
- Give Ss 5 minutes to prepare their own card and think about what they might say to each other. Then allow them to roleplay the meeting.
- Monitor and stop Ss after 10 minutes. Take feedback on what happened and make any comments you want about the language you heard.

Homework or extension option

Set the written homework. Hand out a written follow-up card to Ss. They each write a paragraph summarizing the meeting from their point of view and make recommendations for future meetings and planning.

Photocopiable activity 2.1 (p. 125)

Unit 2 Lesson B

Paired dictation: Exchange your home

Aims: to extend Ss' vocabulary around the topic of house exchange
Time: 20–25 minutes
Grouping: Ideally pairs, although other groupings and 1:1s with the teacher are possible.
Preparation: Copy and cut up a set of cards for each pair.

Procedure

- Explain to Ss they are going to do a dictation.
- Put Ss into pairs and give each one a different card (A or B).
- Explain to Ss they are going to complete a text by dictating it to each other. They should not look at their partner's text.
- Ss work together and complete the text by dictating their text and writing in the missing parts.
- Ss read the complete text together and compare and correct their versions.

Variation: Brainstorm ideas Ss have discussed from the unit. Write these on the board before giving out the cards. This will help Ss to complete the dictation.

> **Key**
> The barter economy is on the up and up – you know, you take my apples, I'll have your old Prada bag. Swapping provides cheap holidays. You offer someone a week in your scruffy home in exchange for a fortnight in somewhere nicer. What began as a way for time-rich, cash-poor teachers to spend summer breaks has boomed with the internet. You only need an open mind and an email address for a gateway to adventure. At least that's what I thought when I tried to exchange my London house for a villa in France. It didn't work. Inflexibility was my problem. I wanted Europe. I was offered Canada and India. Swapping seems to work best for retired people and anyone who doesn't mind staying off the beaten track. But it doesn't matter if your home is embarrassingly ordinary – the worst thing is cleaning it before you go. And apparently people trashing your house isn't the worry you might think – it's your car getting scratched. That's all part of the deal, though – and it's a good one.

Homework or extension option

Write the questions on the board. Ss discuss them in groups.
1 Have you ever had a holiday where you couldn't wait to go home? What happened?
2 How often have you stayed in 5 star hotels/cheap guest houses? Which do you prefer? Why?
3 If I ask you to decide now, where do you think you'll go on your next holiday?
4 What has been your best or worst holiday experience so far? What happened?

Photocopiable activity 2.2 (p. 125)

Unit 2 Lesson D

Pelmanism: Compound nouns

Aims: to practise compound nouns
Time: 10 minutes
Grouping: Ideally groups of 4, although other groupings and 1:1s with the teacher are possible.
Preparation: Copy and cut up a set of cards for each group.

Procedure

- Explain to Ss they are going to make compound nouns.
- Put Ss into groups. Give each group a set of cards and tell them to spread the cards face down on the table.
- Ss take it in turns to turn up two cards. If they make a compound noun, that S keeps them. If they don't make a compound noun, the two cards are replaced in the same position and the next S takes a turn.
- Ss have to identify the compound nouns and also remember where they saw the card that they need on the table.
- When all the cards have been taken, Ss show the cards they have collected. The winner is the S with the most correct compound nouns.

Key

waitress service	flat-screen TV
departure lounge	toothpaste
check-in desk	hair dryer
swimming pool	car park
boarding card	queen-size bed
power shower	conveyor belt
walk-in wardrobe	bathrobe

Homework or extension option

Ss write sentences using the compound nous they have collected.
This activity can be repeated with other vocabulary items, e.g. phrasal verbs.

Photocopiable activity 3.1 (p. 126)

Unit 3 Lesson A

Card matching: Natural spoken English

Aims: to practise natural expressions and idioms
Time: 10 minutes
Grouping: Ideally groups of 4, although other groupings and 1:1s with the teacher are possible.
Preparation: Copy and cut up a set of spoken cards and response cards for each group. (Keep separate)

Procedure

- Explain to Ss they are going to match the response cards (grey) to the spoken cards (white).
- Put Ss into groups. Give each group a set of both the spoken and response cards.
- Ss match the spoken cards and responses.
- Check their answers. If time, Ss practise the exchanges.

Key
1 b **2** d **3** g **4** e **5** f **6** c **7** a **8** j **9** h **10** i

Homework or extension option

Ss write short dialogues practising the expressions and idioms.

Photocopiable activity 3.2 (p. 127)

Unit 3 Lesson D

Situation cards: What do you do?

Aims: to practise language of discussing, agreeing, disagreeing
Time: 10–15 minutes to include class discussion
Grouping: Ideally groups of 4, although other groupings and 1:1s with the teacher are possible.
Preparation: Copy and cut up a set of cards for each group and shuffle them before handing them out.

Procedure

- Explain to Ss they are going to practise discussing, agreeing and disagreeing.
- Put Ss into groups. Ss put the situation cards face down on the table.
- Ss take it in turns to pick a situation card. They discuss and think of different ways of dealing with each situation.
- After the group discussions, discuss the Ss' solutions with the class. Ss can also compare the situations with what would happen in their own culture.

Homework or extension option

Ss choose one of the situations they have discussed. Ss write an email to a friend, describing the difficult situation they were in and explaining what their solution was.

Photocopiable activity 4.1 (p. 127)

Unit 4 Lesson D

Card activity: Accepting and rejecting ideas

Aims: to practise accepting and rejecting ideas
Time: 10 minutes
Grouping: Ideally pairs, although other groupings and 1:1s with the teacher are possible.
Preparation: Copy and cut up a set of cards for each pair. Give them out in order.

Procedure

- Explain that Ss are going to practise responding to suggestions appropriately.
- Put Ss into pairs. Ss put their 2 sets of cards face down on the table. Tell them to keep them in the order they are. They take it in turns to take the top card from each pile and discuss an appropriate response.
- After the activity, discuss possible answers with the whole class.

Homework or extension option

Ss write four-line dialogues beginning with a situation prompt. Ss read their dialogues to the class.

Photocopiable activity 4.2 (p. 128)

Unit 4 Lesson E

Roleplay: The appraisal meeting

Aims: to practise using modal verbs expressing obligation and advice in natural formal situation
Time: 20–25 minutes
Grouping: Ideally pairs, although other groupings and 1:1s with the teacher are possible.
Preparation: Copy and cut up a set of cards for each pair.

Procedure

- Explain to Ss they are going to roleplay a situation. One S will be a boss (manager of a small team of employees) and the other S will be his or her line manager.
- Put Ss into pairs. Give each one a different role card (A or B). Tell them not to look at each other's card.
- Discuss the situation and explain the appraisal system if necessary (see notes below).
- Give Ss 5 minutes to work alone to prepare what they might say to each other.
- Ss roleplay the appraisal meeting.
- Monitor and stop Ss after 10 minutes. Take feedback on what happened and make any comments you want about the language you heard.

Background information

An appraisal is a regular formal meeting between an employee and their line manager, at which they discuss performance and set targets for the future. It is then written up by each person and kept on file as a way of monitoring a person's work and contribution to the company. It is a good way of identifying skills that may be lacking and to address these by recommending courses, etc., and also motivating employees and making them feel valued.

Homework or extension option

Ss write a paragraph summarizing the appraisal meeting from their point of view for the record and identifying the targets set for the future.

Photocopiable activity 5.1 (p. 129)

Unit 5 Lesson A

Card activity: Talking about the past

Aims: to practise using the present perfect and past simple
Time: 15 minutes
Grouping: Ideally groups of 3, although other groupings and 1:1s with the teacher are possible.
Preparation: Copy and cut up a set of cards for each group.

Procedure

- Explain to Ss they are going to practise using the past simple and present perfect tenses.
- Put Ss into groups. Give each group a set of cards and ask them to put the cards face down in a pile.

- Ss pick a card in turn, identify the required tense (past simple, present perfect) and complete the sentence so that it is true for them.
- Ss ask each other further questions about their sentences.

Key			
1	past simple	7	present perfect
2	present perfect	8	past simple
3	present perfect	9	present perfect
4	present perfect	10	past simple
5	past simple	11	present perfect
6	past simple	12	present perfect

Homework or extension option

Ss choose a sentence and write a short paragraph for a blog on a social networking website.

Photocopiable activity 5.2 (p. 129)

Unit 5 Lesson C

Card activity: Small talk

Aims: to allow Ss to practise small talk
Time: 5 minutes
Grouping: Ideally groups of 4, although other groupings and 1:1s with the teacher are possible.
Preparation: Copy and cut up a set of cards for each group.

Procedure

- Explain to Ss they are going to practise small talk.
- Put Ss into groups. Give each group a set of cards and ask them to put the cards face down in a pile.
- One Ss picks a card and starts a conversation about it. The rest of the group join in, asking questions and adding their own thoughts, until the conversation is finished.
- The next S picks up the next card and starts a conversation. Ss continue small talk as before.
- After the activity, ask Ss which topics were easy/difficult to talk about. Make suggestions to help Ss with this topic.

Variation:

Give Ss only 2–3 minutes to talk about each topic. After 2–3 minutes, clap your hands and insist that they move on to the next topic.

You could also regroup the Ss after each 3 topics to provide interest.

Homework or extension option

Ss choose a card and write an email to a friend on that topic.

Photocopiable activity 6.1 (p. 130)

Unit 6 Lesson A

Discussion cards: Social rules

Aims: to practise using verbs of obligation
Time: 15 minutes
Grouping: Ideally groups of 3, although other groupings and 1:1s with the teacher are possible.
Preparation: Copy and cut up a set of cards for each group.

Procedure

- Explain to Ss they are going to talk about situations in which there is an unwritten social rule.
- Put Ss into groups and put the cards in a pile face down on the table.
- Ss take it in turns to pick a card and read out the situation. The other Ss suggest what could be said in each situation. Give Ss the examples below for the first situation to help them.
  You can't smoke inside the building. / You mustn't smoke inside the building. / You should go outside to smoke.
- After the activity, discuss which situation Ss think was the most difficult or embarrassing to deal with.

Homework or extension option

1. Ss work in pairs, pick a card and write a four-line dialogue for the situation. Ss read their dialogue to the class.
2. Ss write an email to a friend describing one of the situations and explaining what they said.

Photocopiable activity 6.2 (p. 131)

Unit 6 Lesson C

Dictation and punctuation: Formal and informal styles

Aims: to practise spelling and punctuation
Time: 10 minutes
Grouping: Ideally pairs, although other groupings and 1:1s with the teacher are possible.
Preparation: Copy and cut up a set of cards for each pair.

Procedure

- Explain to Ss they are going to think about spelling and punctuation.
- Put Ss into pairs. Give each pair a set of cards.
- Ss take it in turns to pick a card and dictate the sentence to their partner without telling them what the punctuation is. Tell Ss that they must read the sentences naturally and not too slowly.
- Ss compare the sentence they have written with the sentence on the card.
- After the activity, discuss the sentences and answer any questions Ss may have about the spelling or punctuation.
- Ask Ss which 3 sentences were more formal.

Key
Formal sentences:
My company is the best in its field because its advertising is excellent.

I'd appreciate it if you would advise me on a personal issue.
The next meeting will be held on Wednesday 5th September, at 4.30.

Homework or extension option

1. Give Ss sentences with no punctuation at all and they have to put the punctuation in the right place.
2. Dictate words to students that sound the same but are spelt differently. Example:
   would/wood   sale/sail   great/grate   here/hear

Photocopiable activity 7.1 (p. 132)

Unit 7 Lesson A

Matching activity: Jobs

Aims: to practise using topic vocabulary
Time: 15 minutes
Grouping: Ideally groups of 4, although other groupings and 1:1s with the teacher are possible.
Preparation: Copy and cut out a set of both the jobs and the skills/qualities cards for each group.

Procedure

- Explain to Ss they are going to match 3 skills and qualities required to different jobs. Point out that there may be more than one possibility. Tell Ss to justify their answers.
- Put Ss in to groups. Give each group a set of jobs and skills/qualities cards and ask them to spread the cards out face up.
- Ss match the skills to the jobs.
- After the activity, ask each group to present their matched cards to the rest of the class and explain their reasons.

Key
Possible answers:
Ss may have other ideas. The important thing is that they can justify their choices.
Waiter: patience/willing to work long hours/good social manner
Car salesperson: confidence/good oral communication skills/persuasive manner
Call-centre worker: patience/a sense of humour/good oral communication skills
Shop assistant: patience/ a sense of humour/flexibility
Teacher: patience/a sense of humour/sensitivity/determination/good organization skills/flexibility/academic qualifications
Managing director: good personnel skills/good writing skills/ambition/good social manner/academic qualifications

Homework or extension option

Ss suggest 2 other skills or qualities that are required for these jobs.

Photocopiable notes

Photocopiable activity 7.2 (p. 132)

Unit 7 Lesson D

Prompt cards: Explaining to others

Aims: to practise using tenses and linkers
Time: 10–15 minutes
Grouping: Ideally groups of 4, although other groupings and 1:1s with the teacher are possible.
Preparation: Copy and cut out a set of cards for each group.

Procedure

- Explain to Ss they are going to tell others in the group about different events. They should try to make their narrative as interesting as possible and tell them it does not need to be the truth. They must use linking words in their narrative, e.g.
  The first thing that happened was …, after that …, so that …, because …
- They must talk for about 2 minutes.
- Put Ss into groups. Give each group a set of cards and ask them to put the cards in a pile face down on the table.
- Ss take it in turns to pick a card and talk about it.
- After 2 minutes the others in the group can ask follow-up questions if they like.

Homework or extension option

Ss write one of the narratives.

Photocopiable activity 8.1 (p. 133)

Unit 8 Lesson C

Matching sentences: If …

Aims: to practise zero, first and second conditionals
Time: 10 minutes
Grouping: Ideally pairs, although other groupings and 1:1s with the teacher are possible.
Preparation: Copy and cut out a set of cards for each group and shuffle them before handing out.

Procedure

Part 1

- Explain to Ss they are going to practise conditional sentences.
- Remind Ss of the form of conditional sentences – *if + present, if + will* and *if + would.*
- Put Ss into pairs. Give each pair a set of cards and ask them to spread the cards out face up.
- Ss match the sentence beginnings to the sentence endings.
- After the activity, ask Ss to read out their complete sentences.

Part 2

- Ask Ss to discuss whether they agree with the sentences or not.
- After the activity, discuss which ones they disagreed with and what they would suggest instead.

Homework or extension option

Ss choose a sentence and write an email to a friend explaining how they feel about it.

Photocopiable activity 8.2 (p. 134)

Unit 8 Lesson D

Card matching: What are you doing?

Aims: to focus on language functions
Time: 10 minutes
Grouping: Ideally pairs, although other groupings and 1:1s with the teacher are possible.
Preparation: Copy and cut out a set of the function cards and the sentences for each pair.

Procedure

- Explain to Ss they are going to think about the function of what people say.
- Put Ss in pairs. Give each pair a set of cards and ask them to spread the cards out face up.
- Ss match the sentences to the language functions.
- After the activity, ask Ss to write short dialogues using one of the functions.

> **Key**
> Asking for suggestions: 1, 10
> Asking for an opinion: 5, 12
> Raising an objection: 4, 7, 14
> Checking understanding: 3, 9
> Making a suggestion: 2, 6, 8
> Making a decision: 11, 13

Homework or extension option

Ss act out their dialogues in front of the class.

Photocopiable activity 9.1 (p. 135)

Unit 9 Lesson C

Pelmonism: Phrasal verbs

Aims: to practise phrasal verbs
Time: 10–15 minutes
Grouping: Ideally groups of 4, although other groupings and 1:1s with the teacher are possible.
Preparation: Copy and cut up a set of cards for each group.

Procedure

- Explain to Ss they are going to match phrasal verbs with sentences.
- Put Ss into groups. Give each group a set of phrasal verb cards and a set of sentence cards.
- Ss put the cards face down on the table.
- Ss take it in turns to turn up two cards. If the phrasal verb fits the sentence, the S keeps them. If the two cards don't match, the two cards are replaced in the same position and the next S takes a turn.
- When all the cards have been taken, Ss read the sentences they have collected, changing the phrasal verb into the correct form to fit their sentence. The winner is the S with the most correct complete sentences.

Key			
1	get through to	6	get back
2	put off	7	hung up
3	put you through	8	call back
4	cut out	9	kept on
5	cut off	10	set up

Homework or extension option

Ss write alternative sentences using the phrasal verbs they have collected.

Photocopiable activity 9.2 (p. 136)

Unit 9 Lesson E

Roleplay: Telephoning situations

Aims: to practise telephone language
Time: 10 minutes
Grouping: Ideally pairs, although other groupings and 1:1s with the teacher are possible.
Preparation: Copy and cut out a set of the cards for each pair.

Procedure

* Explain to Ss they are going to do a roleplay on telephone conversations.
* Put Ss into pairs. Give each pair a different set of cards.
* Ss pick a card, look at it and prepare what they will say.
* Ss roleplay the situation.
* After the activity, Ss exchange their cards with a pair from a different group.
* When all Ss have completed all the cards, discuss any problems.

Homework or extension option

After the discussion of the problems, Ss act out one of the situations in front of the class.

Photocopiable activity 10.1 (p. 137)

Unit 10 Lesson B

Discussion cards: Giving advice

Aims: to practise different ways of giving advice
Time: 10 minutes
Grouping: Ideally groups of 4, although other groupings and 1:1s with the teacher are possible.
Preparation: Copy and cut out a set of the cards for each group.

Procedure

* Tell Ss they are going to practise different ways of giving advice.
* Put Ss into groups. Give each group a set of cards and ask them to put the cards face down in a pile.
* Ss take turns to pick up a card and read the situation out to the group. The group then discusses what the best advice would be.
* After the activity, Ss share their ideas with the rest of the class.

* Discuss the consequences of following the advice given in each case.

Homework or extension option

Ss write a brief report on one of the situations. They should
* describe the situation.
* explain what the best advice is, with reasons.
* explain what the consequences would be.

Photocopiable activity 10.2 (p. 138)

Unit 10 Lesson D

Roleplay: Apologizing and responding to apologies

Aims: to practise different ways of apologizing and responding to apologies
Time: 20 minutes
Grouping: Ideally pairs, although other groupings and 1:1s with the teacher are possible.
Preparation: Copy and cut up a set of both the situation and response cards for each pair.

Procedure

* Explain to Ss they are going to practise making and responding to apologies.
* Put Ss into pairs. Give each pair a set of cards and ask them to put each set face down in a pile.
* Ss take turns to pick a situation and response card, and roleplay the situation.
* After the activity, Ss share their ideas with the rest of the class.

Homework or extension option

Ss choose one of the situations and write an email apologizing for what happened.

Photocopiable activity 11.1 (p. 139)

Unit 11 Lesson A

Card activity: *who, which, where, when, while, whose or that?*

Aims: to practise using relative pronouns
Time: 10 minutes
Grouping: Ideally groups of 3, although other groupings and 1:1s with the teacher are possible.
Preparation: Copy and cut up a set of cards for each group.

Procedure

* Explain to Ss the aim of the activity is to complete sentences using relative pronouns and that the winner is the person who collects the most cards.
* Remind them of the relative pronouns they have studied and write them on the board for reference: *who, which, where, when, while, whose, that*.
* Put Ss into groups. Give each group a set of cards and ask them to put the cards face down in a pile.

Photocopiable notes

- Ss take turns to pick a card and read out the sentence, saying 'bleep' where there is a gap in the sentence. The other Ss have to say which word fits the gap: *who, which, where, when, while, whose* or *that*.
- If they are right, they keep the card. If not, the S who read the sentence keeps it.
- After the activity, find out who the winner was. Check answers and discuss any which Ss got wrong.

Homework or extension option

Ss write sentences of their own using relative pronouns.

Photocopiable activity 11.2 (p. 140)

Unit 11 Lesson D

Matching activity: Networking: responding to others

Aims: to practise responding to something you have been told
Time: 10 minutes
Grouping: Ideally pairs, although other groupings and 1:1s with the teacher are possible.
Preparation: Copy and cut up a set of both the statement/question and the response cards for each pair.

Procedure

- Explain to Ss they are going to match responses to statements and questions with the focus on appropriacy.
- Put Ss into pairs. Give each pair a set of cards and ask them to spread the cards out face up. Ss match the (grey) response cards to the (white) statement/question cards.
- After the activity, ask Ss to read the statements and responses with appropriate intonation and feeling.

Answers:
1 g **2** c **3** i **4** a **5** b **6** h **7** d **8** f **9** e **10** j

Homework or extension option

Ss discuss any alternative responses to the sentences/questions.

Photocopiable activity 12.1 (p. 141)

Unit 12 Lesson C

Card activity: Easily confused words

Aims: to practise topic vocabulary and easily confused words
Time: 10–15 minutes
Grouping: Ideally groups of 4, although other groupings and 1:1s with the teacher are possible.
Preparation: Copy and cut up a set of cards for each group.

Procedure

- Explain to Ss the aim of the activity is to clarify the differences between words that are similar.
- Put Ss into groups. Give each group a set of cards and ask them to put the cards face down in a pile.

- Ss take turns to pick a card and read out the two words at the top of the card. The same S then reads the sentence on the card and the others choose which of the 2 words fits the sentence. If they are right, they keep the card. If not, the S who read the sentence keeps it.
- After the activity, find out who the winner was. Check answers and discuss any which Ss got wrong.

Homework or extension option

Ss write sentences of their own using the other word on each card.

Photocopiable activity 12.2 (p. 142)

Unit 12 Lesson D

Card matching: Making complaints

Aims: to practise responding to complaints and excuses appropriately
Time: 10–15 minutes
Grouping: Ideally groups of 3, although other groupings and 1:1s with the teacher are possible.
Preparation: Copy and cut up a set of both the complaints/excuses and the topic cards for each group.

Procedure

- Explain to Ss the aim of the activity is to identify what a person is complaining or making an excuse about. Tell them that some of the complaints and excuses are quite amusing.
- Put Ss into groups. Give each group a set of both the complaints/excuses and topic cards and ask them to spread the cards face up on the table.
- Ss match the complaints/excuses cards to the topic.
- After the activity, check the answers and ask Ss to write short dialogues responding to each of the complaints/excuses on the cards.

Answers:
 1 Other people's choice of luggage
 2 The behaviour of a member of staff
 3 Failing to get a job
 4 An unsatisfactory day at a theme park
 5 Being ripped-off
 6 Colleagues who take long breaks
 7 Being overcharged
 8 Public transport
 9 An unsatisfactory holiday location
10 Not fulfilling a promise
11 Being late for work
12 Not doing homework

Homework or extension option

1 Shuffle the topic cards and put them face down on the table. Ss work in pairs. One S takes a topic card and makes a complaint. Their partner either apologizes and makes an excuse, or suggests a way of putting things right.
2 Give Ss the following situations. They think of excuses in pairs. Ss share their ideas and vote on the best excuse.
   - Not doing revision for exam
   - Taking too long at lunch
   - Arriving late for an interview

How organized are you?

✂

CARD 1
Interview each group member about their working lives. Find out as much as you can and note their answers below.

		A	B	C
1	Do you enjoy your work?			
2	Do you find it easy to ask for help?			
3	How easy is it to prioritize jobs you have to do?			
4	What work would you like to do in the future?			

✂

CARD 2
Interview each group member about their work–life balance. Find out as much as you can and note their answers below.

		A	B	C
1	How many hours sleep do you get each night? Has this changed since you started work?			
2	Do you work late at night? What did you do the last time you worked late?			
3	Do you think about work at weekends?			
4	Which chore do you dislike most? Why?			

✂

CARD 3
Interview each group member about their free time. Find out as much as you can and note their answers below.

		A	B	C
1	Was your life more or less busy in the past? Why?			
2	How often do you have time to go to the gym?			
3	What are you planning to do this weekend?			
4	What new activity would you like to take up in the future? Why?			

Meeting with lifestyle coach

✂

STUDENT A

You are a lifestyle coach. You are having your first meeting with a new client.

He/She has the following problems:
- doesn't see enough of his/her family
- is concerned about not getting ahead quickly enough at work
- is not a good time manager and often find it difficult to prioritize tasks
- worries about work when away from the office

He/She is good at ...
- working with others
- taking responsibility

Run the first meeting. Listen to what your client has to say and suggest changes he or she can make to their lives.

✂

STUDENT B

You are meeting a lifestyle coach to help you organize your life.

You think that you ...
- are doing a good job and staff like you
- are not rewarded for the effort you put in
- deserve promotion because you spend long hours in the office

You are worried about ...
- feeling tired and putting on weight
- having got your work–life balance wrong, but you don't know how to change it

Explain your point of view and listen to what the lifestyle coach says.

Written follow-up

✂

Record of meeting

Date:

Summary of meeting

_____

_____

_____

_____

Recommendations for future

_____

_____

_____

Exchange your home

✀

STUDENT A

The barter economy is on the up and up – _____ , I'll have your old Prada bag.

_____ . You offer someone a week in your scruffy home _____ .

What began as a way for time-rich, cash-poor teachers _____ has boomed with the internet.

_____ and an email address _____ . At least that's what I thought

_____ for a villa in France. _____ Inflexibility was my problem.

_____ I was offered Canada and India. _____ for retired people and

anyone _____ . But it doesn't matter if your home _____ – the worst thing

is _____ . And apparently people trashing your house _____ it's your car

getting scratched. _____ and it's a good one.

✀

STUDENT B

_____ you know, you take my apples, _____ . Swapping provides cheap

holidays. _____ in exchange for a fortnight in somewhere nicer. _____

to spend summer breaks _____ . You only need an open mind _____

for a gateway to adventure. _____ when I tried to exchange my London house

_____ . It didn't work. _____ . I wanted Europe.

I _____ . Swapping seems to work best _____ who doesn't mind staying

off the beaten track. _____ is embarrassingly ordinary – _____ cleaning it

before you go. _____ isn't the worry you might think – _____ . That's all

part of the deal, though – _____ .

Compound nouns

✀

waitress	service	departure	lounge
check-in	desk	swimming	pool
boarding	card	power	shower
walk-in	wardrobe	flat-screen	TV
tooth	paste	hair	dryer
car	park	queen-size	bed
conveyor	belt	bath	robe

Natural spoken English

Spoken cards:

✄

1 You mustn't tell anyone about the new project.

2 Can I bring a friend with me to the dinner?

3 I didn't get the job.

4 How shall we decide who has the last piece of chocolate?

5 You must make up you mind whether you want the job.

6 Do you know what that Italian dish we had at the restaurant was called?

7 Can I buy you a drink?

8 I wish I could remember her name.

9 What would you like to eat?

10 I'm sorry, but I don't eat meat.

Response cards:

✄

a That's very kind of you, thanks.	**f** I know but I can't decide what to do – I'll have to sleep on it.
b Don't worry – my lips are sealed.	**g** Oh well – better luck next time.
c I haven't a clue.	**h** I'm not really hungry – I'll just have a quick snack thanks.
d Certainly – the more the merrier.	**i** That's no problem – I can rustle up an omelette for you.
e Let's toss for it.	**j** Yes, it's on the tip of my tongue, too.

PEARSON Longman

What do you do?

Situation cards

✂

Your Mexican host offers you worms with burritos at a festival of unusual food. You don't want to try to dish, but you don't want to offend him.	Your Spanish host offers you black rice with squid in ink. You like fish, but have never had squid and you don't like the look of it.	An old friend from university calls you to invite you to his/her wedding. You haven't seen him/her for five years and the wedding is in Australia. You can't afford the airfare.
A friend of your parents invites you to a dinner party to celebrate their wedding anniversary. You find them boring.	Your boss invites everyone in the office out for a drink after work. You don't really get on with your colleagues.	An old friend wants to go to an expensive restaurant. You are saving up for a holiday and don't want to spend the money.
There are ten people in the department where you work who are going to be made redundant. You are not one of them, but feel bad. You wonder whether you should offer to take a pay cut.	Your department is under great pressure and people are getting ill with the stress. Your line manager is not interested.	Your friend has told you that you need to lose weight, but you are embarrassed and don't know what to do.

Accepting and rejecting ideas

Situation cards

✂

1	What about doing something together this weekend?
2	I'm finishing work early tonight. Shall we play tennis?
3	I'd like to have a meal out tonight. What do you think?
4	I propose that our department should run a fun event for the whole company next month to show what we can do.
5	I'd like you to set up a new system for integrating new employees into our work culture.
6	If you come over at the weekend, then I'll cook for everyone.
7	I think that it's best to be fully organized, then it's easier to deal with things that happen unexpectedly.
8	My philosophy is that if you plan too much then it stops you thinking creatively.

Response cards

✂

1	Refuse, giving a reason.	5	Agree and add a further suggestion.
2	Accept, but try to change the time/day.	6	Accept, but refuse the meal giving a reason.
3	Disagree and make a counter suggestion.	7	Agree, but add more detail.
4	Agree, but suggest an alternative.	8	Disagree and make a counter suggestion.

The appraisal meeting

STUDENT A

You are the team manager's line manager and you are having your annual appraisal with him/her.

He/She has the following problems:

- doesn't keep his staff fully informed of what's going on
- is lacking some crucial skills in IT
- is not a good time manager and often takes too long to complete a task
- spends too long away from the office at lunchtime

He/She is good at …
- involving others in making decisions
- giving staff credit when they do well
- creating a good atmosphere in the office

Run the appraisal meeting, using modal verbs of advice and obligation. Explain your point of view and listen to what your appraisee has to say.

STUDENT B

You are in charge of a small team of employees and you are due to have an annual appraisal with your line manager.

You think you …
- are doing a good job and are popular with staff
- perform adequately in the area of IT but are aware that you are not as good technically as others who work under you
- work hard because you spend long hours in the office in the evening
- deserve more money
- lighten the atmosphere in the office by making jokes

Explain your point of view and listen to what your line manager says.

Talking about the past

✂

1 The most interesting place I have ever been to _____ . **Past simple/present perfect?**	**2** I haven't _____ for several years. **Past simple/present perfect?**	**3** I haven't _____ yet. **Past simple/present perfect?**	**4** I have already _____ but I haven't _____ yet. **Past simple/present perfect?**
5 Last year I was very pleased that I _____ . **Past simple /present perfect?**	**6** Last Monday I _____ but I regretted it. **Past simple/present perfect?**	**7** I have _____ since _____ . **Past simple/present perfect?**	**8** I _____ when I was _____ . **Past simple/present perfect?**
9 I have never wanted to _____ but I would have loved _____ . **Past simple/present perfect?**	**10** I _____ recently for the first time. **Past simple/present perfect?**	**11** My company has already _____ but it hasn't _____ . **Past simple/present perfect?**	**12** The best film I _____ was … **Past simple/present perfect?**

Small talk

✂

A television programme I enjoyed	A sporting event I went to	An interesting book I read	A restaurant I would recommend	The weather this month
A place I recommend for a good holiday	The place I live	What I enjoy doing at weekends	A difficult journey I once made	My holiday plans this year
An activity I enjoy and would recommend	Good places to go out in my town	What I do in my job	My family and what they do	Good places to go shopping in my town
An interesting conference I attended	A change I have made in my life recently	A film or play I would recommend	A good place to take the family for a day out	A useful language to learn to speak
A sporting event I enjoyed recently	What I enjoy about my job	What presents are good to take when visiting a company in another country	Clothes that people wear at work	An interesting story from the news or television this week

Social rules

✄

A person is smoking inside a public building. What do you say to them?	You get on the bus and sit next to an elderly passenger. There are lots of empty seats elsewhere. What have you done wrong?	You are sitting on a full bus. A pregnant lady gets on and has to stand. What do you say to the young man sitting down?	Today is your friend's birthday but you have forgotten to send a card. You want to go out and buy one at lunchtime. What do you say?	Your guest tries to pay for your lunch in the staff canteen but it is free. What do you say to them?
A young colleague has just started a new job in your company and has arrived on the first day wearing jeans. This is against company policy. What do you say to him?	You are going to catch a train and plan to walk to the station, which is only 5 minutes away. Your friend who is coming with you wants to take a taxi to the station. Explain why it's not necessary.	Your company insists that all visitors report to Reception to sign in. A visitor is coming to have a meeting with you. What do you tell your visitor before they arrive?	Your company expects all employees to work for 8 hours a day, but the actual time of work is flexible. What do you tell a potential employee about the company?	Staff are advised not to drink too much coffee when they work, as it can make them feel stressed. Your colleague loves coffee! What can you say?
You are going out to a meal with a client and can put the meal on expenses. Your client offers to share the costs. What do you say?	A new employee asks you where to go for lunch and what it costs. Your company has no canteen facilities. What do you say?	There is nowhere to park at your workplace, but a colleague keeps parking in a space reserved for disabled visitors. What do you say?	You are at the theatre. As the lights go down you notice that someone in the next seat has not turned off their mobile phone. What do you say?	There are a lot of speed cameras in your town. A visitor to your company has arrived in a fast sports car. What do you say to them?

Formal and informal styles

✂

Don't go out yet – it's raining. The weather forecast said it'd stop around two o'clock.

I love eating salads when the weather's hot.

My friend Sam's a great footballer, but he's not so good at golf.

I've got a friend who's a real fitness fanatic – she goes to the gym every day!

Let's go out for a meal very soon – I'm hungry and the restaurant opens at six.

I wish I didn't have to work today because it's my sister's birthday.

I've bought a new car, but unfortunately it's not working properly.

I've never been to Rome before, but I'm going next year.

My company is the best in its field because its advertising is excellent.

My brother loves football, but he's never been to a live match.

I'd appreciate it if you would advise me on a personal issue.

Whose car is it in the disabled space? It shouldn't be there!

I'm trying to update my CV, but I don't know how to present my current situation, as I'm actually unemployed right now!

The next meeting will be held on Wednesday 5th September, at 4.30.

Jobs

Jobs

✂

Waiter	Car salesperson	Call-centre worker
Shop assistant	Teacher	Managing Director

Skills/Qualities

✂

patience	good personnel skills	confidence
a sense of humour	good organization skills	willing to work long hours
good oral communication skills	determination	flexibility
sensitivity	persuasive manner	good writing skills
ambition	good social manner	academic qualifications

Explaining to others

✂

Describe what happened in your first English lesson.	Describe the proudest moment in your life so far.
Talk about a time you were learning something new, but did it badly.	Explain what your greatest interest is and how you got into it.
Tell a story that your parents always tell friends about you.	Describe your most exciting day at work so far.
Explain what happened on your first day in your company/organization.	Explain what you were doing before you started your current job.
Describe a misunderstanding you had when you were speaking English.	Explain what your company does.
Describe a time when you did something dangerous, but survived.	Talk about your current job and how you feel about it.

If ...

If I were rich,	I would give a lot of money away to charity.
If I had the opportunity to be 'green',	I would buy an electric car.
She always turns the lights off	whenever she leaves a room.
You will save money	if you turn the temperature of the heating down.
If you share a car going to work,	you will save money and could help the planet.
If you recycle paper,	you save trees.
Unless we address the problem of carbon emissions,	air quality will get worse.
I would behave in a more 'green way'	if I thought it would do any good.
We have to recycle more	if we really want to help the environment in a practical way.
It's not worth doing anything for the environment	unless everyone in the world does the same thing.
If people travelled by plane less,	carbon emissions would be reduced.
If petrol companies put up prices,	fewer people would drive cars.

What are you doing?

Function cards

✂

Asking for suggestions	Asking for an opinion	Raising an objection
Checking understanding	Making a suggestion	Making a decision

Sentences

✂

1	Anyone got any better ideas?
2	It might be an idea to make a long-term plan.
3	So what you're saying is that you don't agree.
4	That's OK as far as it goes, but the problem is the finance.
5	I'd like to hear your opinion on this.
6	It'd be better if we could let everyone know today.
7	That could work, but it would be very expensive and time-consuming.
8	You might want to think about bringing in a consultant.
9	Just to clarify – you think we should implement the plan?
10	Would anyone like to add any other ideas?
11	So that's what we'll do.
12	We could certainly think about that – but how would you feel about increasing the budget?
13	So we'll run with that. Now moving on …
14	That's just not going to be feasible – there's not enough money in the budget.

Phrasal verbs

Phrasal verb cards

✀

hang up	call back	put (someone) through	get through to	cut out
cut off	keep on	get back	put off	set up

Sentence cards

✀

1 I'm trying to _____ Sue, but she's not picking up her phone – is she there?

2 Hello, is that Mr Jones? I'm really sorry, but we've had to _____ the meeting until the 20th as so many people can't make it.

3 Bear with me – I'll try to _____ to him, but I'm not sure whether he's at his desk right now.

4 I was talking to John on my mobile, but as the train went through the tunnel the signal _____ .

5 I do apologize – I pressed the wrong button and we got _____ .

6 I'm not sure what has happened. Leave it with me and I'll look into it and _____ to you.

7 So, I phoned her up to apologize, but she was so angry with me that she _____ the phone before I'd finished speaking.

8 I'm sorry, Peter's not here right now. Could you _____ this afternoon?

9 It was difficult speaking English at first, but I _____ trying and it soon got easier.

10 I'll try to _____ another meeting between the two departments next month, once the budget has been decided.

Telephoning situations

Pair 1

✂

STUDENT A

Call your colleague. Tell him/her you would like to change your meeting on Thursday – suggest Friday morning. You have not yet got the papers for the meeting.

STUDENT B

Your colleague phones you. You are not free on Friday morning and want to leave the meeting as it is. You agree to send your colleague the missing papers.

Pair 2

✂

STUDENT A

You work in the HR department. The phone rings and you pick it up. Someone wants to speak to Helen, but she is away from her desk. When you hear who it is, you know that Helen does not want to speak to them.

STUDENT B

You want to speak to Helen about your recent interview to find out why you did not get the job.

Pair 3

✂

STUDENT A

This is an important call that can't wait. If you can't speak to Claire Jones in the legal department, you have to leave a detailed message. The copy of the contract has been received but has been signed in the wrong place. You will email her a new copy, which she needs to get her client to sign in the right place and return to you by post. If there is any delay, the deal will fall through.

STUDENT B

You are a student on work experience in a law firm. You pick up the phone. Claire Jones is away for two days. Take a message.

Pair 4

✂

STUDENT A

You pick up the phone. Janet Robinson is on holiday for a week. Take a message.

STUDENT B

You need to speak to Janet Robinson urgently. If you can't, you have to leave a detailed message. Your meeting has been changed. Instead of Wednesday it has been brought forward by a day, to Tuesday next week. Someone needs to make arrangements to book the room and refreshments. Could someone please email you the new details as you have to tell the rest of the attendees today?

Giving advice

Discussion cards

✂

My friend wants to borrow some money from me, but I think that lending to friends is a bad idea. What should I do?	I want to move to a bigger flat, but I can't really afford to pay any more rent. What should I do?	My friend is applying for a job in the same company where I work. It's a good job, but I don't think it's the right one for him. What should I do?	I feel very tired all the time and it's difficult to get motivated at work. What should I do?
I'd love to have a holiday this year, but I don't think I can afford to go anywhere expensive. What should I do?	I'm very shy and find it hard to talk when I meet new people. What should I do?	I want to find a new job, but there isn't anything out there. What should I do?	I need to borrow some money to buy a new car. What should I do?
I really wish I had listened when my teacher told me to get some qualifications. If I had listened, I wouldn't find it so difficult to get a job now. What should I do?	I knew that the man sitting next to me on the train hadn't bought a ticket. If I'd told the guard, then he would have been fined. Should I have done that?	I've had a big argument with my best friend. I know it was my fault, but I said some horrible things. I wish I hadn't done that – if I had been nicer, we'd still be friends! What should I do?	I've got an evening job to pay off a debt. I hate it, but if I hadn't taken it, I wouldn't have been able to pay off the debt. What should I do?

Apologizing and responding to apologies

Situation cards

✂

1	2	3	4	5
You arranged a meeting with a new client but overslept. Phone the client, apologize and try to rearrange the meeting.	You have agreed to meet a colleague and go to the cinema after work, but an old friend arrives in town unexpectedly. Apologize but cancel the cinema.	You have had a meal in an expensive restaurant which was not very good. Finally, the waiter brings the bill which is wrong. You are not pleased.	You are visiting a friend but spill water over his laptop by mistake. Apologize and express regret.	You tell a client that you will call them back but forget. Call and apologize, but don't take responsibility.
6	**7**	**8**	**9**	**10**
You promised to help a friend but go away for the weekend instead. Apologize and offer to put things right.	Your friend lends you his expensive bike. You forget to lock it up and it is stolen. Apologize, take responsibility and offer to put things right.	You promise to bring an important book for a colleague who is making a presentation to clients using it, but you haven't got it with you. Apologize and give an explanation.	You are out for a meal with friends and have agreed to share the cost. Unfortunately, you have left your wallet/purse at home. Apologize and give an explanation.	You are rushing up the stairs without looking and knock a smaller colleague over. Apologize and offer to help.

Response cards

✂

1	2	3	4	5
You were looking forward to a meeting with a new company, and don't like being stood up. You don't want another meeting.	Your colleague prefers to cancel a cinema trip with you in order to meet another friend. Accept the apology, but show that you are upset.	You are a waiter in an expensive restaurant. The customer has been very difficult and is now complaining that the bill is wrong. Apologize and explain.	Your friend has spilt water over your laptop while staying in your flat. It was a very expensive computer and important to your work.	You feel that you should not have been forgotten and that it is not your fault.
6	**7**	**8**	**9**	**10**
You expected your friend to help you move to a new flat. You couldn't manage without help and it took you twice as long.	You use your bike regularly and are very annoyed that it has been stolen. You think your friend has been careless.	You feel very upset that your colleague has let you down. You felt embarrassed and unprofessional.	Your friend often 'forgets' to pay when you are together. You are fed up with his/her behaviour.	You have been knocked over on the stairs by a colleague who never thinks about other people. You are upset and annoyed.

who, which, where, when, while, whose or that?

✄

A child _____ enjoys school will do better than one _____ doesn't. **Answer:** who	That's the theatre _____ I saw a Shakespeare play last month. **Answer:** where	I refuse to buy anything from a shop _____ exploits animals. **Answer:** which/that
That's the town _____ I was brought up. **Answer:** where	I have no idea _____ phone this is. I just found it on the bus. **Answer:** whose	It was _____ I was living in France that I really learnt to speak French fluently. **Answer:** when/while
I will support any organization _____ helps others and _____ doesn't have a political agenda. **Answer:** which/that	I have no idea _____ to vote for in the next election – I just can't decide! **Answer:** who	My friend, _____ is a nurse, lives near the hospital. **Answer:** who
I'd love to live in a place _____ there are no taxes to pay! **Answer:** where	Firenze, _____ is its Italian name, is called Florence in English. **Answer:** which	I want to go on holiday to a beach _____ is hot, sunny and romantic! **Answer:** which/that

Networking: responding to others

✂

Statements/Questions	Responses
1 I've just been told that I've been shortlisted for that new job.	**g** Congratulations! That's half the battle! Just the big interview to go – but you'll be fine.
2 Nice to meet you – I'm the Events Manager.	**c** Good to meet you. I'm Charles, the new co-ordinator.
3 Did you hear that Sam has left?	**i** Oh no, I'm sorry to hear that. She was really good at her job.
4 Have you heard that Sarah's having a baby?	**a** Really? So who will be covering her maternity leave?
5 Could you give me a bit of help with this report?	**b** It's not exactly my area, but I know someone who could. Try Jon over there. He's great with that sort of thing.
6 We're all going out tonight after work. Why don't you come?	**h** Thanks for asking, but actually I've already made plans. Maybe next time.
7 Hello, have we met? I'm Suzie from HR.	**d** Didn't we both go to that conference in London? I'm Joe from Accounts.
8 How long are you staying in London? We must meet up for a coffee.	**f** I'm here until Friday. Is that any good?
9 Can I give you my card? It's got my phone number and email address on it.	**e** Thanks – but I'm afraid I've run out of mine. Can I email you with my contact details?
10 Anything happening in your department?	**j** Oh, you know, the usual! I'm looking forward to the weekend though.

Easily confused words

✂

overcharge/refund	**suspect/inspect**	**install/build**
I was furious when the mail-order company refused to _____ my money even though the goods were damaged.	When you buy a new house or flat, you should always get an expert to _____ it in case there are any structural problems.	I called an electrician today to get him to _____ some lights in the living room.
Answer: refund	**Answer:** inspect	**Answer:** install
scams/deals	**rip off/take off**	**unprofessional/amateur**
You have to be careful when you buy things on the internet – there are a lot of _____ about and you can lose a lot of money.	You must be careful in a new city – there are lots of people trying to _____ you _____ and take your money.	This building work is terrible. It looks as if it has been done by an _____ .
Answer: scams	**Answer:** rip (you) off	**Answer:** amateur
prescription/receipt	**recommended/reputable**	**memorize/remember**
I went to the chemist to collect the _____ for my medication, but they hadn't got the medicine in stock.	I wanted to book a holiday with a _____ company – I don't want to find that they go bust after I've paid them!	I went on a fantastic holiday last year. I can still _____ the smell of the sea and the sound of the waves!
Answer: prescription	**Answer:** reputable	**Answer:** remember
cash-in-hand/deposit	**dishonest/disgraceful**	**consumer service/customer service**
The builders wanted to be paid _____ , but we preferred to pay by cheque.	That builder didn't tell the truth – the whole project cost more than he said, and he didn't tell the truth about the cost of the parts . He was really _____ .	If you have any problems with a company, the best thing is to contact their _____ department. If it's a good company, they will always help.
Answer: cash-in-hand	**Answer:** dishonest	**Answer:** customer service

Making complaints

Complaints cards/Excuses

✂

1	There were too many black bags on the carousel at the airport – I couldn't find mine!
2	I have never been treated like that in my life – and I'm old enough to is be his mother!
3	They just don't know talent when they see it – the interview must have been fixed!
4	I got my feet wet on the log flume ride at the amusement park, which ruined my sandals, and the sun was so hot it melted my iced drink before I'd finished it.
5	We bought 'Ray-ban' sunglasses for five euros (£3.50) from a street trader, but to our total amazement we found out they were fake.
6	We're only supposed to have an hour for lunch but some people just don't play fair.
7	I asked for a receipt, which was a good thing as it showed what the price should have been.
8	It's always the same – you wait and wait and then four come at once. Then you have to stand up and there's nowhere to put your bag …
9	The beach was too sandy.
10	I'm sure I emailed it to you yesterday as agreed – it must be somewhere in cyberspace …
11	My dog ate my car keys.
12	I didn't do it because I didn't want to add to my teacher's already heavy workload.

Topic cards

✂

Other people's choice of luggage	The behaviour of a member of staff	Failing to get a job
An unsatisfactory day at a theme park	Being ripped-off	Colleagues who take long breaks
Being overcharged	Public transport	An unsatisfactory holiday location
Not fulfilling a promise	Being late for work	Not doing homework